THE
CABINET-MAKER
AND UPHOLSTERER'S
DRAWING-BOOK

THE
CABINET-MAKER
AND UPHOLSTERER'S
DRAWING-BOOK

BY

THOMAS SHERATON

WITH A NEW INTRODUCTION BY

JOSEPH ARONSON

DOVER PUBLICATIONS, INC.

NEW YORK

Published in Canada by General Publishing Company, Ltd.,
30 Lesmill Road, Don Mills, Toronto, Ontario.
Published in the United Kingdom by Constable and Company, Ltd.

This Dover edition, first published in 1972, reproduces material
from various early editions of *The Cabinet-Maker and Upholsterer's
Drawing-Book* published by the author in London between 1793 and
1802. It also contains several new features, including a new introduction by Joseph Aronson, written specially for the present edition.
For details, see the Publisher's Note opposite.
   The publisher is grateful to Dr. Adolf Placzek, Avery Librarian
at Columbia University, and to Mr. Arthur Whallon, for making
available for reproduction rare early editions of this work in their
collections.

International Standard Book Number · 0-486-22255-1
Library of Congress Catalog Card Number: 72-77998

MANUFACTURED IN THE UNITED STATES OF AMERICA
Dover Publications, Inc.
180 Varick Street
New York, N. Y. 10014

Publisher's Note

The present volume reproduces from the original publications all the material pertaining to furniture to be found in the editions of Sheraton's *Cabinet-Maker and Upholsterer's Drawing-Book* published within the author's lifetime. Material on geometry and perspective that does not pertain directly to furniture has been omitted. The following breakdown shows what has been included here. All inclusions are from the 1793 edition unless otherwise stated.

"Frontispiece Explained."

Frontispiece.

Title page.

"Contents of the Three Parts."

"Directions for finding . . . the Plates" (the original list of plates, showing their original placement within the book; this 1793 list is reproduced in its entirety, and thus includes Plates 1 through 23 of Parts I and II—omitted in the present volume —and fails to include the plates of the Appendix and the Accompaniment—added to the present volume).

"Contents" (the original 1793 listing in its entirety—hence including sections omitted here and excluding sections added here).

[The "List of Subscribers" that originally followed is omitted here.]

"To Cabinet-Makers and Upholsterers in General" (in the 1802 edition this foreword was revised and a section "To the Reader" was added).

[Omitted here are the "Introduction to Part the First"; all of Part I, with Plates 1–13 showing geometrical figures and architectural orders; and most of Part II, including Plates 14–23 showing perspective constructions.]

Plates 24–26 of Part II and the text pertaining to the furniture figures in these plates (this material is on pages 34–47 of the present volume).

Part III in its entirety, with all plates.

[Omitted here are the "Errata," which pertain exclusively to omitted sections of the text, and a second "List of Subscribers"—this second list is perhaps found only in the 1794 edition.]

"Appendix to the Cabinet-Maker and Upholsterer's Drawing-Book" in its entirety, with all 33 plates—omitting only the list of plates and the list of subscribers. Six text pages and eight plates (the so-called Additional Plates) have been added to this Appendix from the 1802 edition. (In one copy of the 1794 edition that we examined, six of these plates were bound in without text. The 1802 edition adds them, with text, to the Appendix, as we have done here.)

"An Accompaniment to the Cabinet-Maker and Upholsterer's Drawing-Book" in its entirety, with all 14 plates—omitting only a further list of subscribers. This Accompaniment is reproduced from the 1794 edition, the first edition to contain it.

Two "Descriptive Indexes" listing the pieces of furniture by genre, reproduced from the 1802 edition, in which they first appear.

New features of the present edition are the Introduction by Joseph Aronson; an additional, consecutive, pagination ("Dover page numbers"); a table of contents and a list of plates showing our specific inclusions and using the Dover page numbers. All this new material appears on pages with roman folio numbers, and precedes the material listed above reproduced from original editions.

Introduction to the Dover Edition

Thomas Sheraton could never in his dreary life have imagined that his name would become the appellation of a furniture style that climaxes the Georgian while it forecasts the Regency and the Victorian of the English sphere of influence. It was certainly not his intention in 1791, when he announced his projected *Cabinet-Maker and Upholsterer's Drawing-Book*, to offer anything beyond a manual of instruction in drafting, geometric representation, the Orders of Architecture and perspective, with suitable comments and examples. As a journeyman cabinetmaker, he would inevitably choose articles of furniture for illustrative examples; as a preacher and pedant, he could not resist adding moralities and mythology within the best eighteenth-century construction of philosophy. Thus the work became, in its final form, a monument of unplanned exposition, a landmark in the history of furniture design and a record of reluctant concessions to the fluctuating vicissitudes of a time of turmoil and swift change—and to the pressures of importunate subscribers. The time, the place and the man were all wrong for each other, and for the molding of a memorable representative style. Yet this is what Thomas Sheraton achieved by inadvertence.

Thomas Sheraton was born in 1751 in Stockton-on-Tees, County Durham, and early fell into his father's trade of cabinetmaking. He seems to have reached London about 1790, but his progress from his birthplace may have been long and indirect. It is possible that as a journeyman cabinetmaker he may have paused to earn his living at various towns along the route, for his first subscription list includes many cabinetmakers whom he may have met in such places. The projected *Drawing-Book* germinated during his first year in London, when he may have issued the prospectus, the title page of which, dated 1791, is here reproduced as Figure A. This was apparently accompanied by ten pages of text (ending page "14") and a remarkable allegorical frontispiece, with the "Frontispiece Explained." The text states the objectives of the work entirely in the future tense.

THE

CABINET-MAKER

AND

UPHOLSTERER's

DRAWING-BOOK,

IN THREE PARTS.

PART I.

Containing fuch GEOMETRICAL LINES and INSTRUCTIONS as are highly ufeful to perfons of both branches; including the methods of finding Lines for Hip and Elliptic Domes for State Beds, of mitring Mouldings of different Projections together, and of finding curved Lines to anfwer the various Sections of irregular Figures.—To which are added, the Five Orders, proportioned by aliquot parts, and exhibited in one large Plate.

PART II.

On PRACTICAL PERSPECTIVE, applied to the Art of reprefenting all kinds of Furniture in different fituations; together with a little of the THEORY for fuch as would know fome of the reafons on which this ufeful Art is founded.

N. B. The Examples in Perfpective are intended to exhibit the neweft Tafte of various Pieces of Furniture, and likewife to fhew the neceffary Lines for defigning them.

PART III.

Is a Repofitory of various ORNAMENTS, confifting of Defigns for Pediments, with Cornices, &c. drawn at large, their Springs fhewn, and the proper gaging marked off to work the feveral Mouldings by.—To which are added, two methods of reprefenting a Drawing-Room, with the proper Diftribution of the Furniture.

By T. SHERATON, CABINET-MAKER.

LONDON:

PRINTED FOR THE AUTHOR, BY T. BENSLEY;

And fold by J. MATHEWS, No. 18, Strand; G. TERRY, No. 54, Paternofter-Row; J. S. JORDAN, No. 166, Fleet-ftreet; L. WAYLAND, Middle-Row, Holborn; and by the AUTHOR, No. 4, Hart-ftreet, Grofvenor-fquare.

1791.

[Entered at Stationers-Hall.]

Fig. A. Title page of Sheraton's 1791 prospectus.

This title page carries a revealing outline of the three parts proposed, with the description of the second part alone containing the rather grudging admission: "N. B. The Examples in Perspective are intended to exhibit the newest Taste of various Pieces of Furniture, and likewise to shew the necessary Lines for designing them."

Part III of the 1793 edition, reproduced here in its entirety, departs substantially from the original program of 1791, and illustrates only furniture. Many of the plates dated 1791 and 1792 adhere to the idea of showing construction lines and some perspective development, but the majority are simple illustrations, mostly in one-point perspective, often without scales, and totally uninformative as to back-leg profiles, depth of seats, etc. For all Sheraton's harangues on perspective, his own drawings leave something to be desired in visual correctness and explicitness of dimension.

The 1793 edition also contains an "Appendix" with plates all dating from 1793. In later editions (1794 and 1802), not only does the tense of the author's foreword change from the future to a mildly complaining past, but an "Accompaniment" of fourteen plates dated 1793 and 1794, and a group of eight "Additional Plates" all dated 1794, are added. Sheraton's designs through these years are remarkably personal and consistent. It is on the group of plates mentioned in this paragraph, and on this group alone, that the fame of Sheraton the designer rests.

The 1791 title page has Sheraton living at "No. 4, Hart-street, Grosvenor-square," while the 1793 edition lists him at "No. 41, Davies-street, Grosvenor-square." The Appendix of same year finds him at "No. 106, Wardour-street, Soho," which agrees with his trade card of somewhat later date (Figure B), while "8, Broad-street" is the location on the title page of his 1803 *Cabinet Dictionary*. It was at this address, apparently, that he "left his family, it is feared, in distressed circumstances," according to the "Obituary, with Anecdotes, of Remarkable Persons" in the *Gentleman's Magazine* for November 1806.

Comparison of dates and places gives eloquent if circumstantial evidence of the exigencies of Sheraton's sixteen years in London. There is nothing to suggest that his hand ever participated in the production of a piece of furniture, nor that he enjoyed at any time the company or patronage of the affluent or the influential, or indeed experienced anything but abject poverty and loneliness. Our sole biographical memoir is the observation by Adam Black, later a distinguished publisher, who worked with Sheraton "for about a week . . . writing a few articles, trying to put his house in order, for which I was remunerated with half a guinea. Miserable as the pay was, I was half ashamed to take it from the poor man." Sheraton died only two years later, in October 1806. Probably Black's "few articles" were entries in the *Cabinet-Maker, Upholsterer and General Artists' Encyclopaedia,* a frenetically ambitious project of which only the A–C folio was completed before the author's death.

Fig. B. Sheraton's trade card.

The *Drawing-Book,* the *Cabinet Dictionary* and the *Cabinet Encyclopaedia,* together forming the "style of Sheraton," make a picture of the desperate struggle of a troubled, bitter personality to compose a wide range of knowledge and emotion into designs saleable to a convulsively fluctuating, nervously revolutionary society. The stable social base of the early reign of George III had deteriorated into economic insurgency at home, social and political turmoil on the Continent, philosophical and artistic dissension everywhere, as the weak-kneed Regency accommodated itself to all shifting tides. Cross-currents of revolutionary fervor and luxurious excesses materialized in the trappings of ancient imperialism. The instructive *Drawing-Book* that Sheraton projected was distinctly not an answer to the demand for exciting new designs in furniture. Pedant-preacher-teacher that he was, he must have become disturbingly aware after the publication of the first two parts of the *Drawing-Book* that his intent may have been somewhat different from the expectations of his subscribers. Complaining in the Introduction to Part III that everybody wanted something new, different and exciting, and that it was impossible to satisfy everybody, Sheraton proceeded to embellish familiar late-Adam basic shapes with the divergent ornamental novelties of a restless period. In one direction, he compounded mechanical trickery, long a delight of Germanic designers like Riesener, Röntgen, Jacob; in another, he discovered the gaudier ornamental vocabulary of the expiring court of Louis XVI. He further stressed the upholsterer's art as it had not been known in England since the Restoration. Finally he came to the classical animal symbolism which, in the hands of more practically realistic designers like Percier and Fontaine and their apostle Thomas Hope, led successively into the French Empire, the English Empire, the Regency and ultimately the Early Victorian styles. To quote Macquoid (in *The Dictionary of English Furniture*), "Up to the opening of the war with France in 1793, the influence of Robert Adam was barely contested but soon after this date a revolution in taste, a closer and more intense classical revival, was taking place both in England and the Continent." Napoleon's expeditions to Egypt and Syria, 1798–1801, included archeologists and artists, whose notes produced the Empire mélange of Egyptian and Greco-Roman which, reaching England, swamped the Adam tradition.

A considerable quantity of furniture survives, safely attributable to this period, which more or less, in this or that particular, resembles designs shown in the *Drawing-Book*. Whether these survivors were the inspiration for Sheraton's exemplars, or whether they were inspired by the publication, will forever remain a subject for speculation. Even more speculative is the possibility that some of this furniture may actually have been designed by Sheraton. His text is full of hints of his familiarity with the London cabinet trade and industry, and their practices and specialties. By this time the Factory System had completed the divorce of the designer from the craft-production process. Presumably Sheraton served the industry as a free-lance designer, circulating among the cabinet shops of the city, earning his meager living by sporadically selling his services as designer or delineator.

There is little in Sheraton's published drawings that would today be construed as definitive instruction to a craftsman. For that matter, no existing drawing of the period would now be considered adequately informative for a working drawing. The perfection of line and proportion of most known late Georgian furniture tells of a uniform understanding of these idiomatic details, a quality of vernacular craft-training that made conventions of such details. Assuming that the specialization of operations by this time was so explicit, it probably fell to the lot of one artisan—a foreman or pattern-maker—to detail to a hair the exact dimensions, the thickness of a leg or a molding, the precise sweep of a curve, the depth of carving. Sheraton speaks of the use of the compass to develop dimensions from the drawings, but this procedure would be only a source of clumsy error unless such detailing were guided by exquisite taste and technique. This bolsters the supposition that Sheraton drew what he *saw*, that he employed familiar details and composed them capriciously into original arrangements. His drawings were thus meant to be schematic or conceptual, with the skill of the working designer to supply the missing minutiae of dimension and shape.

Exported to colonies and neighboring countries, the designs of the late Georgian school were freely adapted to local conventions and skills. There is no way of knowing to what comparative extent the message was carried by exports of books, or of actual furniture models, or by memory, hearsay or rough sketches. Only two foreign subscribers are listed—"Dillon, Cabinet-maker, Russia" and "Stewart, Cabinet-maker, Bengal"—but the *Drawing-Book* themes are found after 1790 in Italy as in Spain, in Germanic lands as in Scandinavia, most pertinently in America. In these ex-colonies an expanding economy drew refugees from revolution and disordered economic systems. Taste and skill and familiarity with changing ideas came with immigrants like Duncan Phyfe and Honoré Lannuier. Phyfe, who probably learned his trade in Albany, opened shop in New York just about the time Sheraton's *Drawing-Book* may have reached there. His early style developed at once along late-Adam-Georgian lines, with a bias toward Sheraton's own details such as reeding on edges and turnings. Later Phyfe leaned to the French influence, with rather more restrained grace than Sheraton himself. Lannuier, on the other hand, used animal forms extravagantly, as in Sheraton's work after 1800. Closest to Sheraton of all American work is a chair by Samuel McIntyre, wood-carver of Salem, virtually a true rendition of Plate 33, with logical corrections. Square-framed back-shapes are recalled in chairs by Henry Connelly of Philadelphia, John Seymour of Boston and numerous unknowns. More remotely inspired is the family of "fancy chairs" which proliferated in the United States after 1810. Tables for games and work, dining and library use, sideboards and desks, drew so heavily on Sheraton detail after 1800 that the Federal style may be said to be the American counterpart of the Sheraton manner.

Back in England, the acceleration of style change dizzied Sheraton. His 1803 *Cabinet Dictionary* gropes for novelty at the expense of design logic. It appears, however, that his *Drawing-Book* was so widely distributed, especially in the provinces that were unaffected by the war hysteria, that it motivated continuously sober, less frantically stylish furniture for many years. Cescinsky (in *The Gentle Art of Faking Furniture*) lists makers of "Sheraton" furniture through 1880: Gillow of Lancaster, the Seddons, Edwards & Roberts, Wright & Mansfield, Jackson & Graham, Johnson & Jeans and Cooper & Holt of Bunhill Row. Such work, ascribed to the Sheraton manner, undoubtedly partook equally of Hepplewhite and Shearer (the *Cabinet-Makers' London Book of Prices* was still in current use well after mid-nineteenth century). George Smith seems to have followed Sheraton's later style quite assiduously, notably in his 1808 *Collection of Designs for Household Furniture*. Smith in 1826 shamelessly appropriated Hepplewhite's title for his *Cabinet-Maker and Upholsterer's Guide,* revealing how sadly Hepplewhite had been forgotten while the whole pre-Regency was attributed to Sheraton.

Future researchers may enjoy tracing the ebb and flow of popularity of the Sheraton manner, by seeking out references to the name during the later nineteenth century. The 1895 Batsford reprint of the *Drawing Book* brought the whole work together in orderly form, not a feature of the original. After this date there were many excellent critiques. The 1946 Towse reprint offered all the furniture drawings, including parts of the *Cabinet Dictionary* and the *Cabinet Encyclopaedia,* and deleting the bulk of the text and the drawing instruction. The present edition limits itself to the part of Sheraton's work that has lived on as a summary, an exemplar and a memorial of the climactic English eighteenth-century epoch in furniture.

JOSEPH ARONSON

BIBLIOGRAPHY

Bell, J. M., ed.: *The Furniture Designs of Chippendale, Hepplewhite and Sheraton* (1938)

Blake, J. P., and Rivier-Hopkins, A. E.: *Little Books about Old Furniture,* Vol. 4 (1912)

Brackett, Oliver: *An Encyclopedia of English Furniture* (1927)

Cescinsky, Herbert: *English Furniture From Gothic to Sheraton* (1929; 2nd ed., 1937, reprinted by Dover)

Claret-Rubira, José: *Muebles de estilo inglés y su influencia en el exterior* (1946). Line drawings of details

Clouston, R. S.: *English Furniture and Furniture Makers of the 18th Century* (1906)

Edwards, Ralph: *Georgian Cabinetmakers* (1955)

Gloag, John: *British Furniture Makers* (1945)

Hayward, Charles H.: *Antique or Fake?: The Making of Old Furniture* (1970)

Hayward, Helena: *The Drawings of John Linnell in the Victoria and Albert Museum* (Furniture History Society, V, 1969). Forerunner of the style

Heal, Ambrose: *London Furniture Makers from the Restoration to the Victorian Era* (1953). Brief biographical listings and trade cards

Jourdain, Margaret: *Decoration and Furniture During the Later 18th Century, 1760–1820* (1922)

——: *Regency Furniture, 1795–1820* (1924)

London Cabinet-Makers' Union Book of Prices, The (1811; 2nd ed., 1824; 3rd ed., 1836; 4th ed., 1866). Drawings by Hepplewhite, Shearer, others

McClelland, N.: *Duncan Phyfe and the English Regency* (1939)

Macquoid, Percy: *A History of English Furniture,* Vol. 4 (1908; Dover reprint)

Meyrick, Sir Samuel Rush: *Specimens of Ancient Furniture* (1836)

Rogers, John C.: *English Furniture* (1923)

Simon, Constance: *English Furniture Designers of the 18th Century* (1906)

Tatham, C. H.: *Etchings of Ancient Ornamental Architecture* (1799). May have influenced Sheraton after the *Drawing Book;* similar foreshadowing and inspiration are suggested in drawings by Albertolli, Piranesi, Linnell, Adam, Henry Holland, Shearer, et al.

Ward-Jackson, Peter: *English Furniture Designs of the 18th Century,* Victoria and Albert Museum, 1958

Contents of the Dover Edition

The page numbers are those of the present edition.

List of Plates in the Dover Edition

The page numbers are those of the present edition. The original plate numbers are shown within parentheses; note that there is some duplication in the numbering system.

List of Plates in the Dover Edition

IN THE "APPENDIX"*

*The last eight plates in the Appendix are the "Additional Plates," which first found their place in the Appendix in the 1802 edition.

FRONTISPIECE EXPLAINED.

To ſhew in as pleaſing a way as I could the ſtability of this Performance, and the ſubject of the book in general, I have, by the Figure on the right hand, repreſented Geometry ſtanding on a rock, with a ſcroll of Diagrams in his hand, converſing with Perſpective, the next figure to him, who is attentive to the principles of Geometry as the ground of his art; which art is repreſented by the frame on which he reſts his hand. On the left, ſeated near the window, is an Artiſt buſy in deſigning; at whoſe right hand is the Genius of Drawing preſenting the Artiſt with various patterns. The back Figure is Architecture, meaſuring the ſhaft of a Tuſcan column, and on the back ground is the Temple of Fame, to which a knowledge of theſe Arts directly leads.

T. Sheraton del.

Hawkins, sculp.

Time alters fashions and frequently obliterates the works of art and ingenuity; but that which is founded on Geometry & real Science, will remain unalterable.

Pub.d as the Act directs Nov.r 20.th 1791. by T. Sheraton.

THE

CABINET-MAKER

AND

UPHOLSTERER'S

DRAWING-BOOK.

IN THREE PARTS.

———————————

BY

THOMAS SHERATON,

CABINET-MAKER.

———————————

LONDON:

PRINTED FOR THE AUTHOR, BY T. BENSLEY;

AND SOLD BY J. MATHEWS, N° 18, STRAND; G. TERRY, N° 54, PATERNOSTER-ROW;

J. S. JORDAN, N° 166, FLEET-STREET, L. WAYLAND, MIDDLE-ROW,

HOLBORN; AND BY THE AUTHOR, N° 41, DAVIES-

STREET, GROSVENOR-SQUARE.

1793.

[Entered at Stationers Hall.]

CONTENTS OF THE THREE PARTS.

PART I.

Containing fuch Geometrical Lines and Inftructions as are highly ufeful to Perfons of both Branches, illuftrated in Seven Copper-plates. To which are added the Five Orders, exhibited in five different Plates, proportioned by Modules, Minutes, and Aliquot Parts, according to the moft approved Authority; together with fome Account of their Antiquity and Origin.

PART II.

On Practical Perfpective, applied to the Art of reprefenting all Kinds of Furniture in different Situations; interfperfed with fomething of the Theory, for fuch as would know the Principles on which this ufeful Art is founded. The Whole illuftrated in Thirteen Copper-plates.

PART III.

A Difplay of the prefent Tafte of Houfehold Furniture; containing alfo ufeful Remarks on the manufacturing Part of difficult Pieces. To which are added, fome Cornices drawn at large; the Method fhewn of Gaging, Working, Contracting, and Enlarging of any Kind; together with two Methods of reprefenting a Drawing-Room.

DIRECTIONS

NOTE: This is the complete list of plates of the 1793 edition, included here for reference. It lists the plates (1–23 of Parts I and II) that are omitted in the present volume, and does not include plates added to the present volume from editions later than 1793.

The page numbers in this listing are those of the 1793 edition. For the Dover page numbers, see the Dover list of plates on page xix.

DIRECTIONS for finding and binding in the PLATES, with an Account of their CONTENTS.

The Frontifpiece faces its Explanation before the Title Page.

PART I. *Of Geometrical Lines.*

PART

7

PART II. *Of Perspective.*

PART III. *Of Pieces of Furniture.*

7   31. A

CONTENTS.

NOTE: This is the complete table of contents of the 1793 edition, included here for reference. It lists sections that are omitted in the present volume, and does not include material added to the present volume from editions later than 1793.

The page numbers in this listing are those of the 1793 edition. For the Dover page numbers of the chief subdivisions, see the Dover table of contents on page xvii.

C O N T E N T S.

PART I. *Of Geometrical Lines.*

b   Geometry

11

S E C T. I. *On Geometrical Lines.*

S E C T. II.

S E C T. III.

The

CONTENTS.

SECT. IV.

SECT. V. *Problems pertaining to the Working Part.*

b 2

Problem

13

SECT. VI.

SECT. VII. *Of the Proportion of the Five Orders.*

What

CONTENTS.

General

PART II. *Of Perfpective.*

SECT. I.

SECT. II.

SECT.

SECT. III.

SECT. IV.

7

Problem

S E C T. V.

Example

18

CONTENTS.

SECT. VI.

Cafe

PART III. *Furniture in general.*

5

Of

CONTENTS.

c 2

TO

CABINET-MAKERS AND UPHOLSTERERS

IN GENERAL.

GENTLEMEN,

I PRESUME, that to publiſh a Drawing-book anſwerable to the preceding title page will not require many words to convince you either of the neceſſity or propriety of the attempt.

Nor will it be requiſite to uſe an oſtentatious preface to recommend it to your notice, or to perſuade you of the utility of ſuch an undertaking. Therefore, what I have further to ſay in this Addreſs ſhall be to give ſome account of my plan, and point out to you the difference between this and other books which have been publiſhed for the aſſiſtance and uſe of Cabinet-makers and Upholſterers.

Books

Books of various defigns in cabinet work, ornamented according to the tafte of the times in which they were publifhed, have already appeared. But none of thefe, as far as I know, profefs to give any inftructions relative to the art of making perfpective drawings, or to treat of fuch geometrical lines as ought to be known by perfons of both profeffions, efpecially fuch of them as have a number of men under their directions. Nor have thefe books given accurate patterns at large for ornaments to enrich and embellifh the various pieces of work which frequently occur in the cabinet branch. Such patterns are alfo highly neceffary to copy from by thofe who would fufficiently qualify themfelves for giving a good fketch, or regular drawing, of any thing they meet with, or are required to draw for others. It is granted that there are books of ornaments already publifhed fufficient for the above ends; but it may alfo be obferved, that thofe ornamental books which are good, are very extenfive, and of courfe very expenfive: on the other hand, thofe that are cheap are either fo fmall and ill drawn, or fo deficient through brevity, or want of examples, as to render them of little ufe to the learner. Befides, were there no other reafon for introducing ornaments into the following work, but the convenience of having a few good examples of this kind always at hand and ready to copy from, it would be fufficient to juftify the attempt. Nor indeed would this performance anfwer fo well to the title of a Drawing-book without them. I hope, therefore,

therefore, that it will be confidered as an enhancement to the real value and ufefulnefs of the Cabinet-maker and Upholfterer's Drawing-Book to compofe and felect fome examples of fuch ornaments as fhall ferve, both for the purpofe of the learner, and alfo to affift the ideas of thofe who have occafion to adorn their work in this way.

As I have alluded to fome books of defigns, it may be proper here juft to fay fomething of them. I have feen one which feems to have been publifhed before Chippendale's. I infer this from the antique appearance of the furniture, for there is no date to it; but the title informs us that it was compofed by a fociety of Cabinet-makers in London. It gives no inftructions for drawing in any form, but we may venture to fay, that thofe who drew the defigns wanted a good fhare of teaching themfelves.

Chippendale's book feems to be next in order to this, but the former is without comparifon to it, either as to fize or real merit. Chippendale's book has, it is true, given us the proportions of the Five Orders, and lines for two or three cafes, which is all it pretends to relative to rules for drawing: and, as for the defigns themfelves, they are now wholly antiquated and laid afide, though poffeffed of great merit, according to the times in which they were executed. But it may here be re-
marked.

marked to his credit, that although he has not given rules for drawing in * perfpective himfelf, yet he was fenfible of their importance and ufe in defigning, and therefore he fays in his preface: " Without fome knowledge of the rules of perfpective, the cabinet-maker cannot make the defigns of his work intelligible, nor fhew, in a little compafs, the whole conduct and effect of the piece. Thefe therefore, referring to architecture alfo, ought to be carefully ftudied by every one who would excel in this branch, fince they are the very foul and bafis of his art."

After Chippendale's work there appeared, in the year fixty-five, a book of defigns for chairs only, though it is called " The Cabinet-maker's real Friend and Companion," as well as the Chair-maker's. This publication profeffes to fhew the method of ftriking out all kinds of bevel work, by which, as the author fays, the moft ignorant perfon will be immediately acquainted with what many artifts have ferved feven years to

* This is ftrictly true of the third edition of Chippendale's book; but the firft edition of it, printed in 1754, has given two chairs, a dreffing table, and a book-cafe in perfpective, fhewing the lines for drawing them. But why thefe examples were not continued in the fucceeding editions I know not. In the laft edition of any work, we naturally expect to fee it in its beft ftate, having received its laft revifal from the author, or fome other hand equal to the tafk; and therefore it can never be thought unfair for a reader to form his judgment of a book from the laft impreffion. I hope, therefore, this will fufficiently apologize for the above obfervation.

know.

know. But this affertion both exceeds the bounds of modefty and truth, fince there is nothing in his directions for bevel-work, which he parades fo much about, but what an apprentice boy may be taught by feven hours proper inftructions. With refpect to the geometrical view of the Five Orders which he has given, thefe are ufeful, and the only thing in his book which at this day is worth notice, as all his chairs are nearly as old as Chippendale's, and feem to be copied from them.

The fucceeding publication to this feems to be Ince's and Mayhew's Book of Defigns in Cabinet and Chair Work, with three plates, containing fome examples of foliage ornaments, intended for the young defigner to copy from, but which can be of no fervice to any learner now, as they are fuch kind of ornaments as are wholly laid afide in the cabinet branch, according to the prefent tafte. The defigns in cabinets and chairs are, of courfe, of the fame caft, and therefore have fuffered the fame fate: yet, in juftice to the work, it may be faid to have been a book of merit in its day, though inferior to Chippendale's, which was a real original, as well as more extenfive and mafterly in its defigns.

In looking over Ince's book I obferved two card-tables with fome perfpective lines, fhewing the manner of defigning them. Thefe, fo far as they go, are a ufeful attempt; but cer-

B   tain

tain it is to me, from fome experience in teaching, that no perfon can have the fmalleft acquaintance with the principles of
perfpective, merely from feeing two or three lines joined to a
plate, without proper inftructions by letter-prefs. It is true,
a defcription is given of thefe lines in the 7th page of his book,
but not equal to what is abfolutely requifite to fuch as have no
previous acquaintance with the art; and thofe that have, will
not require that which can give them no affiftance. Properly
fpeaking then, what is done in this book, relative to perfpective lines, can only ferve as a hint to the workman, that this
art is effential in defigning.

In the year 1788 was publifhed, " The Cabinet-maker's
and Upholfterer's Guide." In which are found no directions for
drawing in any form, nor any pretenfions to it. The whole
merit of the performance refts on the defigns, with a fhort defcription to each plate prefixed. Some of thefe defigns are not
without merit, though it is evident that the perfpective is, in
fome inftances, erroneous. But, notwithftanding the late date
of Heppelwhite's book, if we compare fome of the defigns,
particularly the chairs, with the neweft tafte, we fhall find that
this work has already caught the decline, and perhaps, in a
little time, will fuddenly die in the diforder. This inftance may
ferve to convince us of that fate which all books of the fame
kind will ever be fubject to. Yet it muft be owned, that books

of

of this fort have their ufefulnefs for a time; and, when through change of fafhions they are become obfolete, they ferve to fhew the tafte of former times.

I fhall now conclude this account of books of defigns with obferving, that in the fame year was given a quarto book of different pieces of furniture, with the Cabinet-maker's London Book of Prices; and, confidering that it did not make its appearance under the title of a Book of Defigns, but only to illuftrate the prices, it certainly lays claim to merit, and does honour to the publifhers. Whether they had the advantage* of feeing Heppelwhite's book before theirs was publifhed I know not; but it may be obferved, with juftice, that their defigns are more fafhionable and ufeful than his, in proportion to their number.

Upon the whole then, if the intended publication, which now petitions your patronage and fupport, be fo compiled and compofed as fully to anfwer, and alfo to merit, the title which has been given to it, I think it will be found greatly to fupply the defects of thofe books now mentioned, and will appear to

---

* This is not meant to infinuate any difrefpectful idea of the abilities of thofe who drew the defigns in the Cabinet-maker's Book of Prices. I doubt not but they were capable of doing more than Heppelwhite has done, without the advantage of feeing his book: and it may be, for any thing I know, that the advantage was given on their fide.

be

be on as lafting a foundation as can well be expected in a work of this kind. For inftance, the firft part, which provides the workman with geometrical lines, applied to various purpofes in the cabinet branch, cannot be altered any more than reafon itfelf. The fame may be faid of Perfpective; the fubject of the fecond part. This art, being founded on Geometry and Optics, may be improved in its practice, but its fundamental principles can never be altered, any more than the nature of vifion and thofe immutable principles upon which good fenfe is founded.

With refpect to mouldings and various ornaments, the fubject of the third part, it is granted that thefe are of a changeable kind. Yet it is pretty evident that materials for proper ornaments are now brought to fuch perfection as will not, in future, admit of much, if any, degree of improvement, though they may, by the fkill and touch of the ingenious hand, be varied, *ad infinitum*, to fuit any tafte at any time. It may be neceffary to obferve alfo, that this book will have the advantage of exhibiting the prefent and neweft tafte of work; for, whilft we are teaching the practice of Perfpective, the examples given fhall both fhew the neceffary lines for defigning, and likewife reprefent, in different fituations, fome ufeful or fafhionable piece of furniture. To this advantage we fhall alfo add another, namely, that every example in pieces of furniture will have the geometrical

metrical dimenfions laid down on the ground, or other fcale lines adapted for that purpofe. So that no perfon, however ignorant of Perfpective, fhall be liable to miftake the Perfpective for the geometrical meafurements, or be at any lofs to know the general fizes of fuch pieces as fhall be introduced *. And we may fay, with refpect to changes of fafhions, that he who is properly acquainted with lines, verfed in Perfpective, and fufficiently practifed in ornamental drawing, will, from a few hints, be able, at any time, to turn his hand to any fafhion.

Laftly, I would entreat leave to remark, that, as the publication of this work will be attended with very great expence, the accomplifhment of my defign will principally depend upon

---

* The Cabinet-maker's Book of Prices advertifes thofe who are ignorant of Perfpective to take care how they apply their compaffes to the defigns, left they fhould make any miftake about the fizes. But I do not fee how this can be avoided by fuch as are ignorant of the art, fince there are no directions given how to apply them, nor neceffary fcales for the purpofe of obtaining the true meafurements. They have given a fcale for the front of their defigns, which ferves to give the height and length of fuch of them as are drawn geometrically in front, but can be of no fervice in finding the width of a piece of work drawn in perfpective; becaufe its apparent breadth is much narrower than the real or geometrical one. And it may be further obferved, that we cannot determine the height of a book-cafe merely by a ground fcale, when the book-cafe is drawn in perfpective, becaufe then the top part recedes or falls back from the front, it is therefore in appearance lower than the real height. For which caufe, if any perfon was to apply the compaffes for the height of a piece of work of the above kind, they muft be totally deceived refpecting its height. Therefore, in the following work, every difficulty of this kind fhall be obviated, and proper directions given how to avoid thefe errors, and to apply the compaffes, fo as to obtain every neceffary dimenfion.

the

the encouragement I meet with from you as fubfcribers; and I hope, on my part, that neither care nor affiduity will be wanting to give you all poffible fatisfaction, and to render the book as complete as is in the power of,

GENTLEMEN,

Your humble Servant,

THOMAS SHERATON.

Excerpts from Part II

As explained in the Publisher's Note on page v, all of Part I and most of Part II of *The Cabinet-Maker and Upholsterer's Drawing-Book* have been omitted in the present edition because they do not pertain directly to furniture (the contents of these omitted portions are listed on Dover pages 11–20). The last three plates (24–26) in Part II, however, do contain illustrations of furniture, and these are included here, along with the portions of the text relating to the furniture illustrations (Dover pages 34–47).

Part III, which is here reprinted in its entirety, then follows on Dover page 49.

EXAMPLE VIII. FIG. 35. Plate XXIV.

How to reprefent a Chair, having its Front parallel to the Picture.

AFTER having made a fcale of feet and inches to proportion each part of the chair by, draw A, the profile of the back and fide rail; and draw B on the right, according to the bevel of the feat; and obferve, to diftinguifh the lines of each chair, one is marked with fmall letters, and the other with numerals.

Let H L be the horizon proportioned by the fcale, about five feet high from G R the ground line. Make *a b* equal to the length of the front; from which draw lines to *s*, the center, which, in general, ought to be perpendicular over the middle of the chair, becaufe it affords the moft eafy and natural view of its back. Next, from *q*, the width of the feat, draw a line to the diftance, here out of the plate, cutting the vifual *a s* at *c*;

8   from

from *c* draw a parallel to *e* at pleafure. Take C D, the bevel of the feat, and place it from *a* to *d*; and from *d* draw a line to *s*, cutting *c e* at *y*, which gives the bevel of the feat. From *a* draw a line through *y*, cutting the horizon at V, which will be the vanifhing point to every line originally parallel to *a y*, the fide rail; take *s* V and place the fame fpace to *v*, which will be the vanifhing point to the other fide of the chair; therefore from *b* draw a line to *v*, cutting at *e*, which forms the feat. For the thicknefs of the back rail, draw a line from *p* to the diftance, as the figure fhews. For the height of the back, raife a perpendicular *a g*, and draw a parallel from *r* to *g*; draw alfo a perpendicular from *y*, and a line from *g* to V will cut it at *f*, determining the height of the back. For the bottom of the back foot, draw a line from *u* to the diftance, cutting a perpendicular from *c* at *w*. From *w* draw a parallel, and from *z* draw a line to the vanifhing point V, cutting at *x*, which will determine the place of the back foot*. How every other part is done, muft be evident from infpecting the figure.

* The reader will perceive that the line from *z* to *x* is not accurately drawn, for the engraver did not follow his copy, otherwife the line would have touched the bottom of the back foot tending to V, which the learner may prove, by drawing a line from *z* to V. This inftance may ferve to fhew the trouble there is with engravers, who in general are totally ignorant of perfpective.

R r   EXAMPLE

EXAMPLE IX. FIG. 36. Plate XXIV.

How to reprefent a Chair having its Front perpendicular to the Picture.

IN this example the fame ground line, horizon, center, and diftance, is ufed as in the preceding; therefore let the fpace 7, 1, be equal to the length of the chair front. From 7 draw a line to *s*, and from 1 draw a line to the diftance, cutting at 16. Make 7, 9 equal to the length of the fide rail, and from 9 draw a line to *s*; make 9, 10 the thicknefs of the back foot, and from 10 draw a line to *s*, as before. Draw a parallel line for the depth of the fide rail, and from 8 draw a line to *s*. Next con-fider how much the back foot fweeps off from the perpendicu-lar, which is equal to the fpace 12, 13, or 2, 22; draw vifuals from each of thefe points, as the example directs. To find the bevel of the fides, take C D and place it from 7 to 5, and from 1 to 3; from which draw lines to the diftance, cutting at 11 and 17; from 11 and 17 draw parallels cutting the vifual 9 *s* at 20 and 18; from 7 draw a line to 20, and from 16 draw one to 18, which will finifh the outline of the feat. Laftly, from 18 and 20 let fall perpendiculars, cutting at 24, 25; from which draw parallels to the vifual 13 *s*, which gives the bottom of

8   each

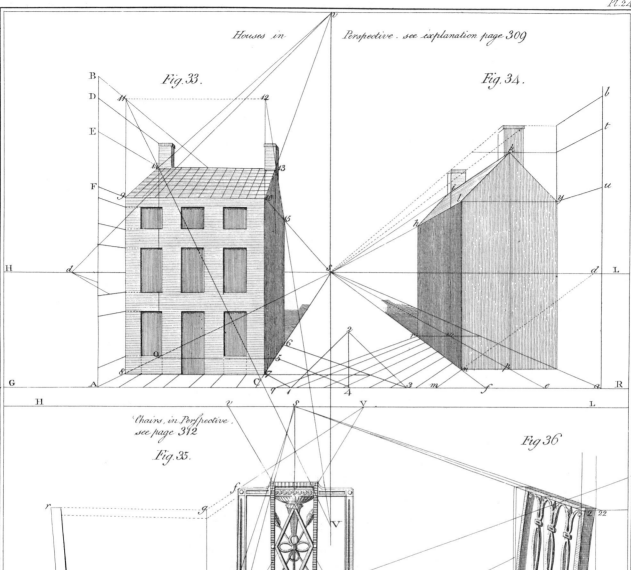

Pl.24.

Houses in   Perspective. see explanation page 309

Fig.33.   Fig.34.

Chairs, in Perspective.
see page 312

Fig.35.   Fig 36

1 Foot

T.Sheraton del

Published by T.Sheraton, Aug. 1, 1792.

G.Terry Sc

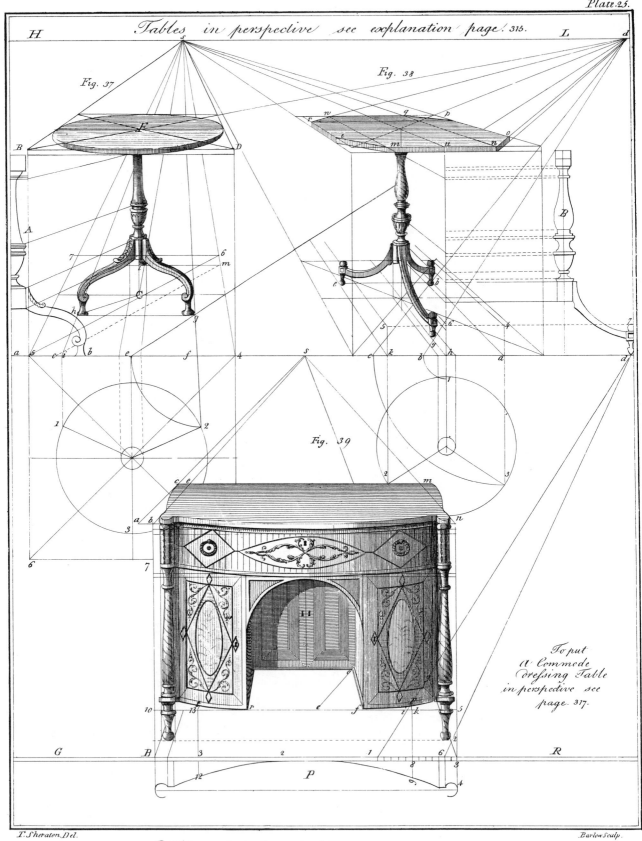

Tables in perspective see explanation page 315.

Fig. 37

Fig. 38

Fig. 39

To put
a Commode
dressing Table
in perspective see
page 317.

T. Sheraton. Del.

Barlow Sculp.

Published as the Act directs. by T. Sheraton. October 1792.

each back foot; and for every other particular, a little reflection and obfervation will be fufficient.

EXAMPLE X.   FIG. 37.   Plate XXV.

*How to reprefent a round Table in Perfpective, having two of
its Claws in front parallel to the Picture.*

DRAW a profile of the pillar and claw, as at A.   Take *a b*,
the fpring of the claw, from the center of the pillar, and with
it defcribe a circle 1, 2, 3; divide the circle into three equal
parts, fo as to fuit the intended pofition of the claws, as 1, 2, 3;
draw from thefe perpendicular lines to *i, e, f.*   Reprefent a
fquare 4, 5, 6, 7, equal to the diameter of the top; draw the diagonals and diameters of the fquare, and from *i f* draw vifuals
to *s*; from C, the center, draw a perpendicular for the pillar;
and having determined the height of the table at B D, from B D
reprefent a circle for the top, as has been taught in page 289,
fee Fig. 23.   Next find the place of the claws; for which make
f e equal *f* 2, and from *e* draw a line to the diftance *d*, cutting at
g; from *g* draw a parallel to *h*, for the other claw.   To find the
place of the back claw; extend the compaffes from *e* to 3, and
make 4 *c* equal to it; from *c* draw a line to the diftance, cutting
at *m*; and from *m* draw a parallel to *i*, which will be the place

R r 2   of

of the claw. For the different parts of the pillar, draw from the profile lines to the diftance, cutting the perpendicular C F, as the figure fhews. It now remains for every part to be finifhed by a good hand and eye accompanied with judgment, as no other rules can be of any fervice in cafes of this fort.

EXAMPLE XI. FIG. 38. Plate XXV.

How to reprefent an octagon Table having one of its Claws in Front perpendicular to the Picture.

DRAW the profile of the pillar and claw, as at B; and, as in the other example, take the fpring of the foot or claw from the center of the pillar, and with it defcribe a circle, and mark out the place of the claws at 1, 2, 3. Draw 1, 2, 3 up to the ground line, and produce 1 up to *u*, for the height of the table. Reprefent a fquare both at top and bottom, and draw the diagonals, finding the center for the pillar. Draw now the dotted lines from the profile to *k u* the perpendicular, and where they cut draw lines to *s*, the center of the picture, cutting the center of the pillar for each refpective moulding. Next find the fituation of the claws; having drawn lines from *k, h, a,* to *s*, make *h h* equal *h i*; and from *h* draw a line to the diftance, cutting at *g*, which will be the place for the firft claw. Make *a c* equal *a* 3, and from *c* draw a line to *d*, as before, cutting at *b*; from *b*

draw

draw a parallel to *e*, then will *b e* be the place of the two other claws. From 5 and 4, produced from 7, the height of the toe, draw lines to *s*; and from *e* and *b* raife perpendiculars cutting thefe, which will be the height of the toes of the back claws. Laftly, we here fuppofe the top to be an irregular octagon, wherefore let *m n* be equal to four of its fides; draw from *n m* lines to *s*, from *n* draw a line to *d*, cutting at *o*; from *o* draw a parallel to *t*; finding the oppofite angle, draw *m t*; and from the diftance draw a line through *w*, cutting at *r*; from *r* draw a parallel to *p*; and draw *p q*, which will finifh the octagon for the top.

Example XII. Fig. 39. Plate XXV.

To put a Commode Table in Perfpective, having its Front parallel to the Picture.

Observe, the ground line for the tables is here ufed as the horizon for the commode.

Make *s d* half the diftance, for want of room on the plate, and make G R the ground line. Draw then the plan P of the front, according to the intended fcale. And, in cutting of each vifual line, ufe one half of a foot inftead of a whole one; becaufe only half the whole diftance is ufed. Therefore, having drawn

drawn the vifuals $3s$, Bs, draw a line from 1 foot on the fcale line to d the diftance, cutting at g; then will $3g$ reprefent a line two feet long, equal to the breadth of the commode. From g raife a perpendicular, cutting at m, finding the apparent width of the top; draw 5, 10 parallel and equal to the height of the foot and bottom of the commode; draw parallel lines, alfo, for the partition below and above the drawer, and for the top, as fhewn by the figure. Proceed now to find the place of the feet and the fweep of the front: for the feet take half 3, 4, and from 3 place it to 6; from which draw a line to d, cutting at 2; from 2 draw a parallel cutting Bs, for the other foot. Find now two points by which to direct the fweep of the front thus: draw perpendicular lines from the plan at 9, 12, and from 13, i, k, where they cut, draw lines to s; then take half 8, 9 and place it from k to i; and from i draw a line to d, cutting at p, finding a point for the curve; from p draw a parallel to t, finding the oppofite point, which will be fufficient for the whole. Laftly, for the recefs draw vifuals from r f, and, fuppofing the recefs to be a foot deep from front, make e f equal half a foot on the fcale; draw from e a line to d, cutting at o; and from o draw a parallel to the oppofite vifual. Every other thing may be learned by obfervation, without going through a minute detail of every particular, which would become an exceeding dry tafk indeed.

EXAMPLE

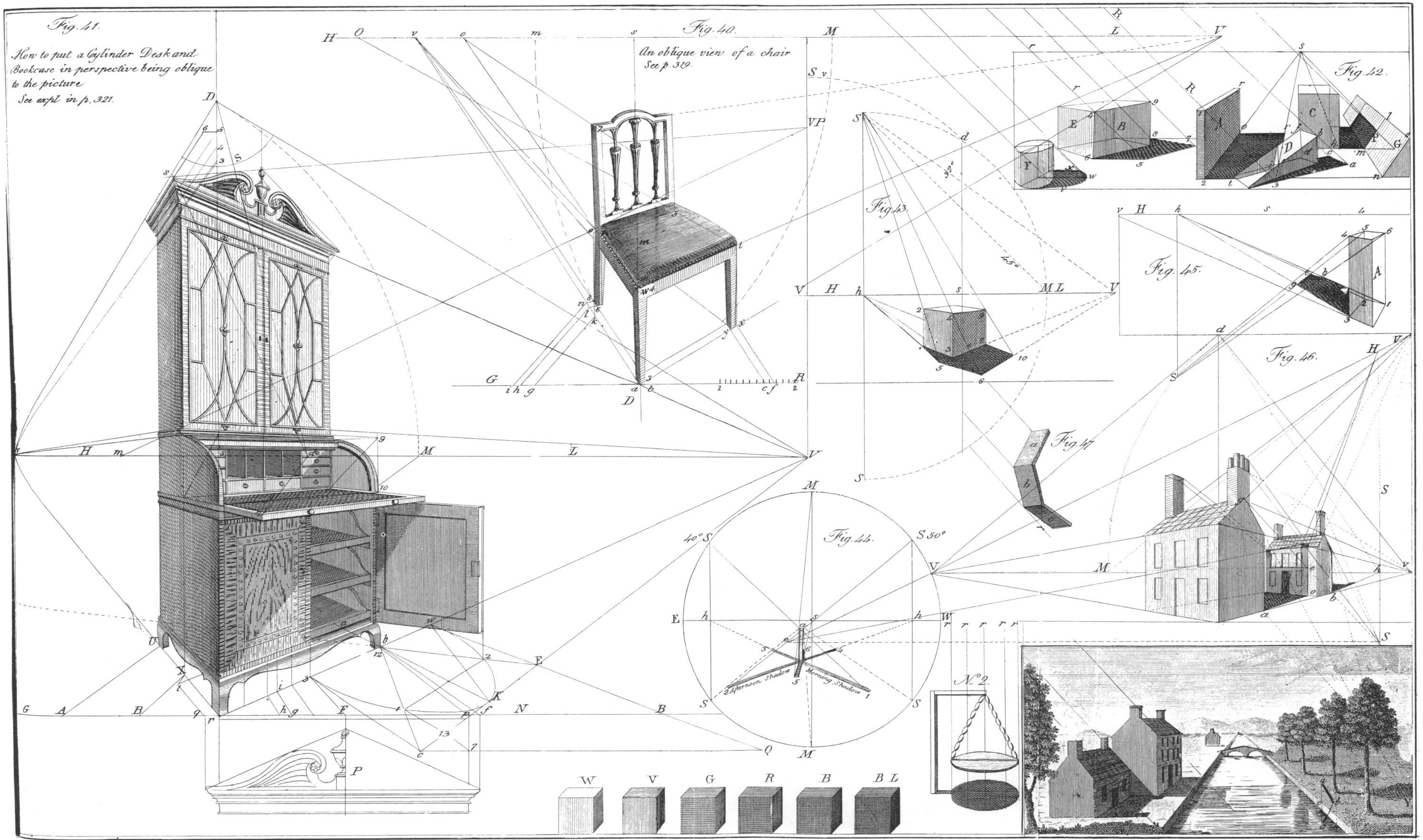
Fig. 41.
How to put a Cylinder Desk and Bookcase in perspective being oblique to the picture
See expl in p. 321.
Fig. 40.
An oblique view of a chair
See p. 319.
Fig. 42.
Fig. 43.
Fig. 44.
Afternoon Shadow
Morning Shadow
Fig. 45.
Fig. 46.
Fig. 47.
No. 2.
W
V
G
R
B
BL

Sheraton, del.
Published as the Act directs by T. Sheraton Novr. 20th. 1792.
Barlow sculp.

EXAMPLE XIII.   Fig. 40.   Plate XXVI.

How to reprefent a Chair obliquely fituated to the Picture.

IN the two former examples of chairs in perfpective, the firft of thefe had its front parallel to the picture, which is the moft ufual way of reprefenting a chair when it is wanted to be viewed as a pattern; for the back being parallel alfo, it gives the moft natural and diftinct view of the banifter and all its parts. The fecond is put with its front perpendicular to the picture, which is a pofition wanted in the reprefentation of internal views of rooms or paffages: and this third example being put oblique, is confidered by painters moft picturefque or fuitable for a picture, in which cafe the pattern of the chair is not much regarded, only its unformal fituation fuiting to the fubject and circumftances of the defign. In this example I fhall therefore confider myfelf as offering fome affiftance to the painter, as well as in a few other inftances in this book.

Obferve, that the vanifhing points *v* V, and meafuring points *m* M, of this example, are all found by laying the diftance downwards to D, for want of room on the plate, and which needs not here be explained, after what has been done

in

in problem VI. page 236, as it makes no difference whether the distance be above or below the horizon. Therefore proceed in confidering G R the ground line, drawn parallel to the horizon H L; on G R make a fcale of inches to proportion every part by. Make *a f* equal to the original length of the front, which in parlour chairs is generally 21 or 22 inches; and let *a g* be equal to the width of the feat from the infide of the back to the front, commonly 16 inches. As *a* is confidered the neareft angle to the picture, from *a* raife a perpendicular at pleafure, on which the original heights of each part muft be laid, as from *a* to *m*, for the height of the feat rail, about 16 inches without the ftuffing. From *a* and *w* draw vifuals tending to V and *v*. From *f c* draw lines to *m*, cutting at *x y*; from *b* do the fame, cutting at 3; from which points raife perpendiculars for each foot. Next, from *g* draw a line to M, cutting at *k*; from which raife a perpendicular to *o*; from *o* draw a line to V; and from 4, the infide of the front foot, whofe thicknefs is fuppofed equal to the bevel of the fide rail, draw a line to *v*, cutting at *p*; then from *w*, the outfide of the foot, draw a line to *p*, produced till it cut the horizon at *o*, which will be the vanifhing point to every line originally parallel to the fide *w p*. From *v* extend the compaffes to *o*, which lay on to O, and O will be the vanifhing point to all lines parallel to the other fide *t* 5. Therefore, from *t* draw a line to O, which will cut at 5, completing the form of the feat. On the perpendicular line from *w*,

lay

lay on 21 inches for the height of the back, and direct a line to
o, and through p draw a perpendicular at pleasure for the joint
of the side rail. Next consider how much the back foot pitches,
which in this example is equal $b\,g$, and $b\,i$ is for the thickness
of the toe. From these draw lines to M, cutting at k, l, n; and
from k, l, n, draw lines to V, which will cut the visual $b\,v$ in
the place for the toe at 8, 6; from 6 raise a perpendicular cutting at 7, and from 7 direct a line to V, for the top rail; and
how the rest is performed must be obvious from what has already been said and done.

EXAMPLE XIV. FIG. 41. Plate XXVI.

*To put a Cylinder Desk and Book-case in Perspective, having its
Front oblique to the Picture.*

DRAW first an elevation of the cornice and pediment, and
proportion the pediment according to Fig. 36, Plate V. by dividing half the length of the cornice into nine equal parts, of
which take four for the pitch. Take one of these parts for the
height of the pedestal, and the remaining three for the vase.
Draw lines up to the ground line at q, r, F, p, f, and the vanish-
ing points having been already found, draw from r lines tending to each; from r, the nearest angle of the book-case, raise a

S f   perpendicular

perpendicular at pleafure, on which the feveral heights muft be laid. From r to A lay on the depth of the lower part, and direct a line to M, cutting at U, and make A B the depth of the book-cafe, and draw a line as before, cutting at X, from which raife a perpendicular. In the fame manner draw lines from F p, tending to m, and cutting at 3, 12, for the length and center of the book-cafe. The feveral original heights for the defk part, doors, and cornice, muft now be placed on the perpendicular, from which lines muft be drawn to each vanifhing point. And here we muft obferve, that as the neareft angle of the book-cafe comes forward to the picture *, confequently the flider is on this fide of it. To project the flider in this cafe, a vanifhing point muft be found, from which, if a line be directed it will pafs through the diagonal of any fquare. Thus: on D, the diftance, fweep the arch S, and bifect it at S, and through S direct a line to the horizon, cutting at d on the fmall drawers; lay from r to g a fpace equal to the projection of the flider; and from g direct a line to m, cutting at i; from i raife a perpendicular to y; and from d, the aforefaid vanifhing point, draw a line through y at pleafure; and from v draw a vifual for the end of the flider, cutting at n; from n draw a line to V, and from v draw one through 10, for the other end of the flider. The opening of the door is next to be confidered. It is evident

---

* When any object is reprefented to touch the ground-line, that part which touches it is faid to be in the picture.

that

that a door turning on its hinges muſt deſcribe a ſemicircle, and
therefore if a ſemi is repreſented, whoſe radius is equal to the
breadth of the door, its circumference will determine any open‑
ing that can be propoſed.

To deſcribe the ſemicircle proceed thus.—From the vaniſh‑
point *v* draw a line through *z*, the center of the book-caſe, and
produce it at pleaſure; then from *d*, the vaniſhing point of any
diagonal, draw a line through 12, cutting at C; from C draw a
line to V; and from *v* draw a line through 12, cutting at K;
and from K draw another diagonal to *d*, cutting at *w*; from *v*
draw a line through *w*, cutting at E, and produced to Q, cutting
a parallel from C; from 12 to E draw a diagonal, and if the
door is intended to be opened 45 degrees more than ſquare, pro‑
duce this diagonal, as ſhewn by the dotted line, till it cut the
horizon, and its interſection with it will be the vaniſhing point
for the top and bottom of the door. Divide C Q into ſeven
equal parts, and from one of which at 7 direct a line to *m*, cut‑
ting at 13; and from 13 draw a viſual to *v*, cutting at 1; from
1 draw a viſual to V, cutting the other diagonal at 2; from 2
raiſe a perpendicular for the apparent breadth of the door in this
poſition; and from the laſt mentioned vaniſhing point found
by the dotted line, draw lines for the top and bottom of the
door, by which it may be completed. For the ends of the cy‑
linder we need not ſay any thing, as this is the ſame as in pro‑

S ſ 2

blem

45

blem XXII. therefore we fhall proceed with the cornice and pediment.

Set off the projection $q\,r$ of the cornice at 6, 5, on a parallel line drawn at the full height of the book-cafe, and draw lines to v, and the line 5 will cut the perpendicular raifed from X, and the line 6 will cut a perpendicular at 8, fuppofed to be raifed from t, the miter point of the cornice, which is found by drawing a line from d, the vanifhing point of the diagonal to X, cutting at t; from t direct a line to V, cutting at a; and from a raife a perpendicular, which will cut a line drawn from 8 to V, at the other miter point; every other part of the cornice muft be finifhed by the reader's judgment, governed by thefe principles, as it would be impoffible to apply every rule in fuch fmall examples.

Laftly, for the pitch of the pediment, a vanifhing point muft be found, according to the principles in Problem IX. Plate XVI. by drawing a line from m parallel to the pitch line at the elevation P, produced to V P, cutting a perpendicular from V; from 8 draw a line to V P, cutting a perpendicular in the center of the front edge of its cornice; from which draw the other fide of the pediment, which, if produced, would cut a point as much below the horizon as V P is above it. Thefe pitch lines being found, the fcroll pediment may be drawn by hand with

8   fufficient

fufficient accuracy; but if the pediment be a ftraight pitch, then the lines for each moulding muft tend to V P, and to a point as much below the horizon. And I would here obferve, that in drawing after thefe examples, it is not intended that the diftances made ufe of in them fhould be a precedent to the learner. Thefe are chofen to fuit the plate; but the learner having fufficient room on his drawing-board, muft choofe his diftance to give the moft natural and pleafing effect to his drawing, by the rules already laid down.

In thefe examples almoft every difficult part of perfpective is introduced, and it is prefumed that, after the learner has made himfelf fully mafter of them, nothing will occur in practice that can give him much trouble, efpecially if he be properly acquainted with the fhort theory that has been given. However I am fully perfuaded, that no cabinet-maker or upholfterer will ever want to practife more; and, if I am not miftaken, there are but very few painters who are at the trouble of practifing fo much. But if the reader's profeffion or neceffities fhould require him to extend his fkill in this art further than what has been advanced in this treatife, I will freely refer him to Mr. Malton's complete Treatife, from which, it is here gratefully acknowledged, I have received confiderable affiftance.

CABINET-MAKER AND UPHOLSTERER'S

DRAWING-BOOK.

PART III.

CONTAINING A DESCRIPTION OF THE SEVERAL PIECES OF FURNITURE. 1. OF THE USE AND STYLE OF FINISHING EACH PIECE. 2. GENERAL REMARKS ON THE MANUFACTURING PART OF SUCH PIECES AS MAY REQUIRE IT. 3. AN EXPLANATION OF THE PERSPECTIVE LINES WHERE THEY ARE INTRODUCED. TO WHICH IS ADDED, A CORRECT AND QUICK METHOD OF CONTRACTING AND ENLARGING CORNICES OR OTHER MOULDINGS OF ANY GIVEN PATTERN.

INTRODUCTION.

THE defign of this Part of the Book is intended to exhibit the prefent tafte of furniture, and at the fame time to give the workman fome affiftance in the manufacturing part of it.

I am fenfible, however, that feveral perfons who have already encouraged the work, will not want any help of this

8   nature;

nature; but it is prefumed many will who are not much converfant in the bufinefs, and who have had no opportunity of feeing good pieces of furniture executed.

For the advantage of fuch, it is hoped that the experienced workman will exercife candour and patience in reading the inftructions intended, not for himfelf, but for thofe now mentioned.

There are few but what may, with propriety, reflect on their own paft ignorance, even in things which afterwards become exceeding fimple and eafy by a little practice and experience. Such a reflection ought, therefore, to promote both candour and good nature in the minds of proficients, when they read the documents neceffary to young beginners. And yet, I hope, it may be faid, without arrogance, that it is probable the experienced workman may derive fome information from the fubfequent remarks, when it is confidered that they are made not merely from the knowledge and experience I have myfelf of the bufinefs, but from that of other good workmen.

In converfing with cabinet-makers, I find no one individual equally experienced in every job of work. There are certain pieces made in one fhop which are not manufactured in another, on which account the beft of workmen are fometimes

ftrangers

ftrangers to particular pieces of furniture. For this reafon I have made it my bufinefs to apply to the beft workmen in different fhops, to obtain their affiftance in the explanation of fuch pieces as they have been moft acquainted with. And, in general, my requeft has been complied with, from the generous motive of making the book as generally ufeful as poffible.

The methods therefore propofed, and the remarks made, may be depended on by thofe who have not yet had an opportunity of feeing the different pieces executed.

This is an attempt which has not yet been made in any book of cabinet defigns, except a very few flight hints; and, though it muft be acknowledged by every impartial mind as highly ufeful, and even in fome cafes abfolutely neceffary, yet I am apprehenfive it will not meet with the approbation of thofe who wifh to hoard up their own knowledge to themfelves, left any fhould fhare in the advantage arifing from it. In fome inftances it may be neceffary for a man to keep knowledge to himfelf, as his own property, and upon which his bread may depend; but I do not fee any impropriety in perfons of the fame branch informing each other. In trades where their arts depend on fecrets, it is right for men to keep them from ftrangers; but the art of cabinet-making depends fo much on practice, and requires fo many tools, that a ftranger cannot

Y y
fteal

51

steal it. But in every branch there are found men who love to keep their inferiors of the same profession in ignorance, that themselves may have an opportunity of triumphing over them. From such I expect no praise, but the reverse. Their pride will not suffer them to encourage any work which tends to make others as wise as themselves; and therefore it is their fixed resolution to despise and pour contempt upon every attempt of this kind, in proportion as it is likely to succeed. But those I will leave to themselves as unworthy of notice, who only live to love themselves, but not to assist others.

Here I would beg leave to observe, that it is natural for every man under a heavy burden to pour out his complaint to the first sympathizing friend he meets with. If the reader be one of these, I will pour out mine, by informing him of the difficult task I have had to please all, and to suit the various motives which different persons have for encouraging a publication like this.

I find some have expected such designs as never were seen, heard of, nor conceived in the imagination of man; whilst others have wanted them to suit a broker's shop, to save them the trouble of borrowing a bason-stand to shew to a customer. Some have expected it to furnish a country wareroom, to avoid the expence of making up a good bureau, and double chest of drawers,

drawers, with canted corners, &c. and though it is difficult to conceive how thefe different qualities could be united in a book of fo fmall a compafs, yet, according to fome reports, the broker himfelf may find his account in it, and the country mafter will not be altogether difappointed; whilft others fay many of the defigns are rather calculated to fhew what may be done, than to exhibit what is or has been done in the trade. According to this, the defigns turn out to be on a more general plan than what I intended them, and anfwer, beyond my expectation, the above various defcriptions of fubfcribers. However, to be ferious, it was my firft plan, and has been my aim through the whole, to make the book in general as permanently ufeful as I could, and to unite with ufefulnefs the tafte of the times; but I could never expect to pleafe all in fo narrow a compafs: for to do this, it would be neceffary to compofe an entire book for each clafs of fubfcribers, and after all there would be fomething wanting ftill.

Y y 2   A DE

A DESCRIPTION OF THE SEVERAL PIECES OF FURNITURE.

Of the Univerſal Table. Plate XXV. *of the Cabinet Deſigns.*

THE uſe of this piece is both to anſwer the purpoſe of a breakfaſt and a dining-table. When both the leaves are ſlipped under the bed, it will then ſerve as a breakfaſt-table; when one leaf is out, as in this view, it will accommodate five perſons as a dining-table; and if both are out, it will admit of eight, being near ſeven feet long, and three feet ſix inches in width.

The drawer is divided into ſix boxes at each ſide, as in the plan, and are found uſeful for different ſorts of tea and ſugar, and ſometimes for notes, or the like. In this drawer is a ſlider lined with green cloth to write on. The ſtyle of finiſhing them is plain and ſimple, with ſtraight tapered legs, ſocket caſtors, and an aſtrugal round the frame.

Of the manufaƈturing Part.

This table ſhould be made of particularly good and well-ſeaſoned mahogany, as a great deal depends upon its not being

8   liable

liable to caſt. In the beſt kind of theſe tables the tops are framed and pannelled; the bed into two pannels, and the flaps each into one, with a white ſtring round each pannel to hide the joint. The framing is three inches broad, and mitered at the corners; and the pannels are ſometimes glued up in three thickneſſes, the middle piece being laid with the grain acroſs, and the other two lengthways of the pannel, to prevent its warping. The pannels are, however, often put in of ſolid ſtuff, without this kind of gluing.

When the pannels are tongued into the framing, and the miters are fitted to, the tops ſhould ſtand to ſhrink as much as poſſible before they are glued for good. There are different methods of ſecuring the miters of the framing. Some make ſimply a ſtraight miter, which they can ſhoot with a plane; after which they put a couple of wooden pins in. Others, again, having fitted the miters to by a plane, they ſlip in a tenon. But the ſtrongeſt method is to mortice and tenon the miters to-gether, having a ſquare joint at the under, and a miter joint at the upper ſide. This method, however, is the moſt tedious of the three, and where the price will not allow of much time, the above methods are more ready, and, if managed with care, are ſufficiently ſtrong. In gluing the miters, it will be proper, firſt, to glue on the outſide of each miter a piece of deal in the ſhape of a wedge, which will take a hand-ſcrew, ſo that when

they

they are putting together, the glue may be brought out, and the miters made clofe.

The frame, as fhewn in the plan, is made exactly fquare, either of faulty mahogany, or of wainfcot veneered. In making this frame a box is formed at each end, about three inches in width, containing two fliders apiece, which run paft each other in the faid box, as fhewn in the plan. In the bottom of each box are put two pieces, with plough grooves in them, and raking contrary to each other. In the line N O, on thofe raking pieces the fliders run, and are ftopped from coming too far out by a pin fixed in the under edge of the flider; which pin runs in the plough grooves already mentioned, denoted in the plan by a dark line. The raking line of the fliders is found by taking the width of the flap, as from S to M, and making the line in-cline in that width equal to the thicknefs of the flap. This may be eafily underftood, by placing a rule from the outer point M of the flap, to S the inner point, which then will be parallel to the raking line. The fliding pieces being in a right line their whole length at the under edge, of courfe their upper edge muft be bevelled off, fo that when they are drawn fully out, they may be even, and in an exact line with the top of the frame.

The frame and tops being thus prepared, they are con-nected together by an iron fcrew and nut, as at A, which is

about

about the fubftance of a bed-fcrew. This fcrew is jointed into a plate, which plate is let into the under fide of the bed, level with it; though I have defcribed it at A with its thicknefs out, merely that the plate might be fhewn. At B the bed A is reprefented on the frame, and the iron fcrew paffing through the rail of the table, is confined to its place by the nut, which is let into the under edge of the rail by a center-bit. And obferve, in making this center-bit hole for the nut, it muft be funk deeper than its thicknefs, that the bed may have liberty to rife a little, and fo give place to the flaps when they are wanted to be pufhed in. It muft be noticed alfo, from the plan of the frame, that there is a middle piece, about five inches broad, and of equal thicknefs with the flaps, fcrewed down to the frame with four fcrews at each end. This middle piece anfwers three purpofes; it fecures the frame, ftops the flaps when they are pufhed in, and prevents the fliding pieces from tilting.

Before the bed is finally fixed to its place, there muft be four pieces of green cloth let into the under fide of it, to prevent the flaps from rubbing as they flide under. Upon the edges of the flaps a hollow is worked all round, leaving a quarter of an inch fquare, for no other purpofe than to take off the clumfy appearance of the two thickneffes when the flaps are

under

under the bed. At the under fide of the flaps muft be goged out finger-holes, to draw them out by.

The drawer is next to be confidered, which is fometimes made with two fronts, and to draw out both ways, as in the plan. On each front of the drawer is a lock, for the conveni-ence of fecuring it at either end; for in cafe one flap be drawn out, then the drawer can be locked or pulled out at the contrary front, without the trouble of pufhing the flap in to come at the drawer.

The covers of each box before mentioned, may have an oval of dark wood, and the alphabet cut out of ivory or white wood let into them, as in the plan; or they may be white ovals and black letters; the ufe of which is to diftinguifh the contents of each box.

Laftly, the flider to write on is made exactly half the infide length of the drawer; fo that when it is pufhed home to either front, there is immediate accefs to fix of the boxes.

And here I would obferve, that fometimes the flaps of thefe tables have round corners, but they do not anfwer the bed fo well when they are in. And, to fave expence, the tops have been found to anfwer the purpofe in folid wood, without being framed.

framed. When they are made in this manner, particular regard should be had to placing the heart side of the wood outward, which naturally draws round of itself, and may therefore be expected to keep true, notwithstanding its unfavourable situation.

N. B. The heart side of a board is easily known by planing the end, and observing the circular traces of the grain, which always tend outwards.

The Perspective Lines explained.

In making designs in perspective, the first thing to be attended to is the scale of feet and inches, by which to proportion the different parts to each other, to determine the height of the horizon, and the distance of the picture.

Having made the scale, take from it about five feet six for the height of the horizon at H L. On this line place the point of sight, so as to give the most favourable view of the design, as at *s*. Next lay on the distance, which is here out of the plate, and being equal to the space *s a*, agrees to the rule for choosing a distance contained in page 281. Draw *a b* perpendicular to the ground line, and from *a* draw a line to the point of sight *s*.

Z z

Next

Next confider how much the top projects over the frame, and as much as this is, lay it from *a* towards *e*, as the firft line fhews, which is directed to the point of diftance. Where this cuts the aforefaid line drawn to *s*, raife a perpendicular anfwering to *a b*. From *b* lay on the fpace *b d*, for the depth of the framing; and from *d* draw a line as before to *s*; and from where the line cuts the fecond perpendicular, draw a parallel for the under edge of the framing. On a parallel line from *b*, lay on the dimenfions of the bed and flap; and from thefe draw lines to *s*, as the defign fhews. Now, as the bed of the table is fquare, nothing more is wanted to find its apparent width than to draw a line from *o* to the diftance which cuts at the oppofite angle; and through this angle draw *r t* parallel, which completes the out-line of the top.

To find the place of the drawer and the boxes in it, proceed thus.—On the ground line make *a e* equal to the whole fpace, from the drawer in the plan to the projection of the middle piece acrofs the frame. Alfo make *e b* the whole length of the drawer, and *g f* the divifions for the boxes. From each of which draw lines to the diftance, cutting at 1, 2, 3, 4; from which draw parallels to 7, 6, 5, 8. Again, from 7 raife a perpendicular, and make *k b*, on *k m*, equal to the height of the drawer; from *b* draw a line to *s*; and from *m*, the height of the covers of each box, do the fame. Laftly, from 6, 5, &c.

8   raife

A Universal Table

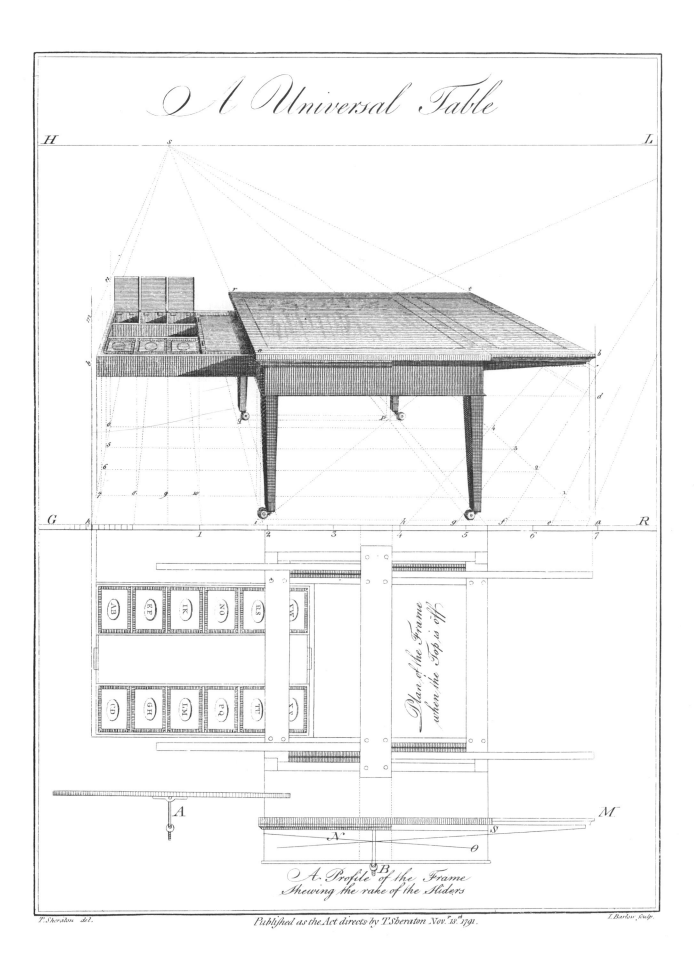

Plan of the Frame
when the Top is off

A Profile of the Frame
Shewing the rake of the Sliders

T. Sheraton del.   Published as the Act directs by T. Sheraton Nov.r 18.th 1791.   T. Barlow Sculp.

Plate 26

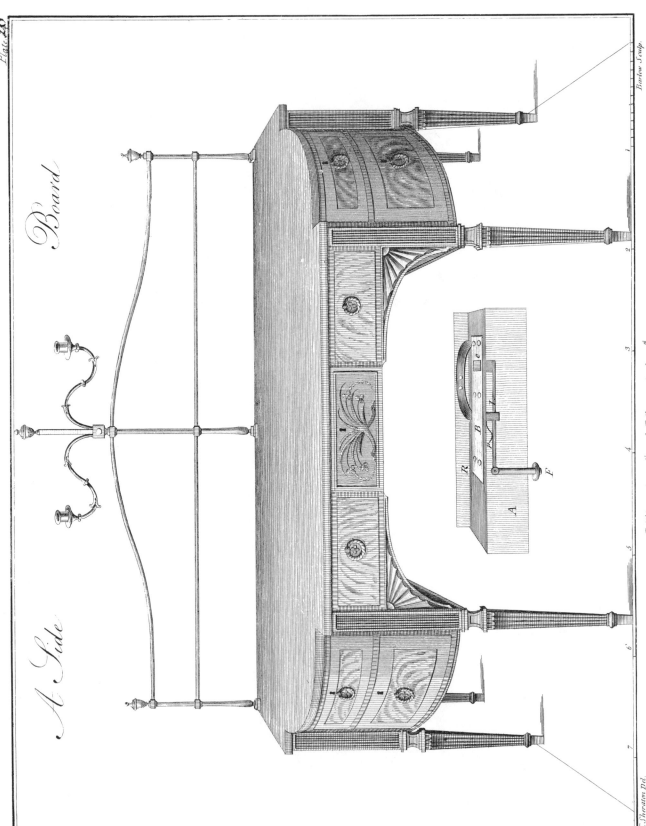

Board

A Side

T. Sheraton. Del.

Published as the Act directs, by T. Sheraton. October 29.ᵗʰ 1792.

Barlow Sculp.

raife perpendiculars, which will cut *b s* in the place for the boxes, and at *n* for the height of the covers. How every other thing is done, muſt be obvious from infpection.

Of the Sideboard Tables, Plate XXVI. *and* XXIX. *and of Tables of this Kind in general.*

THE ſideboard in Plate XXVI. has a braſs rod to it, which is uſed to ſet large diſhes againſt, and to ſupport a couple of candle or lamp branches in the middle, which, when lighted, give a very brilliant effect to the ſilver ware. The branches are each of them fixed in one ſocket, which ſlides up and down on the ſame rod to any height, and fixed any where by turning a ſcrew. Theſe rods have ſometimes returns at each end of the ſideboard; and ſometimes they are made ſtraight, the whole length of the ſideboard, and have a narrow ſhelf in the middle, made of full half-inch mahogany, for the purpoſe of ſetting ſmaller diſhes on, and ſometimes ſmall ſilver ware.

The right-hand drawer, as in common, contains the celleret, which is often made to draw out ſeparate from the reſt. It is partitioned and lined with lead, to hold nine or ten wine bottles, as in Plate XXIX.

Z z 2

The

The drawer on the left is generally plain, but fometimes divided into two; the back divifion being lined with baize to hold plates, having a cover hinged to enclofe the whole. The front divifion is lined with lead, fo that it may hold water to wafh glaffes; which may be made to take out, or have a plug-hole to let off the dirty water. This left-hand drawer is, however, fometimes made very fhort, to give place to a pot-cupboard behind, which opens by a door at the end of the fideboard. This door is made to hide itfelf in the end rail as much as poffible, both for look and fecrecy. For which reafon a turn-buckle is not ufed, but a thumb-fpring, which catches at the bottom of the door, and has a communication through the rail, fo that by a touch of the finger the door flies open, owing to the refiftance of a common fpring fixed to the rabbet which the door falls againft, as is denoted by the figure A. F is for the finger, B is the brafs plate let into the rail, L is the lever, p is the fpring that preffes the lever upwards, and c is the end of it which catches the under edge of the door as it paffes over it and ftrikes into a plate with a hole in it, and s is the fpring fcrewed to the rabbet which throws the door out when F is pufhed upwards.

But the reader muft here obferve, that the fhape of this fideboard will not admit of a cupboard of this fort in the end rail.

rail. Thofe which are fquare at the ends, and only a little fhaped in front, are fitteft for this purpofe.

In large circular fideboards, the left-hand drawer has fometimes been fitted up as a plate-warmer, having a rack in the middle to ftick the plates in, and lined with ftrong tin all round, and on the underfide of the fideboard top, to prevent the heat from injuring it. In this cafe the bottom of the drawer is made partly open, under which is fixed a fmall narrow drawer, to contain a heater, which gives warmth to the plates the fame as in a pedeftal.

In fpacious dining-rooms the fideboards are often made without drawers of any fort, having fimply a rail a little ornamented, and pedeftals with vafes at each end, which produce a grand effect. One pedeftal is ufed as a plate-warmer, and is lined with tin; the other as a pot-cupboard, and fometimes it contains a celleret for wine. The vafes are ufed for water for the ufe of the butler, and fometimes as knife-cafes. They are fometimes made of copper japanned, but generally of mahogany.

There are other fideboards for fmall dining-rooms, made without either drawers or pedeftals; but have generally a wine-cooper to ftand under them, hooped with brafs, partitioned and lined with lead, for wine bottles, the fame as the above-mentioned celleret drawers.

The

The fideboard in Plate XXIX. fhews two patterns, one at each end. That on the left is intended to have four marble fhelves at each end, inclofed by two backs, and open in front. Thefe fhelves are ufed in grand fideboards to place the fmall filver ware on. The pattern on the right is intended to have legs turned the whole length, or rounded as far as the framing and turned below it, with carved leaves and flutes. The divifion beyond the celleret-drawer is meant for a pot-cupboard.

It is not ufual to make fideboards hollow in front, but in fome circumftances it is evident that advantages will arife from it. If a fideboard be required nine or ten feet long, as in fome noblemen's houfes, and if the breadth of it be in proportion to the length, it will not be eafy for a butler to reach acrofs it. I therefore think, in this cafe, a hollow front would obviate the difficulty, and at the fame time have a very good effect, by taking off part of the appearance of the great length of fuch a fideboard. Befides, if the fideboard be near the entering door of the dining-room, the hollow front will fometimes fecure the butler from the joftles of the other fervants.

Of

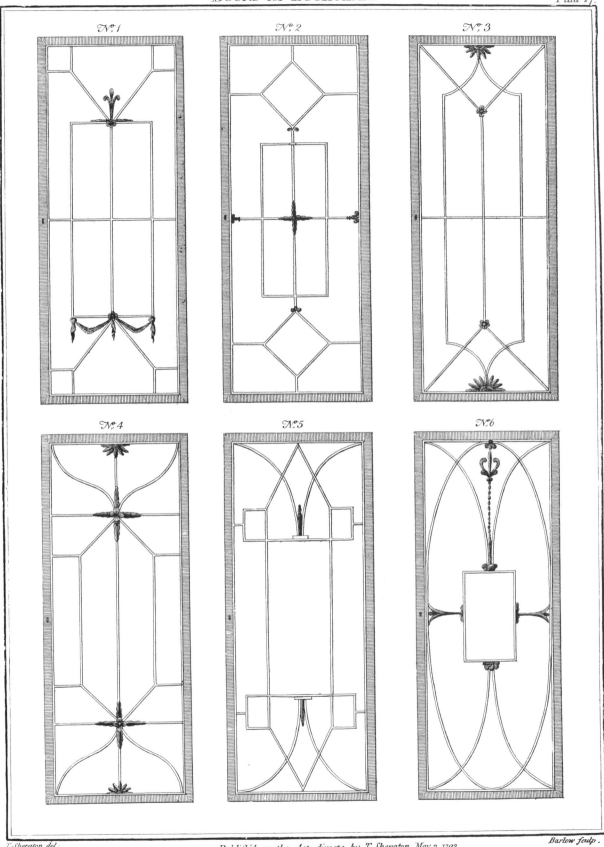

T. Sheraton del:

Publish'd as the Act directs by T. Sheraton, May 3, 1792.

Barlow sculp.

Of *the Perſpective Lines.*

HAVING drawn the plan and adjuſted the height of the horizon by the ſcale, as was mentioned in the univerſal table, repreſent a parallelogram *a, b, c, d,* equal to the length and breadth
of the table; and from every part of the plan draw lines up to
the ground line, and from the ground line direct theſe to the
point of ſight. Take from the plan the ſpace M N, and place it
from 1 to 2; and from 2 direct a line to the point of diſtance, cutting a point next to *y;* from which point draw a parallel for the
place of the front legs. In like manner take the other dimen-
ſions from the plan to find every other correſpondent point in
the repreſentation. To find the repreſentation of the hollow and
round fronts, conſult the treatiſe on perſpective in pages 294 and
295, together with the lines here ſhewn as hints, and it is preſum-
ed that the learner will not be at any loſs in drawing ſuch a table.

Of *the Book-caſe Doors.* Plate XXVII. and XXIX.

IN the execution of theſe doors, the candid and ingenious
workman may exerciſe his judgment, both by varying ſome
parts of the figures, and taking other parts entirely away, when
the door is thought to have too much work.

No. 1,

No. 1, in Plate XXVII. might do for a plain door, if the ornament and fquare part in the middle were taken away.

No. 2 might alfo have the fquare in the middle taken away, and look very well.

No. 4 may have the upright and horizontal bars away, and No. 5 the fmall fquares; and at each angle of the hexagon the ftraight bar might be carried through to the frame.

With refpect to No. 6, it may be ufeful to fay fomething of the method of making it, as well as of fome of thofe in Plate XXIX.

The firft thing to be done, is to draw, on a board, an oval of the full length and breadth of the door. Then take half the oval on the fhort diameter and glue on blocks of deal at a little diftance from each other, to form a caul; then, on the fhort diameter, glue on a couple of blocks, one to ftop the ends of the veneer with at the time of gluing, and the other, being bevelled off, ferves to force the joints of the veneer clofe, and to keep all faft till fufficiently dry. Obferve, the half oval is formed by the blocks of the fize of the aftragal, and not the rabbet; therefore confider how broad a piece of veneer will make the aftragals for one door, or for half a door. For a whole door, which

takes

takes eight quarter ovals, it will require the veneer to be inch and quarter broad, allowing for the thicknefs of a fafh faw to cut them off with. Veneers of this breadth may, by proper management, be glued quite clofe; and if the veneer be ftraight baited, and all of one kind, no joint will appear in the aftragal. Two half ovals thus glued up, will make aftragals for a pair of doors, which, after they are taken out of the cauls and cleaned off a little, may be glued one upon the other, and then glued on a board, to hold them faft for working the aftragals on the edge; which may eafily be done, by forming a neat aftragal in a piece of foft fteel, and fixing it in a notched piece of wood, and then work it as a gage; but before you work it, run on a gage for the thicknefs of the aftragal; and after you have worked the aftragal, cut it off with a fafh faw, by turning the board on which the fweep-pieces are glued on an edge; then having fawn one aftragal off, plane the edge of your ftuff again, and proceed as before.

For gluing up the rabbet part, it muft be obferved, that a piece of dry veneer, equal to the thicknefs of the rabbet, muft be forced tight into the caul; and then proceed as before in gluing two thickneffes of veneer for the rabbet part, which will leave fufficient hiding for the glafs, on fuppofition that the aftragal was glued in five.

3 A

The

The door being framed quite fquare, without any mould-ing at the inner edge, proceed to put in the rabbet pieces. Put, firft, an entire half oval, and fcrew this to the inner edge of the door, and level with it; then jump up the other half oval to it, and fcrew it as before; which completes the center oval. Next, fix the fquare part, having been before mitered round a block, and keyed together; after which, half-lap the other quarter ovals into the entire oval where they crofs each other, and into the fquare part, liping it into the angle of the door; put in the horizontal bars for the leaves to reft on; glue on the aftragals, firft on the entire oval, tying it with pack-thread, to keep it on; then the ftraight one on the edge of the framing, fitting it to the oval; laftly, miter the aftragal on the fquare part, and every other particular will follow of courfe.

With refpect to the doors in Plate XXIX. all of them may be made nearly on the fame principles, at leaft the rabbet parts muft; but the aftragals in No. 1, being all of them portions of circles, fhould be cut out of folid wood, and glued on a deal board and fent to the turner's. The fame may be faid of No. 5, which, in the vafe part, may have a piece of filvered glafs. The center in No. 2, is intended to have a print or painting in it. The fweeps, in No. 6, fhould be cut out of the folid, and worked by a tool. As to fixing any part of the ornaments in-troduced in thefe doors; this is eafily done, by preparing a very

A Secretary and Bookcase

T. Sheraton Del.

Published as the Act directs. by T. Sheraton Dec.r 24.th 1791.

L Barlow sculp.

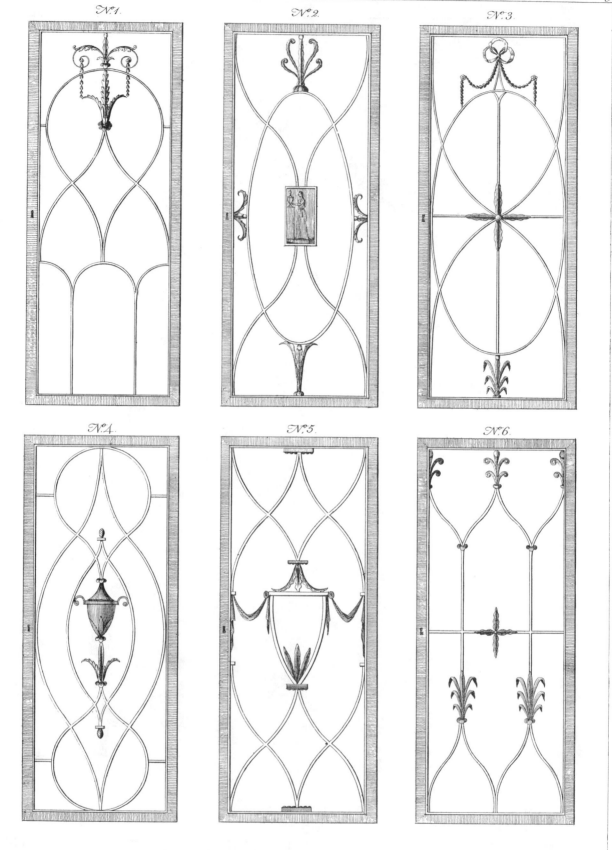

T. Sheraton del

Publish'd as the Act directs, by T. Sheraton.

Terry Sc

very ſtrong gum, which will hold on glaſs almoſt as ſtrong as glue on wood.

Of *the Secretary and Book-caſe.* Plate XXVIII.

THE uſe of this piece is to hold books in the upper part, and in the lower it contains a writing-drawer and clothes-preſs ſhelves. The deſign is intended to be executed in ſatin-wood, and the ornaments japanned. It may, however, be done in mahogany; and in place of the ornaments in the friezes, flutes may be ſubſtituted. The pediment is ſimply a ſegment of a circle, and it may be cut in the form of a fan, with leaves in the center. The vaſes may be omitted to reduce the work; but if they are introduced, the pedeſtal on which the center vaſe reſts is merely a piece of thin wood, with a necking and baſe moulding mitered round, and planted on the pediment. The pilaſters on the book-caſe doors are planted on the frame, and the door hinged as uſual. The top of the pilaſters are made to imitate the Ionic capital.

Of *the Perſpective Lines.*

G R is the ground line, and H L the horizontal line, or height of the eye. Lay on the original heights of the book-

3 A 2

caſe,

cafe, as at *g, h, i, j, k*, &c. and draw a perpendicular line at the angle of the piece, as at A; to which direct parallel lines as fhewn. On the ground line lay *a*, or two feet, for the breadth of the end; and from *b a* direct lines to the diftance, which is here out of the plate, cutting the vifuals at *d e*; from *e* raife a perpendicular, which will determine the front of the book-cafe, provided it be only a foot deep. The perpendicular B is necef-fary, in order to find the perfpective heights of the book-cafe, as fhewn in the figure.

Of the Library Table. Plate XXX.

THIS piece is intended for a gentleman to write on, or to ftand or fit to read at, having defk-drawers at each end, and is generally employed in ftudies or library-rooms. It has already been executed for the Duke of York, excepting the defk-draw-ers, which are here added as an improvement.

The ftyle of finifhing it ought to be in the medium of that which may be termed plain or grand, as neither fuits their fituation. Mahogany is the moft fuitable wood, and the orna-ments fhould be carved or inlaid, what little there is; japanned ornaments are not fuitable, as thefe tables frequently meet with a little harfh ufage.

The

The ftrength, folidity, and effect of brafs mouldings are very fuitable to fuch a defign, when expence is no object. For inftance, the pilafters might be a little funk, or pannelled out, and brafs beads mitered round in a margin, and folid flutes of the fame metal let in. The aftragal which feparates the upper and lower parts might be of brafs; and likewife the edge of the top, together with the patera in the upper pannel, as fhewn on the left hand. The top is lined with leather or green cloth, and the whole refts and is moved on caftors hid by the plinth.

Of the manufacturing Part.

THE top fhould be framed in inch and quarter wainfcot, in the figure of a long hexagon, which beft fuits the fhape of the oval. The pannels, which are tongued in, fhould be of at leaft three quarters hard mahogany, about nine inches fquare, and the ftiles three and an half broad. The top being thus framed of very dry wood, it fhould be planed over, and ftand for fome time at a moderate diftance from a fire, after which it may be glued together, and when hardened it ought to be planed over again, and remain in that ftate till the lower part is finifhed. If thefe methods are not purfued, the pannels will fhrink, and their joints will draw down the leather or cloth, fo that the

figure

figure of the framed top will appear, efpecially when it is lined with leather.

Next, it muft be confidered how to glue on the mahogany on the framing, fo as to make the furbafe moulding appear of folid wood. Firft, plough the four fhort fides of the hexagon, and then tongue in fuitable mahogany lengthways, meeting in a ftraight joint in the center of the top; and, laftly, after the tonguing is dry, glue in ftraight joints pieces on the two long fides of the hexagon, and when dry, the top will be prepared for cutting to its elliptic fhape.

The manner of framing the upper and lower parts of the carcafe muft be learned from the plan.

The upper part, framed in an entire oval, contains the defk-drawers; and, if thought neceffary, two fhort ones may be obtained over the fide niches.

The cupboard part is framed in two, each of which has a niche at the end, and one-third of the fide niches; for the niches are all of them divided into three pannels, and the middle pannels of the fide ones ferve as doors, by which an open paf- fage is gained through the table. There are four cupboards in the whole, divided in the manner fpecified by the dotted lines in

the

the plan, one or two of which may be fitted up in a neft of fmall drawers and letter-holes.

The plinth is framed entire of itfelf, and the bafe-moulding ftands up a little to receive the whole and hide the joint.

In putting on the bafe-moulding there are two or three methods which I would offer as the beft I know of. The frame being made fo thick as to take the projection of the bafe, it muft then be rabbeted out of the folid to receive it. This being done, proceed to glue the bafe in three or four thickneffes, confining them to their place by hand-fcrews, or other devices of that nature; but obferve to let the bafe project further out than the deal plinth, that it may receive the mahogany veneer which is to be glued on lengthways to hide the deal.

After the whole is glued faft to its place, the veneer on the plinth and the bafe muft be cleaned off level with each other. The convex parts of the bafe-moulding may be worked with hollows and rounds; and after thefe are finifhed, the niches fhould be worked down to them, by a tool made on purpofe.

Another method of gluing the bafe-moulding is as follows: —Prepare the inch deal, and make cauls to fit the end and fide niches of the plinth; after which take ftraight baited three-
eighths

eights Spanifh wood, and work the hollow part of the bafe feparate from the torus; then, from quarter ftuff of the fame
kind, cut off flips for the torus; heat the caul well, and both
wet and heat the flips, which will then eafily bend. When the
hollow part is well tempered, and alfo the torus, begin at one
end, and by a thin chip run glue in between them; and as you
go on drive in nails about every inch, having between the nails
and the moulding a thin flip of wainfcot well heated. Obferve
to let the moulding pafs beyond the caul at each end, that a
pack-ftring may be tied to keep it to its place when it is taken
out. The torus may then be worked before it is glued on the
plinth.

A third method is, to make the plinth itfelf the caul, and
firft work the hollows, and foak them in water a whole night.
Next morning take a hand-iron and heat it well, and over the
curved fide of which bend the hollow as near as may be to the
fweep. Having already a ftop fcrewed on the plinth, jump one
end of the moulding to it, and glue as you go on; at the fame
time fixing fmall hand-fcrews to draw it to, or brads may be
put through the fquare part to affift in this bufinefs, if neceffary, for thefe will be covered by the torus. After the hollow
is fufficiently dry, the torus being worked off and well foaked,
and bent round the iron as above, it will glue to the hollow
without the fmalleft difficulty, by firft jumping it againft the

ftop

ſtop before mentioned; and after it is brought pretty near, take another ſtop and ſcrew it againſt the end of the torus, which will draw it down without further trouble. Theſe two methods are founded on experiment; for, at my requeſt, it was performed by ſome cabinet-makers to my full ſatisfaction; therefore, ſhould either of theſe methods fail in the hands of any, it muſt be owing to ſome defect in the management.

Of the Perſpective Lines.

DRAW firſt a plan of the whole, and make G R the ground line, and H L the horizon. From the plan draw perpendicular lines from every part to G R, as ſhewn in the Plate; make ſ the center, and lay on the diſtance, which is here out of the plate. From each perpendicular line drawn to G R draw lines to ſ; then repreſent a parallelogram both at top and bottom, in which the ellipſis may be inſcribed; and draw the diagonal correſponding with that ſhewn in the plan, which will cut the viſua: drawn from the ſaid diagonal in the plan, finding a point to guide the ellipſis. For other particulars relative to the repreſentation of an ellipſis, ſee page 294, and Plate XXI; for the repreſentation of the niche, ſee page 295; and for the deſk-drawer, ſee page 231, Prob. 4.

3 B   Of

Of the Kidney Library Table. Plate LVIII.

THIS piece is termed a kidney-table, on account of its re-semblance to that inteſtine part of animals ſo called. Its uſe, however, is the ſame as that already deſcribed.

The drawers which appear in the deſign are all real, and are ſtrung and croſs-banded, with the grain of the mahogany laid up and down. The pilaſters are pannelled or croſs-banded, and the feet below turned. The view of it below ſhews the ends pannelled, and the back may be ſo too, or it may be plain.

With reſpect to the manufacturing part, I need not ſay any thing after what has been ſaid on the other, except to explain the reading deſk which ſlides out, as ſhewn below. Obſerve, B is the profile of the frame which ſlides out, in the edge of which there is a groove ſhewn by the black ſtroke, and a tongue is put into the edge of the well part to ſuit it. F is the deſk part which riſes by a horſe; and A is a part of that, which riſes at the ſame time to ſtop the book; *b* is a tumbler-hinge let in fluſh with the top, and hid by the cloth or leather; *c* is a com-mon but-hinge let in the edge of F, and upon the frame B; ſo that when F falls to B, A does alſo. The length of the table is four feet, its width two, and its height thirty-two inches.

Of

A Sideboard Table

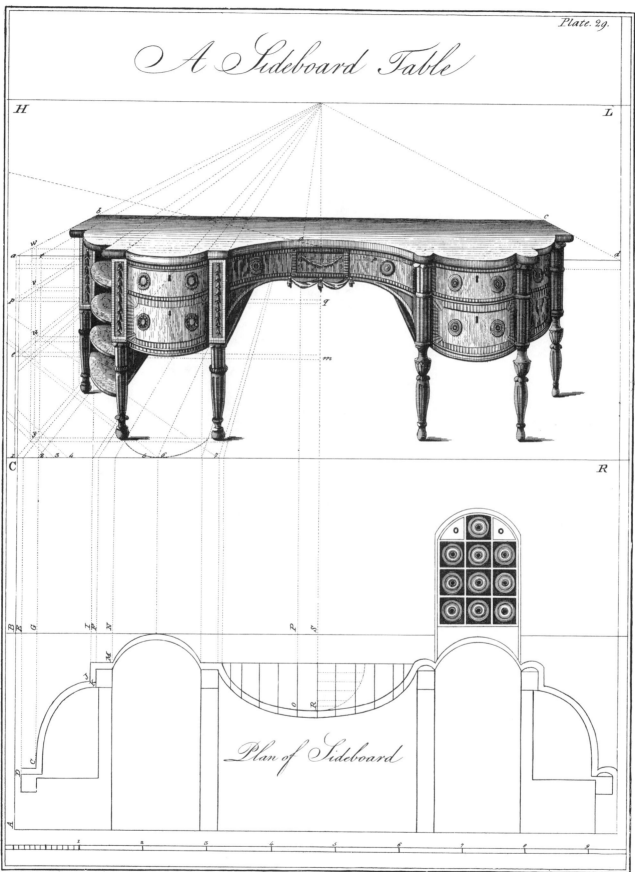

Plan of Sideboard

T. Sheraton delin.

Published as the Act directs, by T. Sheraton Dec.r 7.th 1791.

Barlow sculp.

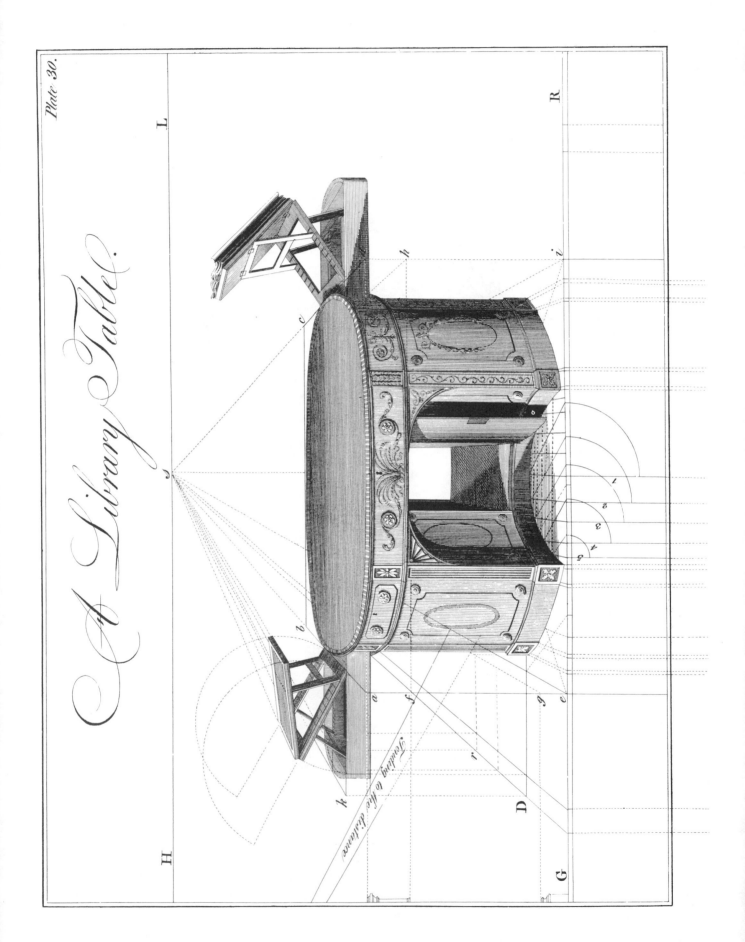

Plate 30.

A Library Table.

Plan

Feet and Inches

1 2 3 4 5

T. Sheraton del.

Publish'd as the Act directs Aug.ᵗ 27. 1791.

G. Terry sculp.

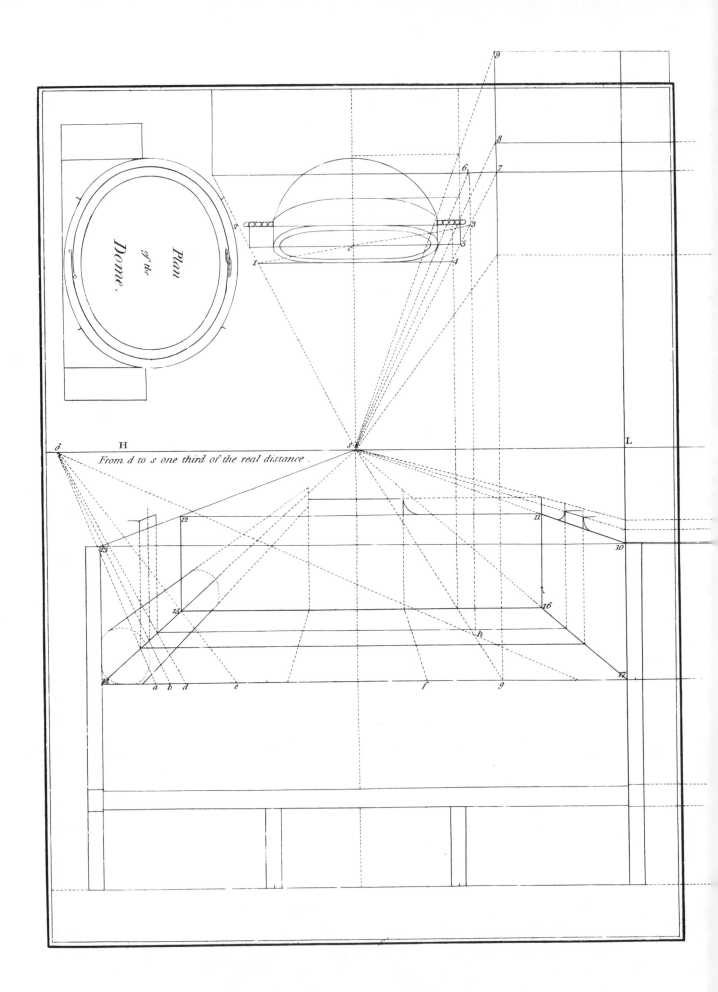

Plan
of the
Dome.

From d to s one third of the real distance.

A SOFA BED.

Plate 31.

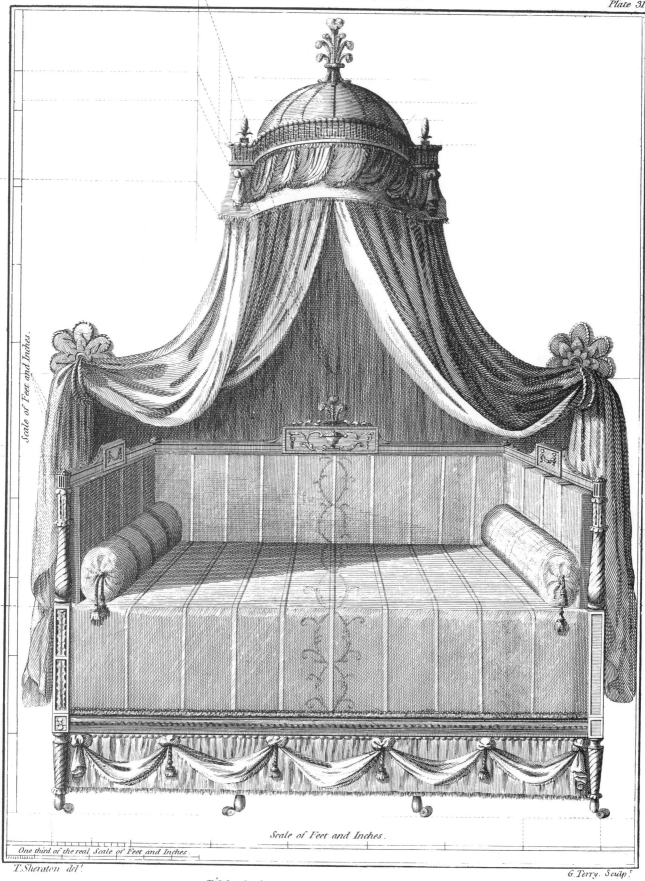

Scale of Feet and Inches.

Scale of Feet and Inches.

One third of the real Scale of Feet and Inches.

T. Sheraton del.

G. Terry. Sculp.

Pub.d as the Act directs. Sep.t 30. 1791 by T. Sheraton.

Plate 32

Drawing Room Chairs.

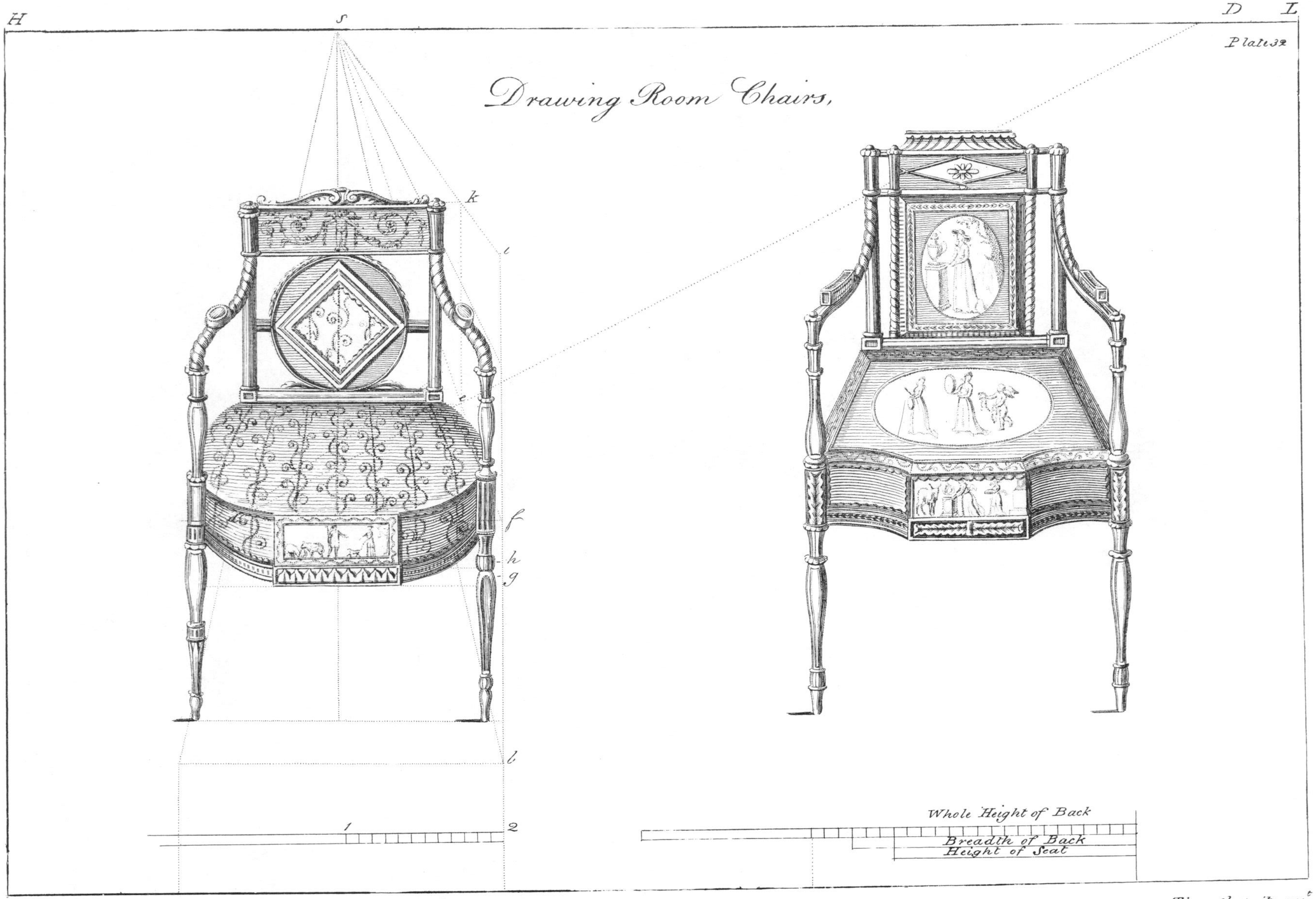

Whole Height of Back
Breadth of Back
Height of Seat

T. Sheraton del.t   Pub.d as the Act directs Jan.y 1.t 1792 by T. Sheraton.   Thornthwaite sc.t

Of the Sofa Bed. Plate XXXI.

THE frames of thefe beds are fometimes painted in ornaments to fuit the furniture. But when the furniture is of rich
filk, they are done in white and gold, and the ornaments carved.
The tablets may have each a feftoon of flowers or foliage, and
the cornice cut out in leaves and gilt has a good effect. The
drapery under the cornice is of the French kind; it is fringed
all round, and laps on to each other like unto waves. The valance ferves as a ground, and is alfo fringed. The rofes which
tuck up the curtains are formed by filk cord, &c. on the wall,
to fuit the hangings; and obferve, that the center rofe contains
a brafs hook and focket, which will unhook, fo that the curtains will come forward and entirely enclofe the whole bed.

The fofa part is fometimes made without any back, in the
manner of a couch. It muft alfo be obferved, that the beft
kinds of thefe beds have behind what the upholfterers call a
fluting, which is done by a flight frame of wood faftened to the
wall, on which is ftrained, in ftraight puckers, fome of the
fame ftuff of which the curtains are made.

The left plate fhews the plan of the tefter, and the manner
of fixing the rods, which are made in two parts to pafs each

3 B 2

other,

other, fo that the curtains may come clofe to each other in the center.

The tefter rods fcrew faft in front, and hook paft each other behind. The manner of fixing the tefter up is by an iron bracket at each end; one arm of the bracket fcrews to the underfide of the tefter, and the other againft the wall, by driving in plugs for that purpofe.

Of *the Perfpective Lines.*

THE left plate fhews thefe lines, and the right fhews the fcales of proportion. Thefe beds feldom exceed twelve feet in height, including the feather at top. Their length is feven feet, and width about five.

The perfpective lines are drawn by a contracted diftance, being only one third of the whole. The front of the fofa is merely a geometrical elevation. For the apparent width of it take five feet from the fmall fcale, which is termed one third of the real fcale of feet and inches; place this meafurement from 14 to *e*, and draw a line to *d*, cutting at 15; *a*, *b*, *d*, are for the tablets at each end; and at *f* is laid on the full meafurement of the back tablet, from which lines are drawn to *s* the center, which

which cuts the back of the fofa at the line 15, 16, and determines its length. The back tablet being the higheft, lay on the
additional height from 10, and draw a line to *s*, cutting a perpendicular at 11; from which draw a parallel as fhewn. The
line drawn through *b* is to find the front of the dome, which
comes forward rather fhort of half of the breadth of the fofa.
The line 4 is the back of the dome, 5 is the center line, and 3 is
its front; 7 fhews the height of the under fide of it, 8 of the top
of the cornice, and 9 the top of the dome; the reft muft be underftood by obfervation.

Of the Alcove Bed. Plate XL.

THE term alcove, in buildings, means a part of a room fe-
parated off from the reft by columns and arches correfponding,
in which is placed a bed: fo that it is not the particular form of
the bed which gives rife to this name, but the place in which it
ftands. The learned inform us, that the word alcove is from
the Arabic *elcauf*, which means a cabinet or fleeping-place.
This defign is reprefented ftanding on a plinth, covered with
carpet, and having a border round it fuppofed to be on the
floor of the room. The fteps are introduced to fhew that beds
of this fort are raifed high, and require fomething to ftep on
before they can be got into. The fteps are generally covered
with

with carpet, and framed in mahogany. Both this, the fofa, and French ftate bed, require fteps. The dome of this bed is fixed in the fame manner as the other; but the rofes to which the curtains are tucked up are different. This is made of tin, and covered with the ftuff of the bed, and unbuckles to take in the curtains behind the rofe. Upon the fluting, as before mentioned, is fixed a drapery in this, as fhewn in the defign; and fometimes in the arch of the alcove a drapery is introduced.

Of the Summer-Bed in two Compartments. Plate XLI.

THESE beds are intended for a nobleman or gentleman and his lady to fleep in feparately in hot weather. Some beds for this purpofe have been made entirely in one, except the bed-clothing being confined in two drawers, running on rollers, capable of being drawn out on each fide by fervants, in order to make them. But the preference of this defign for the purpofe, muft be obvious to every one in two or three particulars.

Firft, the paffage up the middle, which is about twenty-two inches in width, gives room for the circulation of air, and likewife affords an eafy accefs to the fervants when they make the beds.

8

Secondly,

Secondly, the paſſage gives opportunity for curtains to en-
cloſe each compartment, if neceſſary, on account of any ſudden
change of weather.

Thirdly, it makes the whole conſiderably more ornamental,
uniform, and light.

The firſt idea of this bed was communicated to me by
Mr. Thompſon, groom of the houſhold furniture to the Duke
of York, which, I preſume, is now improved, as it appears in
this deſign.

The manufacturing part may eaſily be underſtood from the
deſign by any workman; I ſhall, however, point out a few particulars. The arch which ſprings from the Ionic columns ſhould
be glued up in thickneſs round a caul, and an architrave put on
each ſide afterwards. The arch ſhould be tenoned into the columns, with iron plates ſcrewed on, ſo that it may be taken off
when the bed is required to come down. In this arch a drapery
is fixed, with a taſſel in the center, and a vaſe above. The
head-board is framed all in one length, and the two inner ſides
of the bed tenoned into the head-rail, and ſcrewed. The teſter
is made in one, in which there are two domes, one over each
compartment. It may, however, be made without domes, but
not with ſo good effect. In the middle of the teſter, perpendicular

cular to the fides of the paffage, are fixed two rods, for the curtains above mentioned. Thefe rods are hid by valances, and between the valances is formed a pannel, by fewing on variegated margins to fuit the reft of the upholftery work. The ornamented margins, and the oval with crefts in the center of the counterpanes, may all be printed to any pattern, at a manufactory which has been lately eftablifhed for fuch purpofes.

The fcale fhews the fizes which applies to every part of the end of the bed, it being merely a geometrical elevation.

Of *the French State-Bed.* Plate XLV.

BEDS of this kind have been introduced of late with great fuccefs in England.

The ftyle of finifhing them, with the management of the domes, is already defcribed in general terms, in page 113, &c. I fhall, therefore, omit it here, and proceed to give fome hints relative to the manufacturing part. The dome is fupported with iron rods of about an inch diameter, curved regularly down to each pillar, where they are fixed with a ftrong fcrew and nut. Thefe iron rods are covered and entirely hid by a valance, which comes in a regular fweep, and meets in a point

at

at the vafes on the pillars, as the defign fhews. Behind this valance, which continues all round, the drapery is drawn up by
pulleys, and tied up by a filken cord and taffels at the head of
the pillars. The head-boards of thefe beds are framed and
ftuffed, and covered to fuit the hangings, and the frame is white
and gold, if the pillars and cornice are. The bed-frame is fometimes ornamented, and has drapery valances below.

Obferve, that grooves are made in the pillars to receive the
head-boards, and fcrewed at the top, by which means the whole
is kept firm, and is eafily taken to pieces. Square bolfters are
now often introduced, with margins of various colours ftitched
all round. The counterpane has alfo thefe margins; they are
alfo fringed at bottom, and have fometimes a drapery tied up in
cords and taffels on the fide.

Of *the Perfpective Lines.*

THIS defign is in an oblique fituation, fo termed becaufe
none of its ends or fides are paralled to the picture. I have
here taken the neareft angle of the bed for the center of the picture, from which raife a perpendicular as from feven on the
fcale line. Confider next the height of the horizon, which
fhould be about five feet fix, taken from the fcale you draw the

3 C

bed

bed by. On the perpendicular line now mentioned lay on the diſtance of the piċture from the horizontal line. Then determine the poſition of one ſide of the bed, by drawing a line from the angle E to V; from V draw a line to the diſtance here out of the plate, on the aforeſaid perpendicular; from the diſtance draw a line T U at right angles with this, which produced cuts the horizon, and finds the vaniſhing point for the ends of the bed; conſequently V is the vaniſhing point for the ſides of the bed. From 7 to A is ſeven feet, the length of the ſide; and from 7 to N is the width of the bed. From N A draw lines to D D, the dividing centers, or meaſuring points, found as in Problem VI. Method 2. page 237, which will cut the viſuals for the apparent length and width of the bed. A perpendicular from 5 is the center of the end of the bed; S is the original height of the dome, from which a line is directed to the right hand vaniſhing point, cutting at _d_; a line from _d_ finds the center of the dome, and V the top of the pine-apple; _c a_ give the height of the cornice; the diagonals 1, 3, 2, 4, find the center of the dome, by raiſing a perpendicular from their interſeċtion. Every other thing will follow of courſe to him who has previouſly ſtudied the rules given; without which, it would be impoſſible to make every particular underſtood here.

_Of_

Parlour Chairs

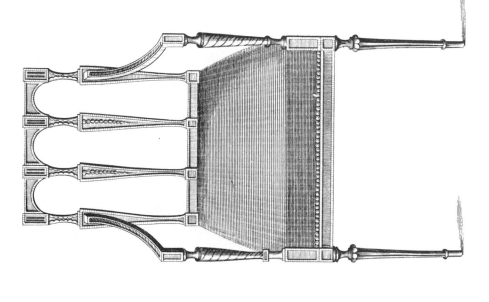

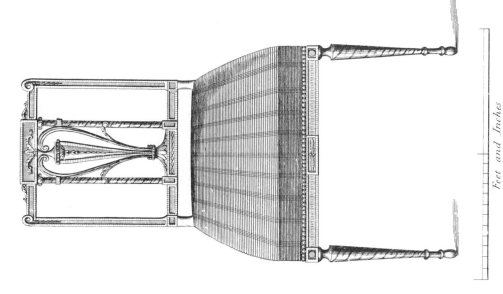

T. Sheraton. Del.

Feet and Inches

Publifhed as the Act directs, by T. Sheraton. September 10. 1792.

J. Barlow. Sculp.

Plate 34

Parlour Chair

Drawing Room Chair

Feet & Inches

T. Sheraton del.

Published as the Act directs by T. Sheraton. May 10. 1792.

G. Terry, Sc.

Pl. 35.

A Sofa.

T. Sheraton, Del.

Towes ſc.

Pub.ᵈ as the Act directs by T. Sheraton, Augᵗ. 20ᵗʰ

Feet & Inches.

7   6   5   4   3   2   1

CHAIR BACKS.

Nº.1.

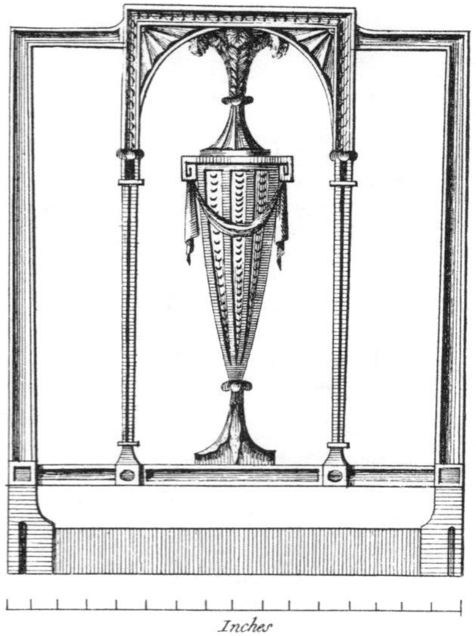

Inches

Nº.2.

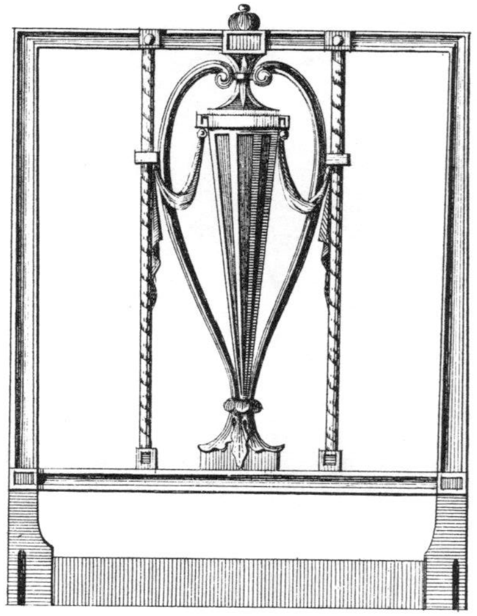

Nº.3.

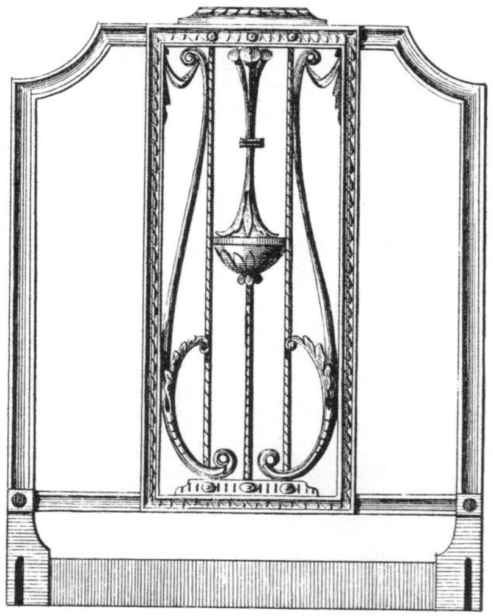

Nº.4.

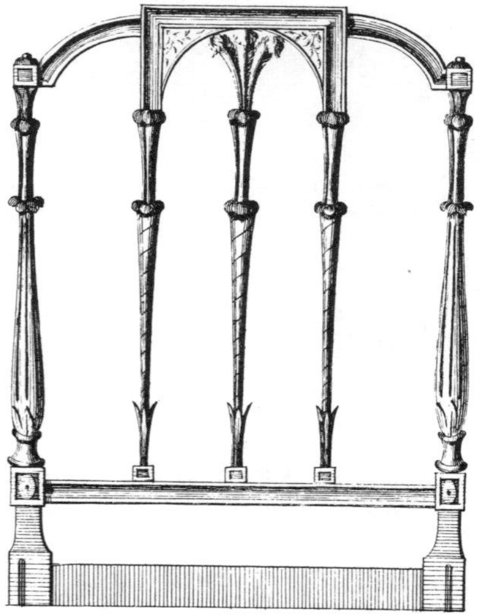

Nº.5.

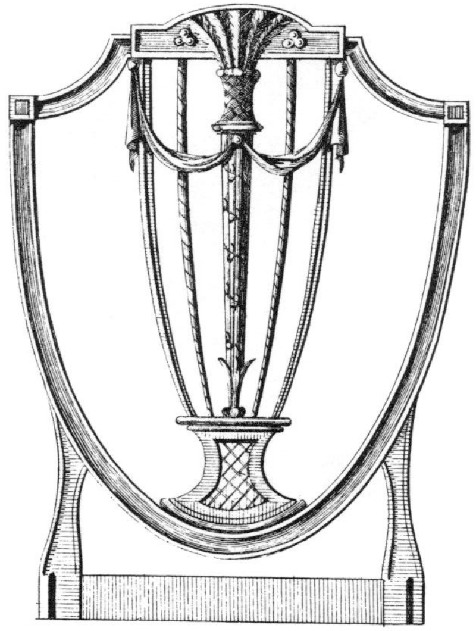

Nº.6.

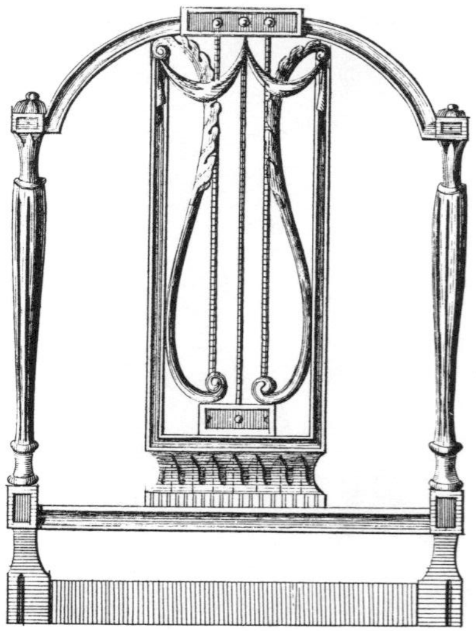

T. Sheraton. del.

Terry Sc.

Publishd. by. T. Sheraton. Aug. 1792.

Of the Drawing-Room Chairs. Plates XXXII, XXXIV.

THESE chairs are finifhed in white and gold, or the ornaments may be japanned; but the French finifh them in mahogany, with gilt mouldings. The figures in the tablets above the front rails are on French printed filk or fatin, fewed on to the ftuffing, with borders round them. The feat and back are of the fame kind, as is the ornamented tablet at the top of the left-hand chair. The top rail is pannelled out, and a fmall gold bead mitered round, and the printed filk is pafted on. Chairs of this kind have an effect which far exceeds any conception we can have of them from an uncoloured engraving, or even of a coloured one.

The perfpective lines in the left chair may ferve as hints; but I need not explain them, fince I have fully done this in Plate XXIV. and XXVI.

The parlour chairs in Plate XXXIII. and XXXVI. need no explanation, as every one muft eafily fee how they are to be finifhed.

3 C 2   *Of*

Of the Sofa. Plate XXXV.

THESE are done in white and gold, or japanned. The loofe cuſhions at the back are generally made to fill the whole length, which would have taken four; but I could not make the deſign ſo ſtriking with four, becauſe they would not have been diſtinguiſhed from the back of the ſofa by a common obſerver. Theſe cuſhions ſerve at times for bolſters, being placed againſt the arms to loll againſt. The ſeat is ſtuffed up in front about three inches high above the rail, denoted by the figure of the ſprig running longways; all above that is a ſquab, which may be taken off occaſionally. If the top rail be thought to have too much work, it can be finiſhed in a ſtraight rail, as the deſign ſhews.

Of the Lady's Writing Table. Plate XXXVII.

THE convenience of this table is, that a lady, when writing at it, may both receive the benefit of the fire, and have her face ſcreened from its ſcorching heat.

The ſtyle of finiſhing them is neat, and rather elegant. They are frequently made of ſatin-wood, croſs-banded, japanned, and the top lined with green leather.

8

The

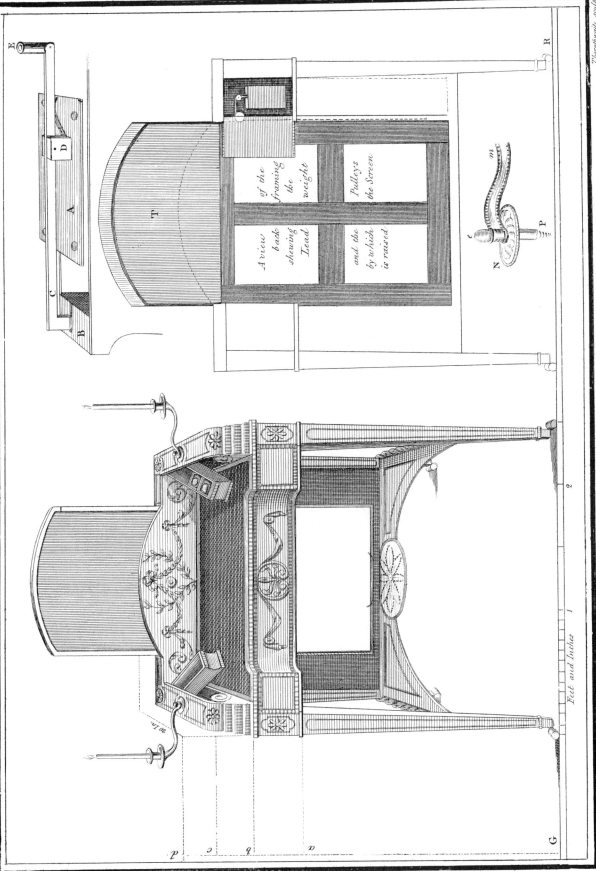

A Lady's Writing Table.

Plate 37.

A view
of the
back
framing
shewing
the
lead
weight

Pulley's
and the
by which
the Screen
is raised

Feet and Inches

T. Sheraton del.t

Published as the Act directs March 4. 1792. by T. Sheraton.

Thornthwaite sculpt

Plate 98

Tripod Fire-screens

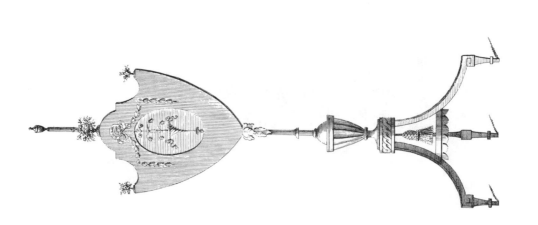

T. Sheraton, delin.

Published as the Act directs by T. Sheraton April 24 1792

G. Terry, Sc.

The manufacturing part is a little perplexing to a ftranger, and therefore I have been particular in fhewing as much as I well could on the plate.

Obferve, that in the fide-boxes the ink-drawer is on the right, and the pen-drawer on the left. Thefe both fly out of themfelves, by the force of a common fpring, when the knob on which the candle-branch is fixed is preffed. Figure A is the fpring which is let in under the candle-branch; C is a lever which is preffed to B, the end of the drawers, by a fpring rifing from D; N is a part of the candle-branch, and *e* is the knob juft mentioned, which is capable of being preffed down; therefore, if P be fcrewed into E by preffing *e*, C rifes and relieves B, which immediately ftarts out, by a common fpring fixed on the infide of the boxes.

Obferve a patera in the center of the back amidft the ornament. This patera communicates to a fpring of precifely the fame kind as A; which fpring keeps down the fcreen when the weights are up: and by touching the faid patera, which has a knob in its center like *e*, the fpring is relieved, and the weights of courfe fend up the fcreen, being fomewhat affifted by a fpring at the bottom, which may be feen in the defign. Figure T fhews the lead weight, how the pulleys are fixed, and the manner of framing the fcreen before it is covered with ftuff.

The

The workman will obferve, that a thin piece of mahogany flides out in a groove, to afford accefs to the weights, and afterwards enclofe them.

There is a drawer under the top, which extends the whole of the fpace between the legs.

The fcale fhews the length of the table, *b* its height, *a* the depth of the drawer, *b c* the depth of the fide-boxes, and *e d* the height of the fwell of the fcreen part; the width of the table is twenty inches.

Of *the Tripod Fire-Screens.* Plate XXXVIII.

SCREENS of this kind are termed tripod *, becaufe they have three feet or legs.

The middle fcreen may be finifhed in white and gold, or japanned; and the other two of mahogany, or japanned. The rods of thefe fcreens are all fuppofed to have a hole through them, and a pulley let in near the top on which the line paffes,

---

* Tripod, of τρεις, *treis*, three; and ποδιον, *podion*, a foot. Anciently the word tripod ufed to be applied to a kind of facred three-footed ftool, on which the heathen priefts were feated to receive and deliver their oracles: from which we may learn how time alters words.

and

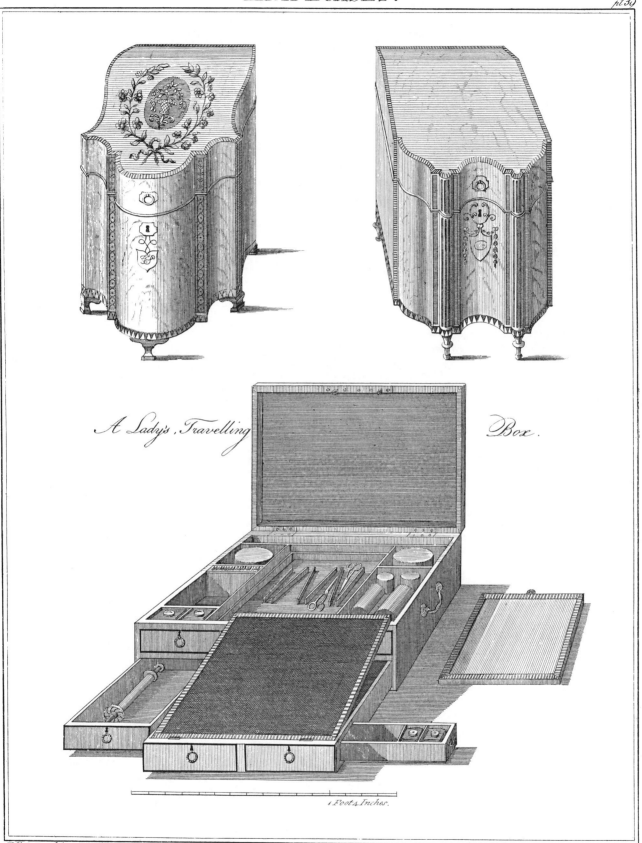

A Lady's Travelling Box.

1 Foot 4 Inches.

T. Sheraton. del.

Publ.ᵈ as the Act. directs by T. Sheraton. Nov. 27. 1792.

G. Terry. Sculp.

T. Sheraton delin.

J. Barlow sculp.

Published as the Act directs, by T. Sheraton Feb.ʸ 4.ᵗʰ 1792.

and a weight being enclofed in the taffel, the fcreen is balanced to any height. The rods are often made fquare, which indeed beft fuits thofe which have pulleys, while thofe that are made round have only rings and fprings.

Such fcreens as have very fine prints, or worked fatin commonly have a glafs before them. In which cafe a frame is made, with a rabbet to receive the glafs, and another to receive the ftraining frame, to prevent it from breaking the glafs; and to enclofe the ftraining frame a bead is mitered round.

Of the Knife-Cafes and Lady's Travelling-Box. Plate XXXIX.

LITTLE need be faid refpecting thefe. It is only wanted to be obferved, that the corner pilafters of the left-hand cafe has fmall flutes of white holly or other coloured wood let in, and the middle pilafters have very narrow crofs-bands all round, with the pannels japanned in fmall flowers. The top is fome-times japanned, and fometimes has only an inlaid patera. The half columns of the right-hand cafe are fometimes fluted out, and fometimes the flutes are let in. The feet may be turned and twifted, which will have a good effect.

As

As thefe cafes are not made in regular cabinet fhops, it may be of fervice to mention where they are executed in the beft tafte, by one who makes it his main bufinefs; *i. e.* John Lane, No. 44, St. Martin's-le-grand, London.

The Lady's travelling-box in the fame plate, is intended to accommodate her in her travels with conveniences for writing, drefling, and working. The front is divided into the appearance of fix fmall drawers; the upper three fham, and the under real. The writing-drawer takes up two of thefe fronts in length, and contains an ink-drawer, and a top hinged to the front, lined with green cloth. The top being hinged at front, by pufhing in the drawer, it will rife to any pitch. The other drawer on the left, which only takes up one front, holds a kind of windlafs or roller, for the purpofe of fixing and winding up lace as it is worked. The middle vacuity, which holds the fciffors and other articles of that nature, takes out, which gives accefs to a convenience below it for holding fmall things. The boxes on each fide hold powder, pomatum, fcent-bottles, rings, &c. The drefling-glafs, which is here reprefented out of the box, fits into the vacuity above the fciffor-cafe.

Of

Plate 41.

A Summer Bed in two Compartiments.

Feet and Inches

Sheraton Del.

Barlow Sculp.

Published as the Act directs by T. Sheraton June 20.th 1792.

Plate 42.

Corner Bason Stands.

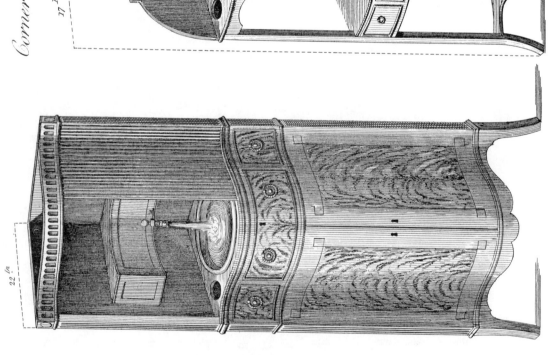

Published as the Act directs by T. Sheraton Nov.r 14. 1792.

J. Barlow sculp.

T. Sheraton delin.

Of the Corner Bafon-Stands.   Plate XLII.

THE right-hand bafon-ftand contains a cupboard and a real
drawer below it; by the top folding down the bafon is inclofed
and hid when it is not in ufe.   The left-hand top is fixed to the
fide of the bafon-ftand by a rule-joint, the fame as the flap of a
Pembroke table; but inftead of iron the hinges are made of
brafs.   The right-hand top is hinged to the other by common
butt-hinges, by which means it will fold againft the other, and
both may be turned down together.   When the tops are in their
place, there then appears a rule-joint on both fides.   The front
edges of the tops are hollowed and beaded, which hang a little
over, fo that the fingers may get hold to raife them up.   Short
tenons are put to the under edge of the right-hand top, to keep
it in its place on the end of the lower part.

The bafon-ftand on the left has a rim round the top, and a
tambour door to inclofe the whole of the upper part, in which
is a fmall ciftern.   The lower part has a fhelf in the middle, on
which ftands a veffel to receive the dirty water conveyed by a
pipe from the bafon.   Thefe fort are made large, and the bafon
being brought clofe to the front, gives plenty of room.   The
advantage of this kind of bafon-ftand is, that they may ftand in a

3 D   genteel

genteel room without giving offence to the eye, their appearance being fomewhat like a cabinet.

Of the Defigns in Plate XLIII.

THE drawer in the wafh-hand ftand is lined with lead, into which the bafon is emptied. The upper part, which contains the ciftern, takes off occafionally. Below the drawer is a cup-board. Obferve, that in the defign the drawer back is fuppofed to be behind the bafon; but before the drawer is wholly taken away, the bafon muft be taken out.

Of the Pot-Cupboard.

THESE are ufed in genteel bed-rooms, and are fometimes finifhed in fatin-wood, and in a ftyle a little elevated above their ufe. The two drawers below the cupboard are real. The par-titions may be crofs-banded, and a ftring round the corners of the drawer. Thefe feet are turned, but fometimes they are made fquare. Sometimes there are folding doors to the cup-board part, and fometimes a curtain of green filk, fixed on a brafs wire at top and bottom; but in this defign a tambour door is ufed, as preferable. The upper cupboard contains fhelves, and is intended to keep medicines to be taken in the night, or to hold other little articles which fervants are not permitted to overlook.

8

Of

A Wash-hand Stand.   A Pot Cupboard

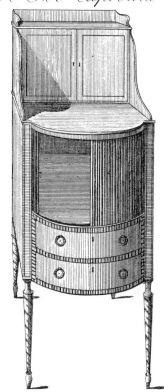

A Lady's Secretary   A Screen Table
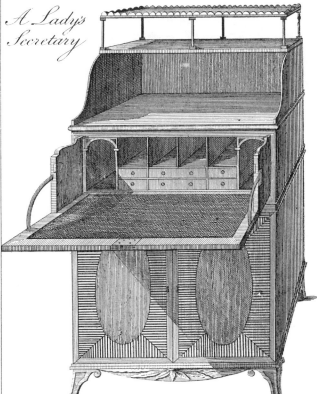
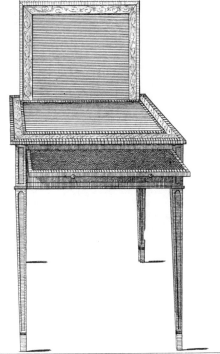

T. Sheraton. del.   Publish'd by T.Sheraton Sep.27.1792.   Terry Sc.

Plate 44

A Reading & Writing Table.

A Writing Table.

2 Feet 4 Inches

1 Foot 9 Inches

Feet and Inches

2

T. Sheraton del.

Published as the Act directs by T. Sheraton. July 16. 1792.

G. Walker Sculp.

Of *the Lady's Secretary.*

THESE are fometimes finifhed in black rofe-wood and tulip crofs-banding, together with brafs mouldings, which produce a fine effect. The upper fhelf is intended to be marble, fupported with brafs pillars, and a brafs ornamented rim round the top. The lower part may be fitted up in drawers on one fide, and the other with a fhelf to hold a lady's hat, or the like.

Of *the Screen-Table.*

THIS table is intended for a lady to write or work at near the fire; the fcreen part behind fecuring her face from its injuries. There is a drawer below the flider, and the flider is lined with green cloth.

The back feet are grooved out for the fcreen to flide in; in each of which grooves is fixed a fpring to balance the fcreen by. The top is firft crofs-banded all round; then a border is put on, fo broad as to fall exactly where the joint of the fcreen will be in the top. Beyond that again is put a narrower crofs-banding. When the fcreen is down the top appears uniform, without any joint, at leaft not fo as to be offenfive to the eye. The ftraining

3 D 2   frame

frame of the fcreen is made of thin wainfcot, and framed in four pannels. When the faid frame is covered in the manner of any other fcreen, flips are got out and grooved and mitered round, and a part of the top which rifes up with the fcreen is glued on to the flip, and as of courfe the top will projed over behind, fo it affords hold for the hand to raife the fcreen by.

Of *the two Tables*, Plate XLIV.

THE left-hand table is to write and read at. The top is lined with leather or green cloth, and crofs-banded. To ftop the book there are two brafs plates let in, with key-holes; and in the moulding, which is to ftop the book, are two pins, with heads and fhoulders, by which the moulding is effectually fecured.

The right-hand table is meant to write at only. The top part takes off from the under part, which, having a bead let in at the back and ends of the top, prevents the top part from moving out of its place. This table being made for the convenience of moving from one room to another, there is a handle fixed on to the upper fhelf, as the drawing fhews. In the drawer is a flider to write on, and on the right-hand of it ink, fand, and pens. The fizes are fhewn by the fcales.

Of

Pl. 45

A FRENCH STATE BED OBLIQUELY SITUATED TO THE PICTURE.

T. Sheraton, delt.

Thornthwaite, sculp.

Pub'ed as the Act directs Feb. 9th 1792 by T. Sheraton.

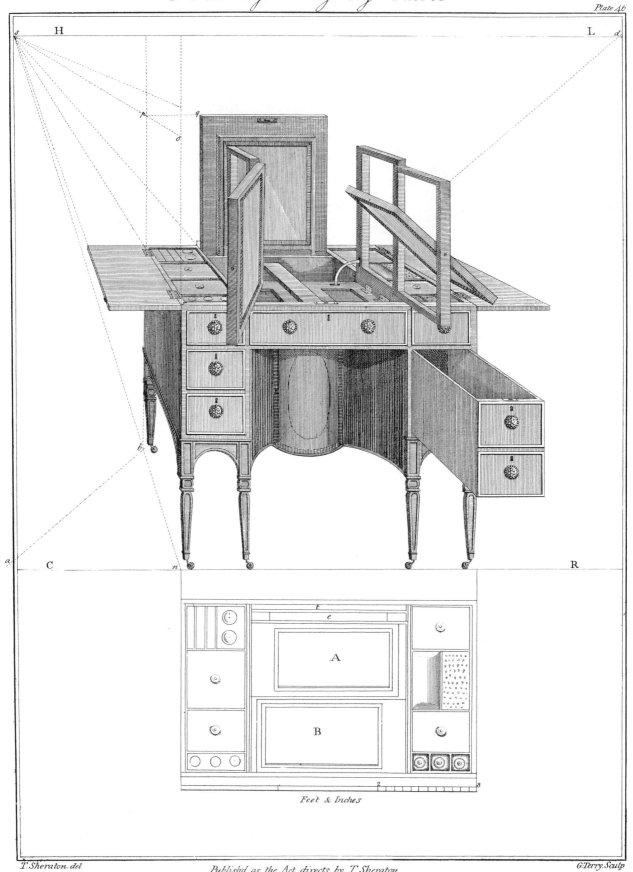

Feet & Inches

T. Sheraton. del.   Publish'd as the Act directs by T. Sheraton.   G.Terry. Sculp

Of *the Lady's Dreſſing Table.* Plate XLVI.

THE ſtyle of finiſhing theſe tables is neat. They are often made of ſatin-wood, and banded; but ſometimes they are made of mahogany. The ſize of this table, which is here three feet, ſhould be increaſed in its length near ſix inches when theſe folding ſide-glaſſes are introduced. The reaſon of this is, that a lady may have more room to ſit between them to dreſs. It ſhould, in this caſe, be made about two inches wider. But, obſerve, the ſize here given is that which is uſed when only the riſing back-glaſs is introduced; and this has been the common way of finiſhing them. Theſe ſide-glaſſes are an addition of my own, which I take to be an improvement; judging that, when they are finiſhed in this manner, they will anſwer the end of a Rudd's table, at a leſs expence.

The glaſs behind riſes up like that of a ſhaving ſtand. Thoſe on the ſide, fold down paſt each other, being hinged to a ſliding ſtretcher, which is capable of being puſhed backward or forward. If the right-hand glaſs be puſhed to the back it will then fold down, and the other keeping its place will do the ſame. A and B, in the plan, ſhew theſe glaſſes in their place; *e* is the back-glaſs, and *t* is the top, which is hinged to a piece

of

of wood, which runs in a groove at each end, fo that when the top is drawn fully up, it will fall down on the frame. The other folding top on each fide have each of them a fmall tenon near the front, as may be feen at the edge of the left-hand one. Thefe tenons being let into the middle part, are the means of fecuring each fide-top, when they are folded down, and the middle part is put down upon them, fo that the lock in the middle fecures the three tops. The drawer on the right is the depth of two fronts, as is eafily feen; the ufe of which is to put caps in. The left-hand fronts are in two real drawers, for the purpofe of laying fmall things in. The cupboard in the knee-hole has its front reeded in the hollow part to imitate tambour, and the circular door in the center is veneered and quartered. This cupboard will take a lady's hat as they wear them now. The other dreffing conveniences are obvious in the plan.

Of the Perfpective Lines.

THESE I only confider as hints or memorandums to fuch as have already gone through the regular treatife on the fubject. *a n* is the width of the table; and a line from *a* to *d*, the diftance, cuts the vifual *n s* in *b*, which gives the apparent width at that diftance. The front of the table is fuppofed to be in the picture, and therefore every meafurement is purely geometrical; that is, they are taken from the fcale. From *r* to *o* is the width

of

of the top, except the flip behind. Therefore by drawing a perpendicular at *p*, and directing a line from *o* to *s*, the center, it will cut at *p*, and give the height of the top, suppofing it to be raifed quite up, ready for turning down.

Of the Cylinder Defk and Book-cafe. Plate XLVII.

THE ufe of this piece is plain, both from the title and defign. The ftyle of finifhing them is fomewhat elegant, being made of fatin-wood, crofs-banded, and varnifhed. This defign fhews green filk fluting behind the glafs, and drapery put on at top before the fluting is tacked to, which has a good look when properly managed. The fquare figure of the door is much in fafhion now. The ornament in the diamond part is meant to be carved and gilt, laid on to fome fort of filk ground. The rim round the top is intended to be brafs; it may, however, be done in wood.

Of the manufacturing Part.

THE manufacturing part of this piece is a little intricate to a ftranger, for which reafon it will require as particular a defcription as I can give to make it tolerably well underftood.

Firft,

First, observe the slider is communicated with the cylinder by an iron trammel, as I, so that when the former comes forward, the latter rises up and shews the nest of the small drawers and letter holes, as appears in the design. When, therefore, the slider is pushed home even with the front, the cylinder is brought close to it at the same time. In this state the lock of the long drawer under the slider secures both the drawer itself and also the slider at the same time, in the following manner:—D is the long drawer under the slider, P the partition above it, and S is the slider; C is a spring-bolt let into the partition. When, therefore, the drawer lock-bolt is out, as it rises it drives C, the spring-bolt, into the slider; and when the drawer is unlocked, then C falls down to its place in the partition, and the slider can be pulled out. The trammel I, is a piece of iron near a quarter thick, and inch and quarter broad, with grooves cut through, as shewn at I. S, in the profile, is the slider; and *g*, 12, *h*, the cylinder. The trammel T is fixed to the cylinder at *h* by a screw, not drove tight up, but so as the trammel will pass round easy. Again, at the slider S a screw is put through the groove in the trammel, which works on the neck of the screw, and its head keeps the trammel in its place; so that it must be observed, that the grooves or slits in the iron trammel are not much above a quarter of an inch in width. When the slider is pushed in about half way, the trammel will be at *u*, and its end will be below the slider, as the plate shews; but when the slider is

home

home to its place, the trammel will be at T and *g*. The center piece with four holes is a fquare plate of iron, having a center-pin which works in the upper flit of the trammel. It is let into the end of the cylinder, and fixed with four fcrews. To find the place of this center, lay the trammel upon the end, as T *h*, in the pofition that it will be in when the flider is out, and, with a pencil, mark the infide of the flits in the trammel. Again, place the trammel on the end as it will be when the flider is in, as at T *g*, and do as before; and where thefe pencil marks interfect each other will be the place of the center-plate. The figures 1, 2, 3, 4, fhew the place of the fmall drawers. The triangular dotted lines with three holes, is a piece of thin wood fcrewed on to the end, to which is fixed the neft of fmall drawers, forming a vacuity for the trammel to work in. F is a three-eighth piece veneered and crofs-banded, and cut behind to give room for the trammel. This piece both keeps the flider to its place, and hides the trammel. The next thing to be obferved is, that the lower frame, containing two heights of drawers, is put together feparate from the upper part, which takes the cylinder. The ends of the cylinder part are tenoned with the flip tenons into the lower frame and glued. The fhaded part at A fhews the rail cut out to let the trammel work. The back is framed in two pannels, and the back legs are rabbetted out to let the back framing come down to the lower drawer. The flider is framed of ma-hogany, with a broad rail at each end about nine inches, and

3 E   one

one at the front about three and an half. In the infide of the
framing a rabbet is cut to receive a thin bottom. The bottom
being fixed in, a flip is put at each end to receive the horfe
which fupports the defk part. The ink and pen drawers at each
end of the flider have a fmall moulding mitered round them to
keep them faft, without their being glued on. Obferve, there is a
fham drawer-front faftened on to the flider, which of courfe goes
in with it, and which contains the depth of thefe ink and pen
drawers, fo that they are not required to be taken out when the
flider goes in. The cylinder is jointed to its fweep in narrow flips
of ftraight-baited hard mahogany, and afterwards veneered. If
the veneer be of a pliable kind it may be laid with a hammer,
by firft fhrinking and tempering the veneer well, which muft
not be by water, but thin glue. If the veneer be very crofs and
unpliable, as many curls of mahogany are, it is in vain to attempt the hammer. A caul in this cafe is the fureft and beft
method, though it be attended with confiderable more trouble
than the hammer. To prepare for laying it with a caul, proceed as follows.—Take five or fix pieces of three-inch deal, and
fweep them to fit the infide of the cylinder. Fix thefe upon a
board anfwerable to the length of the cylinder. Then have as
many cauls for the outfide of the cylinder, which may be made
out of the fame pieces as thofe for the infide. Take then quarter
mahogany for a caul to cover the whole veneer, and heat it
well. Put the caul fcrews acrofs the bench, and flip in the
board

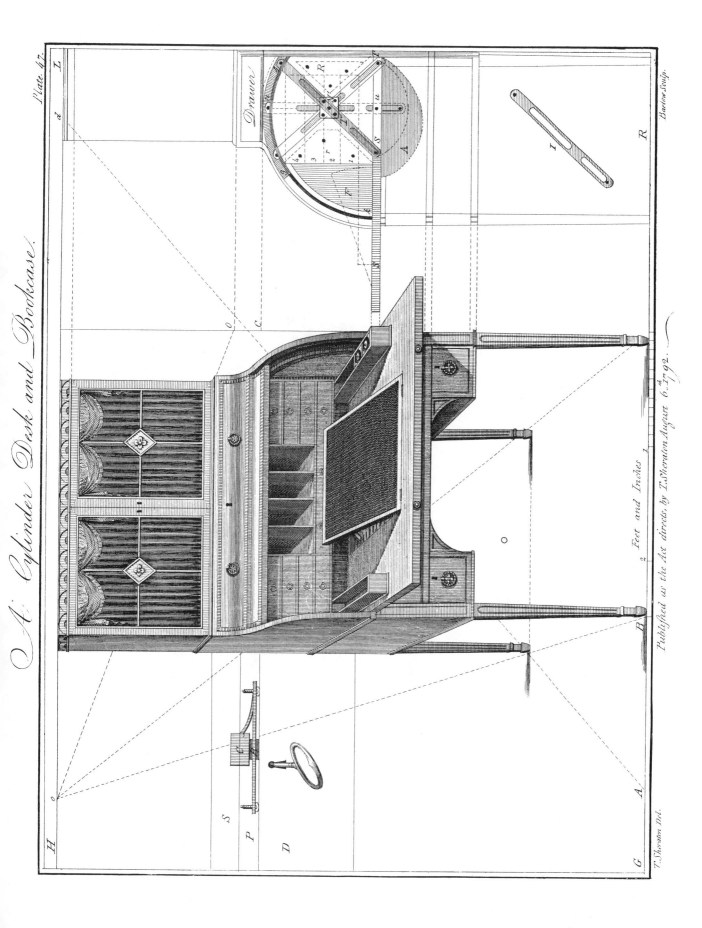

A Cylinder Desk and Bookcase.

Drawer

Feet and Inches

Published as the Act directs, by T. Sheraton, August 6.ᵗʰ 1792.

T. Sheraton Del.

Barlow Sculp.

A Cabinet.

From S to d is only half the whole distance.

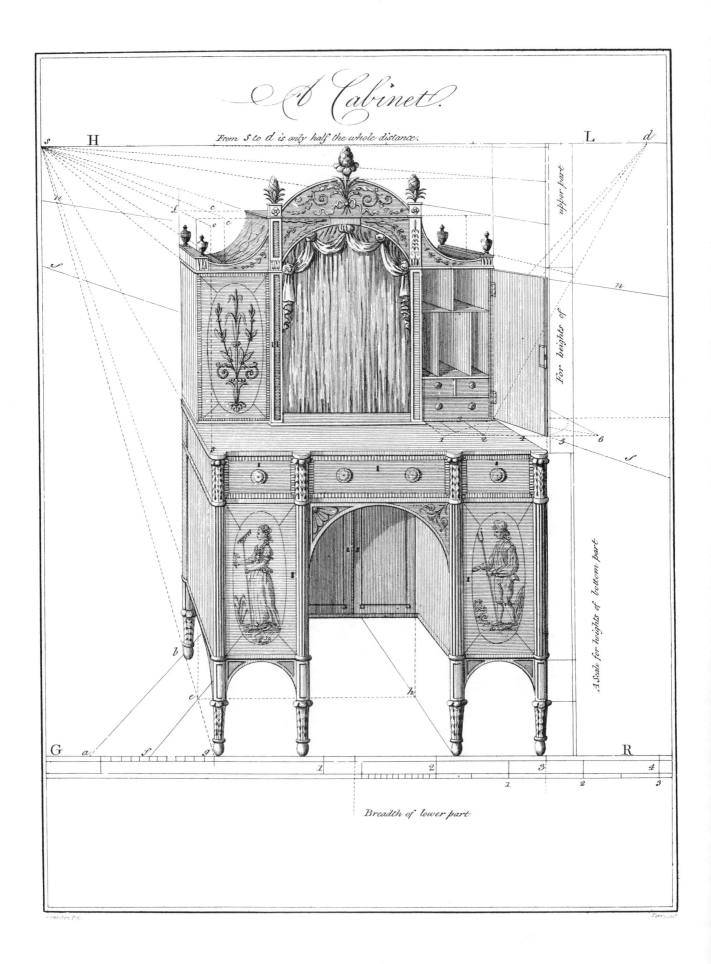

For heights of upper part

A Scale for heights of bottom part

Breadth of lower part

board with the round cauls fcrewed to it; and proceed, in every other particular, as the nature of the thing will neceffarily dictate.

Of the Perfpective Lines.

G R is the ground line, and H L the horizon; *s* the center, and *d* the diftance of the picture. A B, on the ground line, is the breadth of the ends; from which a line is drawn to *d*, cutting the vifual B *s*, for the perfpective breadth of the end. O is the height of the lower part, and the upper part being level with the horizon, appears in one line, and therefore fhews no breadth at the top.

Of the Cabinet. Plate XLVIII.

THE ufe of this piece is to accommodate a lady with conveniences for writing, reading, and holding her trinkets, and other articles of that kind.

The ftyle of finifhing them is elegant, being often richly japanned, and veneered with the fineft fatin-wood.

The manufacturing part is not very difficult, but will admit of the following remarks.—The middle drawer over the

3 E 2

knee-

knee-hole has a flider to write on, and thofe on each fide are plain. The doors under them are hung with pin-hinges, and in the infide there is one fhelf in each. The cupboard within the knee-hole is fitted up in fmall drawers, and fometimes only a fhelf. The pilafters or half columns are put on after the carcafe is made. The corner ones are planed fquare firft, and then rabbetted out to receive the angle of the carcafe, and afterwards deal is glued in a flight manner into the rabbet, that it may be eafily taken out after the column is turned.

The center door of the upper part is fquare at the top, opening under the aftragal which finifhes the cove part. The pilafters are on the door frame, and the drapery is formed and fewed to the filk, and both are tacked into a rabbet together. Behind the filk door are fliding fhelves for fmall books. The wings are fitted up as fhewn in the defign on the right, or with more fmall drawers, having only two or three letter holes at the top.

Of the Perfpective Lines.

G R is the ground line, H L the horizon, and sd only half the full diftance of the picture; wherefore ga is only half the original meafurement of the ends of the cabinet. A perpendicular from e determines the front of the upper part, and all thofe

thofe vifuals drawn to *s* are obvious in themfelves. The perpendicular lines *c c,* at the cove, fhew the centers for drawing
it. The right-hand door opens more than fquare, confequently it is oblique to the picture ; and being oblique, the top
and bottom of it tend to fome vanifhing point out of the center
of the picture, as is denoted by the lines *n n, s s.* Thefe two, if
produced, would meet in a point on the horizon, and that point
is termed the vanifhing point of all lines parallel to the top and
bottom of the door. The door turning on its hinges defcribes
a femicircle, as is fhewn ; and, confequently, every opening
of the door muft come within the circumference of that femicircle.

Of the Lady's Cabinet Dreffing-Table. Plate XLIX.

THIS table contains every requifite for a lady to drefs at.

The ftyle of finifhing them is neat and fomewhat elegant.

With refpect to the manufacturing part, and what it contains, thefe may be learned from the defign itfelf, which here
fhews the parts entirely laid open. I fhall therefore only mention two or three particulars. When the wafhing-drawer is in,
a flider which is above it may be drawn out to write on occafionally. The ink and fand are in the right-hand drawer under

8   the

the center dreffing-glafs. Behind the drapery, which is tacked
to a rabbet, and fringed or gimped, to cover the nails, is a fhelf,
on which may ftand any veffel to receive the dirty water. Above
the drapery are tambour cupboards, one at each end, and one
in the center under the drawer. Above the tambour at each
end are real drawers, which are fitted up to hold every article
neceffary in dreffing. The drawers in the cabinet part are intended to hold all the ornaments of drefs, as rings, drops, &c.
Behind the center glafs is drapery; it may be real to fuit that
below, or it may only be painted in imitation of it. The glafs
fwings to any pofition, on center pins fixed on the fhelf above
the candle-branches. The fide-glaffes fold in behind the doors,
and the doors themfelves, when fhut, appear folid, with ovals
in the pannels, and ornamented to fuit the other parts. Obferve, the whole plan of the top is not in the plate, it being required to be two feet over.

The perfpective lines fhewn at the circular end, are as follows.—When the plan is made, divide the curve into parts, as
fhewn; and from thefe divifions on the ground line, draw lines
to the center s. Then turn up the ordinates to the ground line;
and from the points where they cut on that line, draw lines to
the diftance, as fhewn, which will cut the vifuals at 6, 7, 8, 9,
and fo on, finding points to direct the curve by.

Of

A Lady's Cabinet Dressing Table

Plate 49.

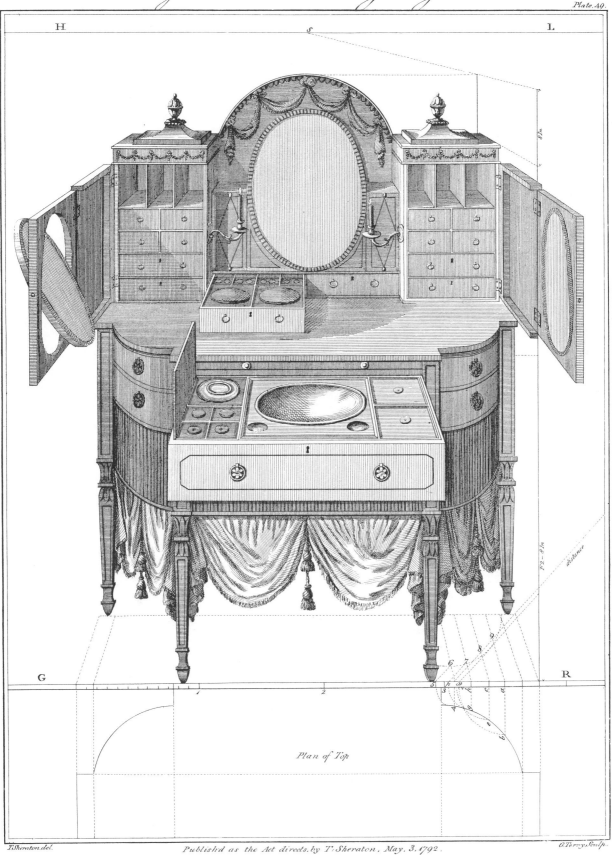

Plan of Top

T.Sheraton.del.   Publish'd as the Act directs, by T. Sheraton, May. 3, 1792.   G.Terry Sculp.

Plate 50.

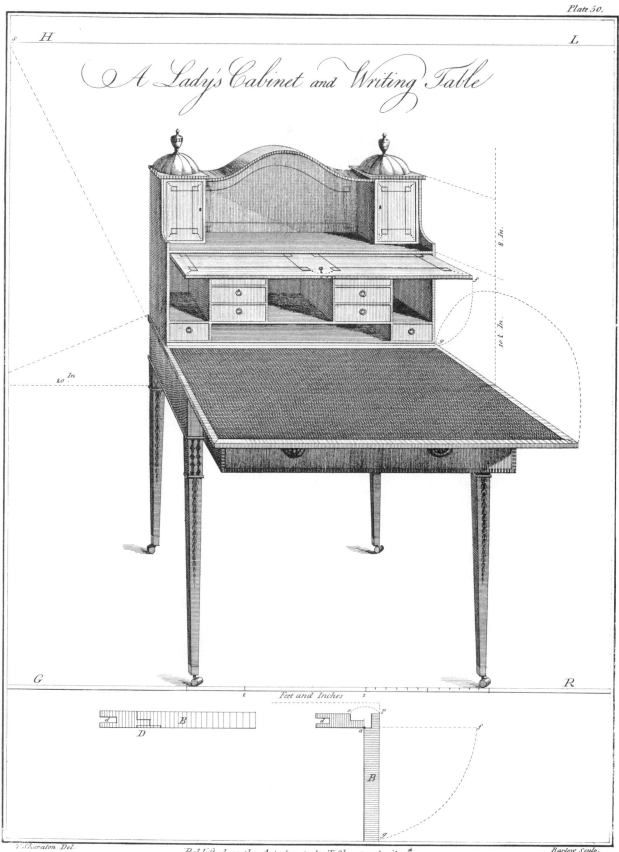

A Lady's Cabinet and Writing Table

T. Sheraton Del.

Published as the Act directs by T. Sheraton April 10.ᵗʰ 1792.

Barlow Sculp.

Of the Lady's Cabinet and Writing-Table. Plates L.

THIS table is intended for writing on, and to hold a few
fmall books in the back of the upper part. Within the door at
each end, under the domes, are formed fmall cabinets of
drawers, &c. The front of the upper part, which inclofes the
neft of drawers and letter holes, flides in under the top, and
when drawn fufficiently out falls down in the curve *f g*, and
locks into the folding top.

The method of hinging this front is thus :—Suppofe B D to
fhew it up, as it is in the defign, ready for pufhing home.
Then obferve, D *d* is a flip which runs in a groove cut at each
end. The front B is rabbetted out, and alfo the flip D. Thefe
are hinged together, and are both of one thicknefs, fo that when
B is drawn out, the flip having a tenon at *d*, ftops it from coming entirely out. The other figure fhews the front when it is
let down, which cannot fail of making it underftood. The
dotted curve line *o* P fhews that the under fide of the top muft
be hollowed out fo that the angle of the falling front may
clear itfelf as it turns.

Obferve,

Obferve, the writing part folds over like a card-table, and when it is open, is fupported by the drawer in the frame. Every other part muft be plain to the workman.

N. B. Upon the fame principles the top of the dreffing-table, Plate XLVI. is managed.

Of *the Drapery.* Plate LI.

LITTLE can be faid of this, as every part explains itfelf, as reprefented in the drawing. It is, however, neceffary to ob-ferve, that the French ftrapping and taffels in the right-hand defign is no part of the cornice, as fome cabinet-makers have already miftaken it to be. It is the upholfterer's work, and is fewed on within the valance or ground of the drapery.

Thefe curtains are drawn on French rods. When the cords are drawn the curtains meet in the center at the fame time, but are no way raifed from the floor. When the fame cord is drawn the reverfe way, each curtain flies open, and comes to their place on each fide, as they are now reprefented. The cord paffes on a fide pulley fixed on the right-hand.

To

Plate 51

Cornices, Curtains & Drapery for Drawing Room Windows.

Terry Sc

T. Sheraton del.

Published as the Act directs, by T. Sheraton, June 11, 1792.

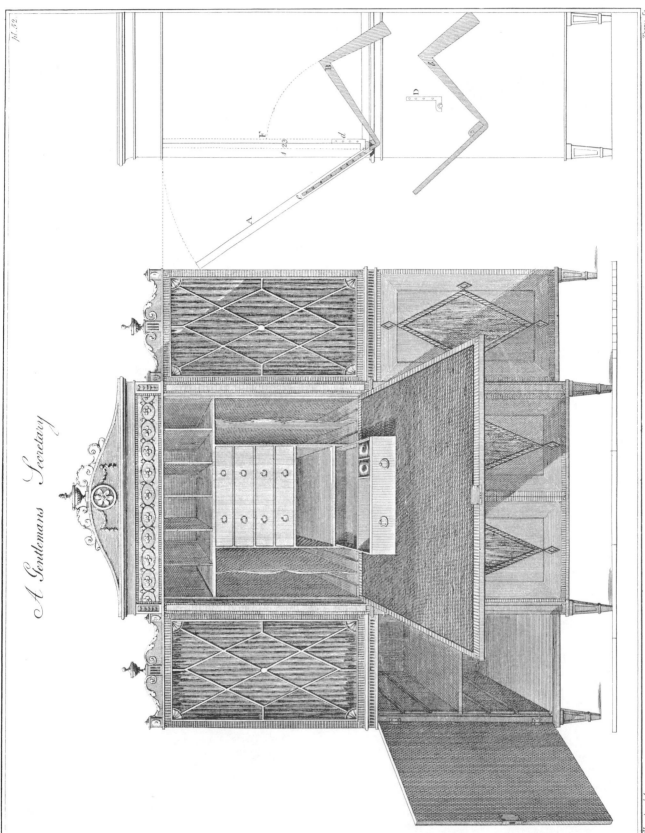

A Gentlemans Secretary

Pl. 52.

Published by T. Sheraton. Sep. 11. 1792.

Terry. Sc.

T. Sheraton. del

To effect this, the rod is made in a particular manner, having two pulleys at one end, and a fingle one at the other, which cannot well be defcribed in words without a drawing of it.

Of *the Gentleman's Secretary.* Plate LII.

THIS piece is intended for a gentleman to write at, to keep his own accounts, and ferve as a library. The ftyle of finifhing it is neat, and fometimes approaching to elegance, being at times made of fatin-wood, with japanned ornaments.

Of *the manufacturing Part.*

THE great thing to be obferved in this, is the management of the fall A, or writing part, which is lined with green cloth. This fall is hung by an iron balance-hinge B, fo that when the fall is raifed up by the hand a little above an angle of forty-five degrees, or in the pofition it is fhewn at A, it falls to of itfelf by the balancing power of B.

When A is in a horizontal pofition, B is at F, the infide of the pilafter, on which is glued a piece of cloth to prevent the

3 F   iron

iron from rattling. B ſtopping at F it is evident how firmly the fall is ſupported by that means; for the hinge is made very ſtrong, about three quarters thick at the dove-tail end, and tapered off to about a quarter thick at the joint, and where it is ſcrewed to the fall. The hinge is made in two parts, as D and *b*. D has a center pin, and is ſcrewed on to the inſide of the pilaſter, as at *d*; *b* is all in one piece, and is ſcrewed on to the fall, having a center hole to receive the abovementioned pin in the other part of the hinge.

It is neceſſary to obſerve, that there is a vacuity behind both the upper and lower pilaſters in which the iron balance operates, ſo that nothing is ſeen but the mere joint of the hinge.

Again, it is requiſite to obſerve, that a hollow muſt be worked on the upper ſide of the under carcaſs, to give place to the circular motion of the under angle of the fall, as it turns upon its hinge from a perpendicular to a horizontal form. This hollow may be obſerved in the plate. The ſpace 1 contains the fall when it is up; 2 is an open ſpace, which affords room for the rings on the ſmall drawers; and 3 is the pilaſter. The ornamented freeze under the cornice is, in reality, a drawer, which ſprings out when the bolt of the fall-lock is relieved. This is done by a ſpring-bolt let into the partition under the

drawer,

drawer, which is forced up by the bolt of the fall-lock into the under edge of the drawer; and when the fall is unlocked this fpring-bolt returns to its place in the partition, and a common fpring fcrewed on to the drawer-back fends it forward, fo that it may be drawn out independent of a ring or handle.

When the fall is up, there appear two pannels in the form of thofe below. As for any other particular, it muft be under-ftood by a workman.

Obferve, the dimenfions of every part may be accurately taken from the profile by the fcale.

Of *the Cylinder Wafh-hand Table.* Plate LIII.

THESE are always made of mahogany, and having a cy-linder to rife up to hide the wafhing apparatus, they look neat in any genteel dreffing-room.

They alfo contain a bidet on the right near the front, and D, a water-drawer on the left near the back, fo that when the two are pufhed home they pafs by each other. The drawer on the front, which appears partly out, runs above the bidet and the water-drawer. The two heights of fham drawers above contain the cylinder, and the two heights of fham drawers be-

3 F 2 low

low contain the bidet and water-drawer. The bafon has a plug-hole at the bottom, by which the water is conveyed off into the drawer D, which is lined with lead. The top of the ciftern is hinged, and can be turned up at any time to fill it with frefh water. The glafs rifes up behind, in the fame manner as that of a fhaving-ftand. And when the glafs is down, the top can be turned down alfo; and the cylinder being raifed to meet it, the whole is enclofed. The motion of the cylinder is guided by two quadrant pieces, one at each end of it, which are hinged to the top in which the bafon hangs. This is fhewn by A in the profile; which, when the cylinder is let fall to its place, will be at B. When the cylinder is raifed up to A, it catches at C, which is a fpring of the fame kind as thofe put on to fecretary drawers. The bidet-drawer is fometimes made to take quite out, having four legs to reft on. The end of the piece of work is cut out fo as the feet can go in without being folded up. This, in the defign, is ftopped from coming quite out, and the framed legs, which appear, fold under the drawer and flip in along with it.

Of the Pembroke Table and French Work Table. Plate LIV.

THE ufe of this piece is for a gentleman or lady to break-faft on.

The

Plate 53.

A CYLINDER WASH-HAND TABLE

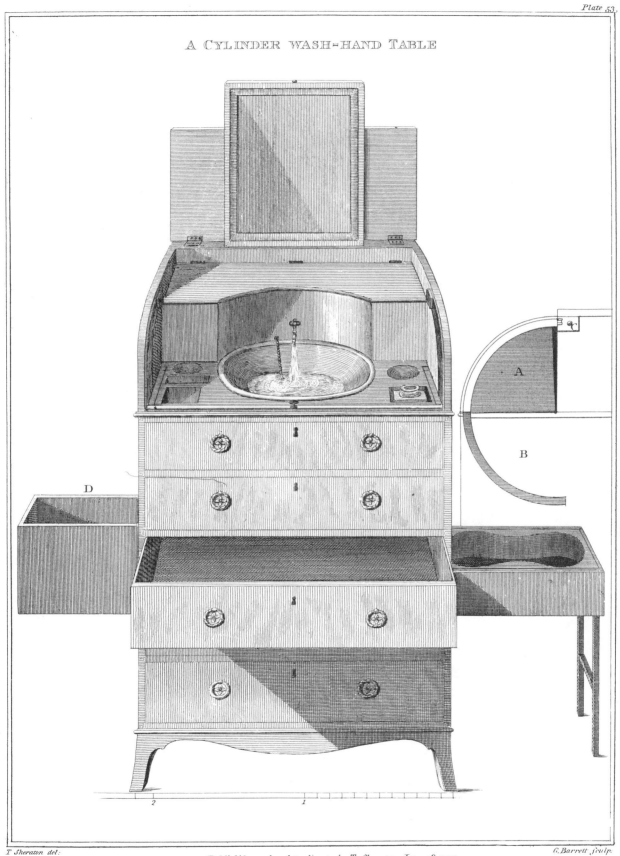

T. Sheraton del:

Publish'd as the Act directs by T. Sheraton, June 28.1792.

G. Barrett sculp:

A Pembroke Table.   A Lady's Work Table.

T.Sheraton.del.   Publish'd as the Act directs by T.Sheraton. Nov.5.1792.   G.Terry Sc.

The ftyle of finifhing thefe tables is very neat, fometimes bordering upon elegance, being at times made of fatin-wood, and having richly japanned borders round their tops, with ornamented drawer-fronts.

The manufacturing part of this table differs but very little from thofe in common ufe.

The fly brackets which fupport the flaps are made and fixed in the fame manner as any other, only I apprehend it beft to make a dove-tail groove in the front for the drawer fides, at a diftance from each end of the drawer-front equal to the thicknefs of the bracket and the inner lining; fo that the front laps over and covers the whole, as appears in the defign. In this cafe the lock-bolt fhoots up into the top of the table. The top and frame may be connected to the pillar and claws, either by a fquare block glued up, or by a couple of pieces, about four inches broad, half-lapped into each other at right-angles, and double tenoned into the pillar, and fcrewed to the bottom of the frame, as the profile of the pillar and claw is intended to fuggeft.

The workman is defired to obferve, that the top of the table, as fhewn in the defign, is not meant to reprefent a regular ellipfis, as they are generally made a little fuller out at each

corner

corner of the bed. The reaſon of this is, that the flaps, when turned down, may better hide the joint rail.

Of the French Work Table, Plate LIV.

THE title of this table ſufficiently indicates its uſe. The ſtyle of finiſhing them is neat, being commonly made of ſatin-wood, with a braſs moulding round the edge of the rim.

The front part of the rim is hinged to the top, in the ſame way as the front of a ſecretary or deſk-drawer; ſo that when it is turned up, it faſtens by two thumb-ſprings as they do. The braſs moulding is mitered upon the edge of the rim when the front is up, and after it is hinged; which being cut through with a thin ſaw, the moulding, on the return of the front, will be fair with that on the end.

The ſhelf below is ſhaped ſomething like a boat. The bottom of it is made of inch ſtuff, and double tenonned into the ſtandards, as the profile plainly ſhews. The top of each ſtand-ard has alſo double tenons, to which croſs-bars are morticed and ſcrewed to the under-ſide of the top.

The ſcale ſhews the proportions of the ſtandard, and the height of the table; its breadth is fourteen or fifteen inches.

7 The

The boat part, which ferves as a convenience for fewing imple-
ments, is fix inches over the middle, and three at each end.

I have, in thefe two defigns, introduced ftrict fhadowing,
that the learner may better judge of its effects in fuch cafes.—
But I muft obferve the fhadows here are rather too faint, becaufe I was afraid to make the plate look heavy. The fun's
rays are here confidered parallel to the picture, which is fully
illuftrated, by different cafes, in the Treatife on Shadowing,
fee page 328. And, therefore, I fhall only obferve here to the
learner, that, in making out the fhadows of objects, a harfh outline ought carefully to be avoided. In fact, there ought to be
no outline at all, except thofe firft drawn by a pencil to determine the boundaries of the fhadow; after which a large hair
pencil fhould be ufed to fill up the fhadow. We may likewife
remark, that if Nature be obferved duly, fhe teaches us that the
fhadows of objects are ftronger neareft the foot or place where
they reft, and grow fainter the further they recede from the
foot of the object. The reafon of this is: becaufe if fhadows are
very long, as from a houfe, there is a ftrong reflection of light
towards the boundaries, which mixes with the fhadow, and
confequently weakens it. It is fomewhat fimilar to what aftro-
nomers term a penumbra, or imperfect fhadow accompanying a
total one.

Laftly,

Laſtly, it may alſo be obſerved, that when an object is totally immerſed in the ſhadow of another, as the table claws are in the ſhadow of the top, there is a ſort of additional ſhadow, occaſioned partly by reflection, and partly by the contact of the two ſurfaces, but theſe are ſhort and imperfect in their boundaries.

Of the Tripod Candle-Stand.   Plate LV.

THESE are uſed in drawing-rooms, for the convenience of affording additional light to ſuch parts of the room where it would neither be ornamental nor eaſy to introduce any other kind.

The ſtyle of finiſhing theſe for noblemen's drawing-rooms is exceeding rich. Sometimes they are finiſhed in white and gold, and ſometimes all gold, to ſuit the other furniture. In inferior drawing-rooms they are japanned anſwerable to the furniture.

Perſons unacquainted with the manufacturing part of theſe ſtands may apprehend them to be ſlight and eaſily broken; but this objection vaniſhes, when it is conſidered that the ſcrolls are made of ſtrong wire, and the ornaments cemented to them.

I could

Feet & Inches

T. Sheraton Del.

Published as the Act directs. by T. Sheraton. July. 24.th 1792.

Barlow Sculp.

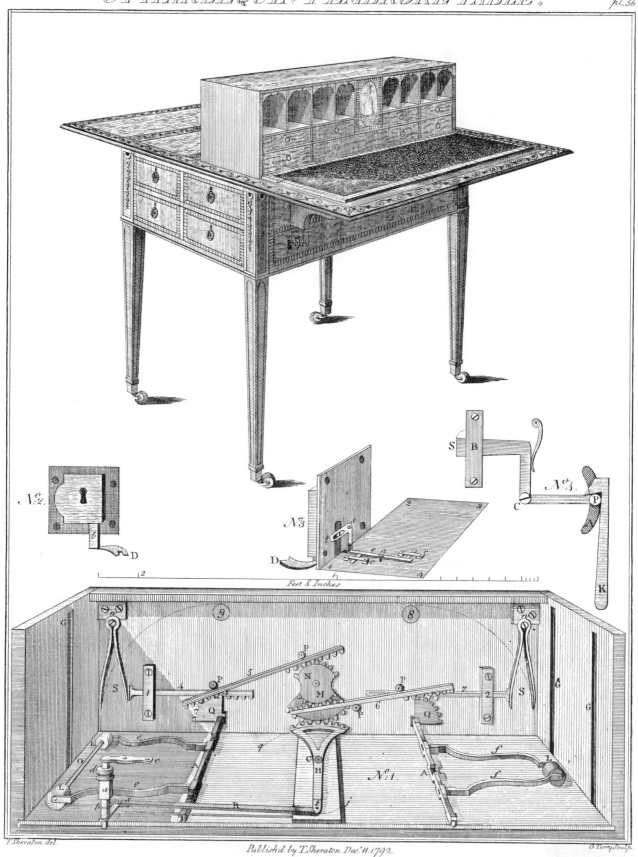

T.Sheraton.del.   Publish'd by T.Sheraton Dec.ʳ 11.1792.   G.Terry Sculp.

I could not fhew to advantage more than three lights, but, in reality, there are four; one at the center, and one at each angle. The top of the left ftand is a round vafe, which can be turned and have the fquare handles put on afterwards. The handles fhould be placed parallel to two of the feet. The top of the right one is a concave fpherical triangle, having all its fides equal.

As to any other part, the workman's own notions will fug-geft every thing neceffary in their manufacture.

Of *the Harlequin Pembroke Table.* Plate LVI.

THIS piece ferves not only as a breakfaft, but alfo as a writing table, very fuitable for a lady. It is termed a Harlequin Table, for no other reafon but becaufe, in exhibitions of that fort, there is generally a great deal of machinery introduced in the fcenery.

Tables like this have already been made, but not according to the improved plan of the machinery here propofed.

In this, however, I affume very little originality or merit to myfelf, except what is due to the manner of fhewing and

3 G   defcribing

defcribing the mechanifm of it : the reft is due to a friend, from whom I received my firft ideas of it.

The particular advantages arifing from the machinery are as follows :

Firft, the neft of drawers, or till, fhewn in the defign, can be raifed to any height, gradually, until at length the whole is out.

Second, when the whole is out, as reprefented in the defign, it cannot be taken away, becaufe of three ftops which keep it in; two at one end, and one at the other, according to the grooves in No. 1.

Thirdly, but if neceffity require that the till fhould be taken quite away from the reft of the table, in order to come at the machinery, then one of thefe ftops at one end is fo conftructed that it can be flipped back, and, the till being raifed up at the fame end where the ftop is flipped back, the two at the other end of courfe will relieve themfelves, fo that the till can be taken quite away.

Fourthly, when the till is replaced, the ftop can be pufhed into the groove again by the finger, which returns again into the groove by the force of a fmall fpring.

Fifthly,

Fifthly, The till being let down again until it is perfectly even with the reft of the table-top, it can then be fecured in its place by means of another ftop at the bottom, fo that if the whole table were turned upfide down the till would ftill keep its place.

Sixthly, although the till be raifed and lowered by turning the fly-bracket which fupports the flap, yet the bracket is made to lofe this effect or power by the turn of a key, and the bracket may then be drawn out to fupport the flap without raifing the till, and the table can then be ufed, as in common, to breakfaft upon.

Thefe are all the advantages that are neceffary, or that can be looked for, in tables of this fort, to render them complete, and to obtain the approbation of the ingenious.

But it will now be requifite to fhew in what manner the machinery operates fo as to effect thefe; and, likewife, to give fome defcription of its parts, that the workman may be able to form a proper idea of the whole.

The firft and great thing to be attended to is, to fhew the manner of raifing the till by turning the fly-bracket. To ac-

3 G 2   complifh

117

complifh this, I have given a perfpective view of the whole machinery at No. 1. Suppofing the till to be taken out, and the fly-brackets and inner lining away from the framing; *a b* is an upright iron axis, made in two parts, and connected together by a round pin at the joint *b*; of courfe, if the winch *c* be turned round, the axis *a* will turn round with it by the above pin, without moving the lower part of the axis *b*. Whence it is evident, that if the winch *c* be fcrewed to the under edge of the fly-bracket, which bracket is fhewn in the defign, it will turn round without affecting any part of the machinery. This is the caufe why the flap of the top can be up whilft the till is down. But if the fquare focket *a* be preffed down paft the joint *b*, the two parts of the axis will then be confined together, and therefore if the winch *c* be moved this way, it is evident that the machinery will inftantly be put in motion in the following manner :

The winch *c* being fcrewed to the fly-bracket, and turned fquare out, it defcribes by its paffage a quadrant of a circle; and the arm *s* of the crank-rod being fixed faft into the fame axis *a b*, confequently it will defcribe the fame curve as the bracket : and as the crank-rod R is jointed into its arm at *s* and at *t*, in moving the arm the rod R is pufhed forward to *j*, and the horizontal cog-wheel H of courfe turns to the left-hand on the center C. It being then turned to the left, as expreffed by the

dotted

dotted line at q, it follows that the upright cog wheel N muſt be turned to the right-hand ; and if this be turned to the right-hand, then muſt alſo the quadrant cog-wheel Q on the left turn to the right with it : and, becauſe the axis A is fixed faſt in the wheel Q, and the crooked levers ee into A, conſequently the rollers L L, fixed by the rod o to theſe levers, will deſcribe a quadrant of a circle, as denoted by the dotted line and the roller 9; becauſe the connecting cog-rod 5 makes Q move in the ſame curve as N does. Again, if N, the upper part of the upright cog-wheel, move to the right, then muſt M, the lower part of it, move to the left; and, being con-nected with the cog-rod 6, and it again to the right-hand qua-drant cog-wheel Q, it follows, as before, that the levers ff, and the roller L, will deſcribe a quadrant of a circle to the left-hand, as at 8. The reader muſt eaſily ſee now, that when the winch c is turned by the fly-bracket, that every part of the machinery will be put in motion, and that the levers and rollers, in ap-proaching gradually to 8 and 9, muſt neceſſarily raiſe up the till. But it muſt alſo be obſerved, that the motion of the levers ff and ee is greatly promoted by the power of the common ſteel-ſprings S S; for, when the till is down, theſe are always charged; that is, the ſides of the ſprings are nearly cloſe to each other, and theſe being connected with what may be termed the auxiliary, or aſſiſtant cog-rods, 4 and 7, and conſequently preſſ-ing againſt their ends, the quadrant cog-wheels Q Q are there-by made to revolve, and the levers and rollers are raiſed almoſt

as

as much by this means as by the other machinery. It muſt alſo be noticed, that as theſe ſprings and auxiliary rods greatly aſſiſt the other power in raiſing the till, ſo do they alſo check the ſudden fall of it, by a conſtant reſiſtance againſt the preſſure of it, ſo that the paſſage of the till downwards is made by this mean ſmooth and eaſy.

Obſerve, *p,p,p,p*, are braſs pulleys fixed to keep the cog-rods in their place, and *w w* are pieces of wood to keep the ſprings firm to their center.

The reaſon why there are but three rollers, and two of them at one end, is obvious; becauſe the till muſt reſt truer on three points than on four. It cannot totter on this account when it is fully raiſed, becauſe there are two ſtops at that end where there is only one roller, which run in the grooves G G; and if the ſtops chuck up to the end of the grooves when the till is up, it is impoſſible that it can totter, conſidering that the other end is upon two rollers. And here let it be noted, that if the work-man find any inconvenience owing to the double roller *o* being at the ſame end with the axis *b b*, it can be removed by putting the double roller where the ſingle one is, which makes no dif-ference with any other part of the machinery. And obſerve, that when the rollers are nearly perpendicular to their axis A A, they enter upon an inclined plane, or on thin pieces of wood

planed

planed off like a wedge, of the width of the rollers, and whofe thin end is glued to meet the rollers as they rife, fo that the till can thereby be raifed as high as we pleafe. Thefe wedges being glued on the under fide of the till to fuit exactly the place of the rollers, the projection of the wedges below the till makes it neceffary that there fhould be a vacuity in the axis A A, for them to fall into when the till is down; becaufe, in this fitua-tion, the till refts on the three rollers, which are nearly on a level with the axis A A. And as the wedges above mentioned muft lie acrofs the axis A A when the till is down, every work-man muft fee the neceffity of a vacuity, or otherwife the till would not fettle to its place.

The next thing in order is to fhew how one of the ftops can be relieved, or flipped back, fo that the till may be taken quite away. The conftruction of this ftop is fhewn by No. 4, which fuppofes that we fee the under-fide of the till. A is a hole cut through the till, which hole is drawn by a compafs, having one foot at C the center. P is a round pin, which comes through to the infide of the bottom of the till. K is a tin key which hooks this pin. In applying this key to the pin, the writing flider, fhewn in the defign, muft be pufhed in, and the front-part which covers the letter holes turned up to its place; and there being a groove acrofs the under fide of the flider, exactly

8   where

where the pin comes, and the flider giving a little way for the thicknefs of the aforefaid key, the groove juft mentioned admits the key over the head of the pin P; then, when the key is drawn back again, P moves toward A by the center C; and S, the ftop which projects beyond the till, is by this mean drawn within. B is a plate fcrewed on to the till to keep the ftop firm. Again, when the till is down to its place, it is neceffary that it fhould be ftopped there alfo, as has been already faid. The apparatus for this is fhewn at No. 3, which is a different view of the fame lock as at No. 2. 1, 2, 3, 4, is fuppofed to be a part of the bottom, not of the till, but that whereon the machinery is placed at No. 1. $t\,s$ is a kind of trammel with flits in it, moving on a center at s. A pin is fixed to the bolt of the lock, and there being a paffage for the pin cut out of the lock-plate, as fhewn in the defign, this pin moves up and down, according as the key is turned. a is a kind of lever, with two arms, moving at the center a. $c\,c$ are ftaples which are faftened to the under-fide of the till, and as the bolt of the lock fhoots downwards, the trammel $t\,s$ throws the arms of the lever out of the ftaples which are fixed to the underfide of the till; by which means the till is relieved, and can then be raifed by drawing out the fly-bracket. And here the workman muft be careful to ob-ferve, that when the bolt b, No. 1, is fhot, as it now appears, the till is always relieved, and the bracket at the fame time has

power

power to raife the till; becaufe the fork D works in the groove *d* of the axis *a b* at No. 1, and thereby preffes the focket *a* to *b*, and gives the winch *c* power over the machinery. And obferve further, that when the bolt *b* at No. 2 is up, as it is fhewn at No. 3, then it is evident that the arms of the ftop-lever will pafs through the beforementioned ftaples at the underfide of the till and fecure it, while, at the fame time, the bracket will lofe its power over the machinery; becaufe the focket *a*, at No. 1, is thereby raifed above *b*, and of courfe as *b* turns on a pin, the winch *c* cannot affect the crank-rod *s* R, and therefore no part of the machinery is moved. Thus it is, I think, fufficiently clear that the till can be ftopped and relieved when it is either up or down, and alfo that the bracket can be drawn out to fup-port the flap, while, at the fame time, the till is both down and ftopped, fo that the whole may be ufed as a common breakfaft table.

It remains now to give fome hints refpecting the manufac-turing part.

Of the Table Top.

THE fize of the table when opened is four feet, and two feet feven inches long; and the rails eight and a quarter deep.

3 H   The

The whole top is divided into four compartments, to anfwer the opening for the till. Round thefe compartments is a japanned border, to fill up the fpace which lies between the end of the table and the end of the till. This border muft be continued all round alike, to make the pannels appear uniform and of equal fize. The bed of the top fhould be framed in two pannels of three-quarters mahogany well feafoned, and the breadth of the ftiles to fuit the opening of the till. A pannel of half-inch ftuff fhould be tongued into the other part of the bed where the till does not rife. Then, for the fake of the aftragal which is to be worked on the edge of the top all round, a piece fhould be tongued in, the long way of the grain, into each end of the bed. And obferve, that as the bed of the table will frequently have to be taken off in the courfe of the work, it is beft to put fmall tenons into the under fide of it, and mortices into the rails all round; by which means the bed will be kept to a certain place, and taken eafy off at any time. A black ftring is put next the till, all round the infide of the border, to hide the joint. In putting this black ftring on at the opening of the till, the infide of the mahogany frame fhould be rabbetted out to take a flip of black veneer about three-eighths wide; and it being left to ftand above the framing the thicknefs of the veneer, this black flip can be fhot by a rabbet-plain to the thicknefs of a neat ftring, and the veneer muft be jumped to it. The ufe of this is, that when the till rifes it may not take any part of the ftring away

7

with

with it, which it certainly would do if it were put on merely as a corner ftring.

Of the Till.

THE carcafs of the till is made of half-inch mahogany; the partitions and letter-holes of thin quarter ftuff, and black beads put on their edges, all of which muft be kept back about half an inch from the edge of the carcafs, to give place to the writing-flider; part of which turns up as a front to the infide of the till, and part of it remains in it: and, as a part of the writing-flider remains in the bottom of the till below the drawers, confequently there muft be a joint in the flider to anfwer it; which joint is hinged at each end, before the crofs-band is put on for the green cloth. The workman may make the hinges himfelf to fuit that purpofe. They may be made as common defk-fall hinges, only the knuckles of the hinge are made a little higher than common to receive a thin veneer; which, when fcrewed on, the veneer for the band of the cloth lies upon and covers the ftraps, fo that a part of the knuckle is only feen: but obferve, that the ends of the veneer, each meeting at the knuckle, muft be cut in a floping direction, fo that they and the brafs knuckle between them will be exactly in the form, and of the fame nature, as the rule-joint of a fly-bracket for a Pembroke

3 H 2   table;

table; and therefore it muſt be evident to every workman that the front will turn up ſquare. The ſlider is ſtopped into the till by a couple of pins which run in grooves; and when it is puſhed home, before it can turn up, a hollow muſt be worked in the bottom of the till, to give room for the angle of the riſing part of the ſlider to turn in. When the ſlider is turned up, it is kept in its place by a ſpring-catch, which ſtrikes into a plate put on at the under ſide of the top of the till. And obſerve, that when the front is up, it ſhould be rather within the carcaſs of the till, both for the purpoſe of letting the till go eaſy down, and to admit of a ſlip of thin green cloth at each end, ſo that when the front is turned upon the top of the Pembroke table it may not ſcratch it.

Another method may, however, be propoſed, and which will be attended with leſs trouble; only with this diſadvantage, that it takes off a little of the height of the drawers.

The ſlider, being made in two parts, may be hinged in the manner of a card-table top, which, when it is folded over, can be puſhed to its place. But obſerve, that the under top muſt be made ſo much broader than the upper one, as will admit of its being ſtopped in after the manner of the other; ſo that when it is drawn out, the upper top will riſe and clear the drawer fronts. If the ſlider be made in this manner, the drawers can
then

then be brought within a little of the front edge, and what remains ferves to give place to a couple of thumb-nail holes to draw out the flider by.

N. B. The profpect door is made to run in at the top like a drawer, upon the fame principles as the front of the cabinet in Plate L.

Of *the Frame of the Table.*

THE legs are made a little ftronger than ufual, becaufe the table is pretty heavy altogether.

Both the end rails are divided into four drawers each, in appearance; but, in reality, there are but two in the whole: for obferve, that, for the fake of ftrength in the frame, the lower drawer of the left hand is made real, and that above it is a fham; but at the other end, which is not feen in the defign, the upper drawer is real, and the under one a fham. A middle rail is tenonned, of inch ftuff, into each end rail. Againft this rail the upright part of the machinery is fixed, as fhewn at No. 1; and as this rail ftands within the edge of the top-framing about an inch, it contains the whole projection of every part of the machinery, fo that the till paffes without obftruction.

The

The inner lining for the fly-brackets to fall againft, is not
lefs than three quarters thick when planed; and it muft be the
whole breadth of the end rails, i. e. eight and a quarter. The
fly-bracket makes up the remaining thicknefs of the foot, and
comes down low enough to anfwer the height of the upper
crofs-band of the lower drawer. The part remaining below the
bracket is veneered the whole length with fatin-wood, and
crofs-banded, to match the drawer fronts. The workman, in
making the fly-bracket to which the winch *c* is fcrewed, muft
obferve to make a fhoulder pin on the turning part of it at the
under edge: and this fhoulder will require to be double the
ufual thicknefs, that the iron winch *c* may be let into the bracket
without injuring the rule-joint, or interfering with the wire of
its center.

The lock, at No. 2 or 3, is put on at the infide of the inner
lining, fo near to the axis *a b*, at No. 1, as that the fork D of the
lock fhall extend to the groove *d* in the focket of the axis *a b*,
which then will determine the place of the key-hole, as fhewn
in the defign.

Of

Ornament for a Frieze or Tablet.

G. Terry sculp.

Published as the Act directs, Oct.10.1791. by I. Taylor.

I. Thornton delin.

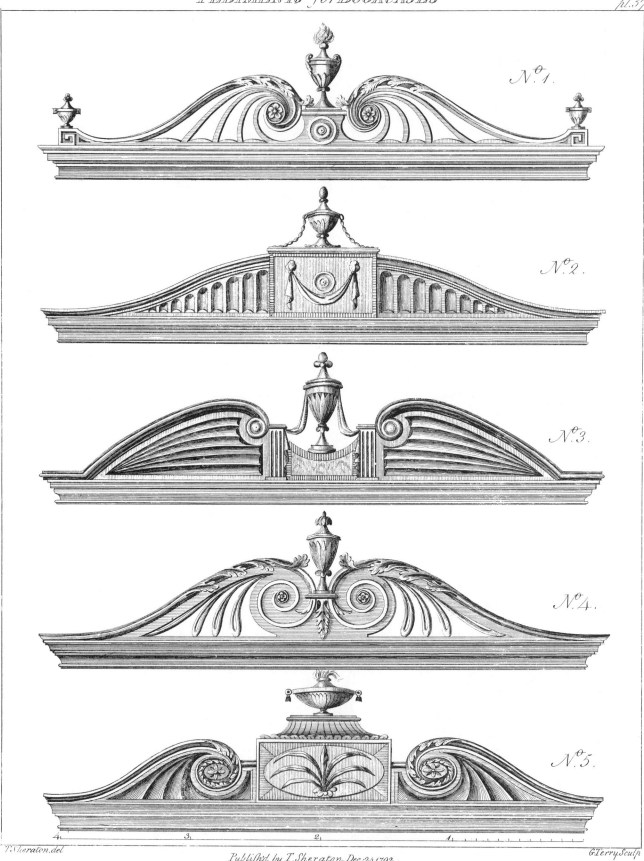

Nº 1.

Nº 2.

Nº 3.

Nº 4.

Nº 5.

T. Sheraton. del

G. Terry. Sculp

Publifh'd by T. Sheraton. Dec. 24 1792.

Of the Pediments. Plate LVII.

WITH refpect to thefe pediments little can be faid, as the defigns themfelves fhew in what manner they fhould be executed.

No. 1. Should have the facia, or ground board, glued up in three thickneffes, having the middle piece with the grain right up and down. The foliage ornaments are cut out along with the aftragal, and planted on; and the whole may eafily be made to take off from the cornice, by having a tenon at each end and one in the center.

No. 2. The tablet part is intended to have a crofs-band round it, and the drapery may be japanned. The aftragal on the top of it is meant to return over the ogee. The fquare of the ogee may come forward, level with the tablet, to prevent too great a projection.

No. 3. In the center there are two pilafters to project a little from the ground, which are fluted. The pannels at each end are intended to be fanned the reverfe way, or with the rounds out.

No. 4.

No. 4. The ſcrolls are continued in one piece from the foliage, and planted on.

No. 5. The center is intended to be veneered and croſs-banded, with an oval let in, and japanned. The pedeſtal above is intended to be thrown back in a hollow carved in leaves. The foliage on the ſcrolls is meant to lap on the aſtragal, and to finiſh off at the patera. The ground of the facia is fanned out.

Of the Cornices. Plate LIX.

IN theſe cornices the ſpring is ſhewn, and the proper gaging is pointed out. The width and thickneſs alſo of the mahogany is ſhewn. The aſtragal, in No. 3 and 5, can be worked ſeparate, and glued on afterwards. The pateras, in No. 6, are turned and planted on.

Of the Method of gaging and working Cornices.

THE explanation of this may be thought, by ſome, an unneceſſary buſineſs; but from the bungling manner in which I have ſeen many workmen proceed to ſtick cornices, I am certain

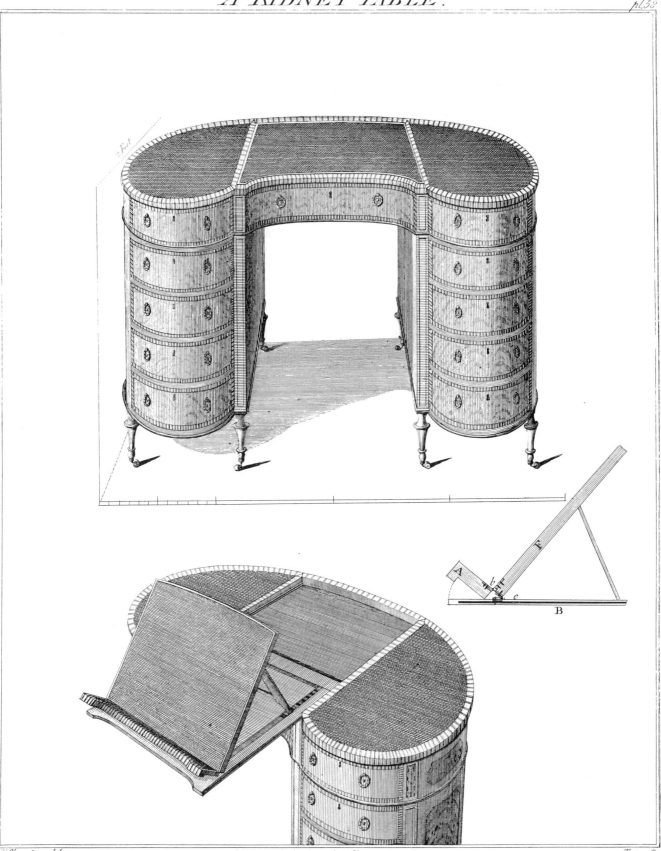

T.Sheraton.del.   Publish'd as the Act directs, by T.Sheraton. Oct.11.1792.   Terry.Sc

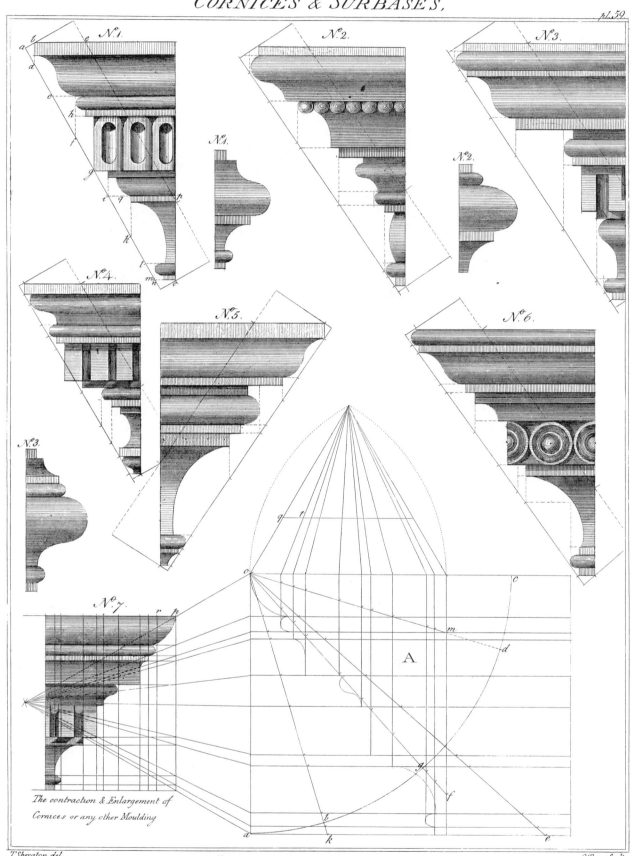

The contraction & Enlargement of
Cornices or any other Moulding

T. Sheraton. del

Publishd as the Act directs, by T. Sheraton. Oct. 26. 1792.

G. Terry Sculp.

tain that a few hints will be of fervice, efpecially to the inexperienced. For this purpofe I have, in No. 1, lettered each gage-point, and I fhall proceed as fuppofing that it is neceffary that the whole fhould be taught.

When the pattern of any cornice is given to be worked, take the drawing and ftrike a line *a n* to touch as near as may be each member. From this front line ftrike one at each end fquare from it, fo as to take in the whole extent of the cornice. Then draw another line parallel to that on the front, to fhew the neceffary thicknefs of the mahogany, and proceed as follows:

Let the ftuff be fawn out broad enough to plane to *b o*; after which, plane it true on both fides, and glue on deal of the breadth of *e p*, and thick enough to make out the whole fpring of the cornice. After the glue is dry, plane the mahogany to the exact breadth of *b o*. After ftriking a fquare line acrofs the mahogany, extend the compaffes from *a* to *a*, and to *c, f, g,* &c. and lay all thefe points on the fquare line, and run a gage thro' each of them. Run then a gage from *a* to *b*, and from *n* to *o*; and taking a bevel, fix the handle of it exactly by the front line, and let the infide of the blade of it correfpond with *o p*. With the bevel thus fixed, plane down the wood behind till it fit the bevel in every place, and be brought down to *o*. Take

3 I

then

then a fquare, and plane down the wood at *b* and *e* till the fquare fit in every place, and the wood is brought down to *b*. After this lay the cornice on the fide *o p*, and fhoot off the wood *a, a, b*; then lay it on the fide *b e*, and fhoot off the wood at *n o* to *m*. The cornice being thus properly fprung, faften it down on the fide *a p*, and proceed to rabbet out the feveral fquares. Begin at *c* and rabbet down to *f*; at *h* run on a fide gage, and, entering in by a fnipe's-bill, work down to *i*, the fluting being laid on afterwards; at *q* run on a fide gage each way for the fquare of the ovalo. From *i* rabbet down to *k*, and at *l* down to *m*; and thus it is evident that the whole cornice, of whatever kind, cannot fail of being correctly worked.

Of the Method of contracting and enlarging Cornices.

Suppose A to be a cornice already drawn or worked, and it be required to draw and work one a third, fourth, or any other proportion narrower than A, and, at the fame time, to contract its projection in proportion to its height :

Take the compaffes and extend them to *a o*, the whole height of the cornice A, and with this opening fweep an arch each way, and where they interfect, to that point draw right-lines from *o* and *a*, forming an equilateral triangle. In the fame

manner

manner proceed with the projection of A, as fhewn in the figure. To the fummits of thofe triangles draw lines from the feveral heights and projections of each member. If the cornice to be drawn is to be one third lefs, then divide any one fide of the triangles into three equal parts, and take one part from o to p, and let fall a perpendicular from p; and from where this perpendicular cuts each line draw parallels, which will give the height of each member in exact proportion. For the projections: $o q$ is one third of the fide of the triangle, as before; draw a parallel line at q, which will give the feveral projections fought. Take $q t$, and transfer this to $p r$, and fo of the reft, till you have laid on each projection; after which let fall perpendiculars, as fhewn at No. 7, and proceed to draw the outlines of each member within their proper fquares, and the cornice will be contracted in the moft accurate manner.

Of enlarging Cornices.

Suppose now the cornice A is required to be higher than what it is at prefent. Draw parallel lines from each member, and having fixed the compaffes to the height propofed, fix one foot at o, and move the other till it touch any where on the line $a k$, as at k; draw a line from c to k, and where this line interfects with each parallel before drawn, will be the feveral heights

3 I 2 of

of the mouldings as required. To find the projection, proceed thus:—fweep the arch *a c*, cutting *o k* at *b*; take *a b* and place it from *c* to *d*, and from *d* draw a line to *o*, and *o m* will then be the whole projection of the cornice proportionable to the height *o k*; confequently where the line *o m* interfects, each perpendicular raifed from the feveral projections of A, will be the feveral projections fought. *o m* is then a fcale line for the projections, and *o k* for the heights of each member; and having thefe, the cornice can then be drawn on a feparate paper, in the fame manner as A was drawn at firft.

By continuing the parallel lines of A to the right, as fhewn in the plate, and by letting fall its perpendiculars to any length, it is evident that A may be enlarged as much as we pleafe, by drawing the line *o k* more oblique, as at *e*, which then makes it rather more than one third higher. Then, by extending the compaffes from *a* to where *o e* cuts the arch, and by replacing this opening from *c* to *g*, and ftriking a line from *o* to *g* through to *f*, *o f* will be its projection as before; on which principles *o f* will be in a ratio with *o e*. This the workman can prove, for by comparing *o f* with the length of the projection of A, he will find it rather more than one third longer; and by compairing *o e* with *o a*, he will find it rather more than one third longer alfo.

8   Thus

Thus it is evident that any cornice or moulding whatever, and however complex, may be contracted and enlarged as we pleaſe, and that with the greateſt mathematical nicety.

Of the Lady's Drawing and Writing Table. Plate LX.

THESE tables are finiſhed neat, either in mahogany or ſatinwood, with a braſs rim round the top part. The upper part is made ſeparate from the under part, and fixes on to it by pins.

The riſing deſk in the middle may be made to ſlide forward*, which will then ſerve to draw upon; and the ſmall drawers below the coves at each end, will be found convenient for colours.

The drawer in the middle of the front ſerves to put the drawings in.

The top is lined with green leather or cloth.

The ſcale ſhews the ſize of every part in the front, and the breadth is two feet three inches.

The height of the upper part is eight inches.

* See the directions given for the Kidney Table.

Of

Of the Dining Parlour. Plate LX.

THIS method of reprefenting a dining or drawing-room has its advantages; though the moft general method is by a plan and fection, as the drawing-room in Plate LXI. In this method the end wall neareft the eye is fuppofed to be laid level with the floor, without which the infide of the room could not be feen. The advantage of this is, that the walls, furniture, and every particular, are fhewn in their natural pofition, except the firft end, fo that the effect of the whole may be better judged of than in the other method.

The advantage of the method in Plate LXI. is, that the fides and ends of the room being turned down, from a geometrical plan, every thing on the walls is fhewn geometrically, and therefore the parts are more diftinct; but with this difadvantage, that it muft be viewed at four different times, by turning each end and fide to the eye; whereas, in the other way, the whole is feen at one view.

In proceeding to draw after the method of Plate LX, make a fcale of feet as there fhewn, and draw G R for a ground line, and H L for the horizon. Let the center of the picture be in the

Plate 60.

A Ladys Drawing and Writing Table.

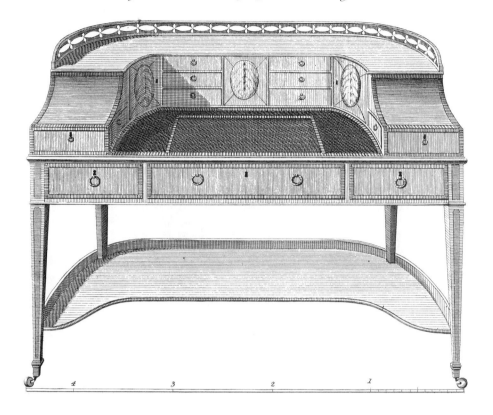

4	3	2	1

A Dining Parlour in imitation of the Prince of Wales's.

feet

T.Sheraton Del.   Barlow sculp.

Published as the Act directs, by T.Sheraton Jan.ᵗ 16,1793.

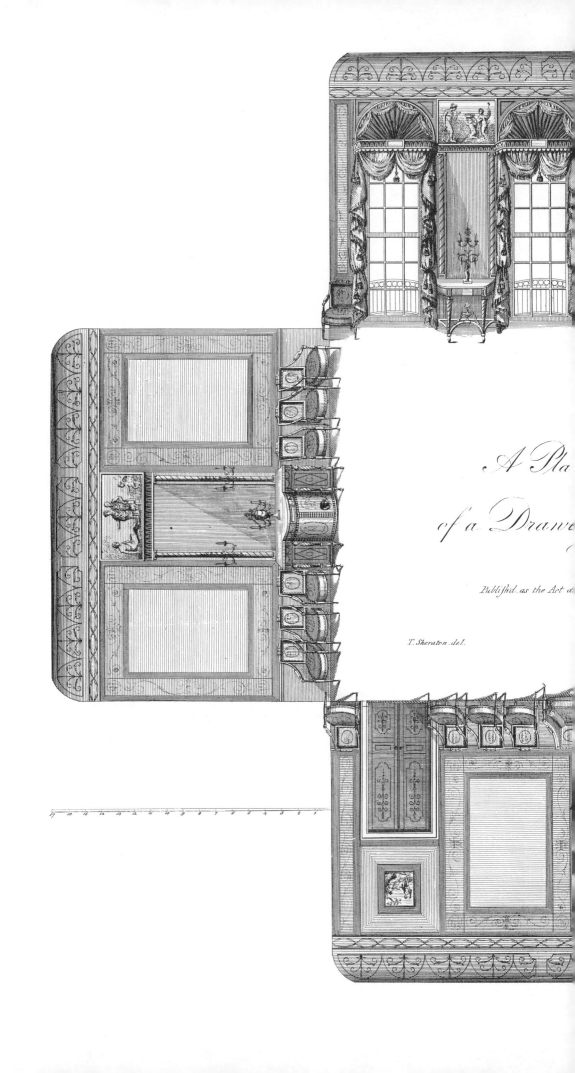

A Pla
of a Drawe

Publiſh'd, as the Act d

T. Sheraton. del.

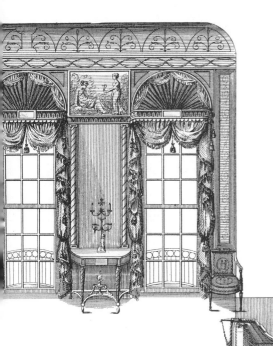

ction

om *pl.61.*

n. Feb.1.1793.

G.Terry. Sculp.

the middle of the end; and, as thefe are views of a fhort diftance, extend the compaffes from the center to *o*, and turn it up
to *d*, which will be the fhorteft diftance that can be applied.
Draw vifuals from *o*, *c*, *b*, *a*, to the center. From *o* to 1 lay on
the fize of the firft pier, and draw a line to *d*, which, cutting
the vifual drawn from *o* to the center, gives the perfpective of
it. Then lay from 1 to 2, the breadth of the window, and draw
a line to *d*; and in like manner find the appearance of all the
piers and windows. Obferve, that a line from R to *d* finds the
whole length of the room. How every other part muft be
drawn will be obvious to every one who underftands perfpective, and no other with any propriety can attempt it.

This dining-parlour gives a general idea of the Prince of
Wales's in Carlton Houfe; but in fome particulars it will be a
little varied, as I had but a very tranfient view of it..

The Prince's has five windows facing St. James's Park. This
alfo has five, one of which is hid by the left column. His windows are made to come down to the floor, which open in two
parts as a double door, leading to a large grafs plat to walk in.
If I remember right, there are pilafters between each window;
but this is intended to have glafs. In his is a large glafs over
the chimney-piece, as this has. To thefe glafs frames are fixed
candle-branches. At each end of his is a large fideboard, nearly

twelve

twelve feet in length, ftanding between a couple of Ionic co-lumns, worked in compofition to imitate fine variegated marble, which have a moft beautiful and magnificent effect. In the middle are placed a large range of dining-tables, ftanding on pillars with four claws each, which is now the fafhionable way of making thefe tables. The chairs are of mahogany, made in the ftyle of the French, with broad top-rails hanging over each back foot; the legs are turned, and the feats covered with red leather.

I could not fhew the curtains of each window without con-fufion, but they are of the French kind.

Many dining-rooms of the firft nobility have, however, only two columns and one fideboard; and thofe of lefs note have no columns.

The general ftyle of furnifhing a dining-parlour fhould be in fubftantial and ufeful things, avoiding trifling ornaments and unneceffary decorations. The pillars are emblematic of the ufe we make of thefe rooms, in which we eat the principal meal for nature's fupport. The furniture, without exception, is of mahogany, as being the moft fuitable for fuch apart-ments.

Of

Of the Drawing Room. Plate LXI.

IN drawing a room of this kind very little perfpective is wanted. All that is required is a horizontal line on each wall. And I would not advife drawing every object on each wall to one point of fight, as thofe at the extremities will thereby become exceedingly diftorted and unnatural. For, upon fuppofition that the fpectator moves along to different ftations as he views any one fide of the room, perfpective will admit that the defigner have as many points to draw to as the fpectator had ftations to view from. If a room of this fort be narrow, fewer points may do for the furniture at each end, with a little management; but the furniture on the fide walls fhould have almoft as many points as pieces of furniture. The line that marks out the boundaries of the floor, ferves as the proper ground line to each horizon, and the geometrical meafurement of each piece being taken from the fcale and laid down on the wall, the perfpective is drawn from each point backwards, or into the room.

A drawing-room is of that fort which admits of the higheft tafte and elegance; in furnifhing of which, workmen in every nation exert the utmoft efforts of their genius.

3 K   To

To affift me in what I have here fhewn, I had the opportunity of feeing the Prince of Wales's, the Duke of York's, and
other noblemen's drawing-rooms. I have not, however, followed any one in particular, but have furnifhed my ideas from
the whole, with fuch particulars as I thought beft fuited to give
a difplay of the prefent tafte in fitting up fuch rooms.

It may not be amifs to mention fome particulars refpecting
the Prince's room, that the reader may form fome idea of its
tafte and magnificence.

Its proportions are as follows:—forty-eight feet fix inches
long, thirty-four broad, and between eighteen and nineteen feet
high, including the cove of the ceiling.

It has five windows in length, a fire-place at each end, and
five doors. Two doors are at each end, one of which is fham;
and a large arched double door nearly in the center oppofite the
windows.

Oppofite each window is a large glafs, with a circular top,
to fuit the arches above the windows; and over each fire-place
there is alfo a glafs. In the piers between each window there
are no glaffes, but a couple of richly finifhed Corinthian pilafters, with their architrave and impofts to fuit the tops of each

3   window.

window. On the fide oppofite to the windows the fame pilafters are employed; for, as the before-mentioned glaffes each occupy a fpace equal to the width of a window, and are directly
oppofite to them, this preferves a regularity in the pilafters on
both fides. In like manner each end of the room has its pilafters of the fame order, one on each fide of the fire-place, and of
the doors. The cove and ceiling are richly ornamented in paintings and gold.

A room of this defcription is not, however, a proper precedent for drawing-rooms in general, as it partakes principally
of the character and ordinance of a ftate faloon-room, in which
are entertained ambaffadors, courtiers, and other perfonages of
the higheft ftations.

In the drawing-room which is here fhewn, every thing
will appear eafily underftood to a workman in town, who is
accuftomed to fee fuch apartments; but for a ftranger, and
thofe workmen who refide in the country, it will be proper to
point out a few particulars.

The pier tables have marble tops and gold frames, or white
and gold. The glaffes are often made to appear to come down
to the ftretcher of the table; that is, a piece of glafs is fixed in
behind the pier table, feparate from the upper glafs, which
3 K 2 then

then appears to be the continuation of the fame glafs, and, by reflection, makes the table to appear double. This fmall piece of glafs may be fixed either in the dado of the room, or in the frame of the table.

The arches above the windows are merely artificial, being only wooden frames put up, ftrained with canvas; after which the fame kind of ftuff which the curtains are made of is formed to appear like a fan, and drapery tacked on to it.

The pannelling on the walls are done in paper, with ornamented borders of various colours.

The figures above the glaffes are paintings, in clare-obfcure. The fofas are bordered off in three compartments, and covered with figured filk or fatin. The ovals may be printed feparately, and fewed on. Thefe fofas may have cufhions to fill their backs, together with bolfters at each end. In France, where their drawing-rooms are fitted up in the moft fplendid manner, they ufe a fett of fmall and plainer chairs, referving the others merely for ornament.

The commode oppofite the fire-place has four doors; its legs are intended to ftand a little clear of the wings; and the top is marble, to match the pier tables. In the freeze part of the commode is a tablet in the center, made of an exquifite compofition

pofition in imitation of ftatuary marble. Thefe are to be had, of any figure, or on any fubject, at Mr. Wedgewood's, near Soho-fquare. They are let into the wood, and project a little forward. The commode fhould be painted to fuit the furniture, and the legs and other parts in gold to harmonize with the fofas, tables, and chairs.

To fupply the Defect of Figure 32, Plate V.

IT is there fhewn how to find the miter of the fides of a comb-tray at any pitch, and of any given projection; but it was omitted to fhew how the miter is obtained in the thicknefs of the ftuff, as it rifes to any pitch.

Having found the breadth of the fides *b c*, Fig. 32, Plate V, with this opening of the compaffes defcribe a femicircle, fee Plate XXII, and make *a e* equal to the perpendicular height of the fide of the tray. Draw a line from *e* to the center; and parallel to this, fet off a line for the thicknefs of the tray fides, and the bevel of the under edge will be at 4. Draw a fquare at the center, the length of whofe fides fhall be equal to the thick-nefs of the tray fides, as 3, 1, 2. Next draw the line B, A, E, pa-rallel to the diameter; and take *a e*, the fine of the angle of the tray fides, and transfer it to E A. From A draw a line to the center, cutting the fmall fquare at 1, and the fpace 1—2 will be the miter fought for; that is, when the fides are mitered in

their

their breadth, according to Fig. 32, Plate V, fet a gage to 1—2, and run the gage along the miter, and plane it off to the gage from the outfide, and the miters will all come exactly together. If the tray fides were raifed to *b*, *b i* would then be the fine of their angle; and which being transferred to B, a line from B to the center cuts the fquare at 3; then is the fpace 3—2 the length of the miter fought. And thus it is evident, that as *b* advances to E the perpendicular, fo will the miter point B approach to D, the full miter. It is alfo evident, that by this figure the miter of any thing not exceeding the diameter E of the femicircle may be found. For inftance, if the fides of any tray be half an inch thick, and it is required to be mitered and keyed together, draw a fquare of that dimenfion, as the fecond fhewn in the figure; and if the fides bevel in an angle equal to the line *e*, then 1—2 of the fecond fquare will be the length of the miter. I proved the truth of this theory by practice, and therefore the workman may depend on its infallibility; but he may eafily make the fame experiment himfelf.

T H E   E N D.

APPENDIX

TO THE

CABINET-MAKER AND UPHOLSTERER'S

DRAWING-BOOK.

CONTAINING

A VARIETY OF ORIGINAL DESIGNS FOR HOUSEHOLD FURNI-
TURE, IN THE NEWEST AND MOST ELEGANT STYLE;

ALSO,

A NUMBER OF PLAIN AND USEFUL PIECES, SUITABLE EITHER FOR
TOWN OR COUNTRY;

TOGETHER WITH A DESCRIPTION AND EXPLANATION TO EACH PIECE.

BY

THOMAS SHERATON,

CABINET-MAKER.

LONDON:

PRINTED FOR THE AUTHOR, BY T. BENSLEY;

AND SOLD BY J. MATHEWS, N° 18, STRAND; G. TERRY, N° 54, PATERNOSTER-ROW;
J. S. JORDAN, N° 166, FLEET-STREET; L. WAYLAND, MIDDLE-ROW,
HOLBORN; AND BY THE AUTHOR, N° 106,
WARDOUR-STREET, SOHO.

1793.

[Entered at Stationers Hall.]

APPENDIX.

Of the Elliptic Bed. Plate I. of the Appendix.

As fancifulnefs feems moft peculiar to the tafte of females, I have therefore affigned the ufe of this bed for a fingle lady, though it will equally accommodate a fingle gentleman.

The elliptic fhape of the frame of this bed contracts its width at each end confiderably, on which account it will not admit of more than one perfon.

On the manufacturing part of it I would offer a few hints to affift the workman.—The frame of the bedftead fhould be glued up in wainfcot three or four thickneffes, with the jump-joints croffing each other, as in the method of gluing the frames of circular card-tables, which fome ufe. For which purpofe, draw the full fize of the ellipfis upon a board, and make the diameters each way, by which one quarter will be found.

found. A thin mould muſt then be made to agree with the quarter of the ellipſis, which will ſerve for cutting out the whole by, when different portions of it is ſo taken as to form croſſing-joints. The frame being thus made an entire ellipſis, as Fig. A, in Plate XXX. it is propoſed to half-lap the pillars into the frame, and to have a ſtretching rail at each end to tenon in oppoſite to each pillar; into which ſtretcher the ſcrews are to work which fix the pillars to the frame, as ſhewn at *a*, *b*, *c*, *d*, in Fig. A. The workman will eaſily ſee that the frame made in this manner will not be defective in ſtrength, nor inconvenient to move from one room to another.

The ſtuffed head-boards at each end are framed ſeparate, and grooved into the pillars, with a tenon in their center to ſlip into the bed-frame, which can be eaſily done when the pillars are ſcrewing to.

The firſt teſter which fixes on the pillars, ſhould form an entire ellipſis to ſuit the frame, and muſt be glued up in two thickneſſes of good deal or wainſcot; to the·edge of which ſhould be glued two thickneſſes of clean ſoft mahogany, of which to work the cornice, as expreſſed by Figure B, in Plate XXX.

Z.

The

T. Sheraton. del.

G. Terry. Sculp.

Publish'd as the Act directs by T. Sheraton Mar. 1. 1793.

T. Sheraton Del.

Published by T. Sheraton March 1. 1793.

J. Caldwall Dirext

The fecond, or falfe tefter, is that to which the ribs of the dome part are fixed, as *e* in Fig. B; and *f* is an architrave which is bent round the infide of the firft tefter, and rifes fo high above it as to receive nearly the thicknefs of the falfe tefter; fo that the architrave is a guide to the whole dome, and is fufficient of itfelf to keep it firm in its place.

With refpect to the dome, it will be beft to make it in two parts. The cove part feparate, and the round or fpherical part feparate. This can eafily be done, by repeating the fame operations as were neceffary for fixing and managing the cove part; for it muft be obferved, that there is a light cornice or moulding where the circular part of the top begins, and which fixes on a tefter in the fame manner as the other. To the under fide of this cornice is the drapery, which hangs in the cove, tacked all round, as is the valence to the under cornice. The curtains are drawn up by pulleys fixed in the under tefter, and thus forms a drapery, by being tied to the pillars with cords.

The circular part of the top is intended to be pannelled out in gilt mouldings, which cannot fail of producing a fine effect, particularly fo if the furniture and covering of the dome be light blue. The foliage ornament that runs round the under cornice may be made either of compofition metal, or it may be cut in

B

wood

wood and fixed on wire, in the fame manner as the tops of ornamented glaffes are managed.

Of *the Ducheffe.*

THE French have what they term ducheffe beds, whence I fuppofe we have derived our ideas of a ducheffe. What is fome-times named a ducheffe amongft us, is merely two barjier chairs faftened to a ftool in the middle; fometimes, indeed, we add a flight tefter and covering, but even this is very different from theirs. The French ducheffe beds are more ftately. The tefter is full and fixed to the wall, with drapery hanging down to the bedding and floor. The head part is formed fomething like the back of a chair; at the foot there are fhort ftump pillars; and the whole frame of the bed being detached from the tefter, may be moved to any part to loll upon. The ducheffe which is here given, is intended to anfwer three different purpofes. The ends, when detached from the middle ftool, may ferve as fmall fofas. When they are connected together without the tefter, and a fquab or cufhion made to fit over the whole, it will then ferve to reft or loll upon. When it is ufed as a bed, four fhort pillars are fcrewed to each back foot, and a ftraight lath extends acrofs from pillar to pillar at each end. From thefe pillars are fixed the fweep iron rods which form the tefter, and which fupport the

A LIBRARY CASE

T.Sheraton.del.   Publish'd as the Act directs by T.Sheraton.March.9.1793.   G.Terry.Sculp.

T.Sheraton.del.

G.Terry.Sculp.

Feet

Publiſhd by T.Sheraton. March.27.1793.

the drapery and covering which is thrown over the whole. The little dome or top is made feparate and entire of itfelf, with the cornice mitered round, and the taffels fixed to it as fhewn in the defign, and the whole is placed loofe on without any faftenings.

They are made narrow, between two and three feet wide, and feldom above it. Every thing is made exceeding light about the tefter. The ftool is fixed to each chair with ftraps and buttons, and the whole thus finifhed makes a pleafing appearance.

Of the Library Cafe. Plate III. of the Appendix.

THE elliptic breaks of this bookcafe will produce a good effect in the whole.

The doors in the upper part are intended to have fluted green filk behind, and a drapery at top.

The pilafters are fuppofed to be glued to the ftile of the door, and are hinged as in common.

The lower middle part contains clothes-prefs fhelves, and every other part may be fitted up for books; or the lower elliptic

tic breaks may be formed into a neft of drawers, as there is depth enough.

The half columns on the lower doors are glued to the ftile, and the doors hinged as in common; but for the fake of fhewing the defign to advantage, the open door is drawn as if the columns were feparate.

The young workman fhould obferve, that the whole is to be made in fix carcafes, and fcrewed together, and then the plinth fhould be made to fit it, of one entire frame; alfo the furbafe and its freeze are made all in one frame, and fcrewed down on to the carcafes; as alfo is the cornice and its freeze.

Of the Pier Tables. Plate IV.

As pier tables are merely for ornament under a glafs, they are generally made very light, and the ftyle of finifhing them is rich and elegant. Sometimes the tops are folid marble, but moft commonly veneered in rich fatin, or other valuable wood, with a crofs-band on the outfide, a border about two inches richly japanned, and a narrow crofs-band beyond it, to go all round. The frames are commonly gold, or white and burnifhed gold. Stretching-rails have of late been introduced to thefe

3   tables,

tables, and it muſt be owned that it is with good effect, as they take off the long appearance of the legs, and make the under part appear more furniſhed; beſides they afford an opportunity of fixing a vaſe or baſket of flowers, which, with their re-flection when there is a glaſs behind, produce a brilliant ap-pearance.

Some, in place of a ſtretcher, have a thin marble ſhelf, with a braſs rim round it, ſupported by a light frame; in which caſe the top ought to be of marble alſo.

Of *the Library Steps and Table.* Plate V.

THIS deſign was taken from ſteps that have been made by Mr. Campbell, Upholſterer to the Prince of Wales. They were firſt made for the King, and highly approved of by him, as every way anſwering the intended purpoſe. There are other kinds of library ſteps which I have ſeen, made by other perſons, but, in my opinion, theſe muſt have the decided preference, both as to ſimplicity and firmneſs when they are ſet up. The ſteps may be put up in half a minute, and the whole may be taken down and encloſed within the table frame in about the ſame time. The table, when encloſed, ſerves as a library table, and has a riſing flap, ſupported by a horſe, to write on. The

C   ſize fize of the table is three feet ten inches long, thirty-three inches high, and two feet one inch in width. When the steps are out they rife thirty-three inches perpendicular from the top of the table frame, and the whole height of the last step is five feet five perpendicular from the ground. The perpendicular height of the hand-rail is three feet one inch above the last step; and observe, that on *g*, which is iron, is fixed a small flap on which a book may rest, fo that a gentleman, when he is looking at any book in his library, may note down a passage from it without the trouble of going down again. The method of folding the whole up is as follows:

The triangular iron bracket *g* is unlocked by a catch which keeps it firm to the hand-rail, and the desk-flap fixed to it being turned over to the inside, the whole comes forward, and lies level upon the upper steps. The standard *b* may then be raised out of its socket, and, having a joint at the top, it turns up to *d*, as shewn by the dotted curve line. The short standard *d e* is then, by relieving a spring, pressed down below the edge of the table-top; and the hand-rail and standard *b* having been folded together, as mentioned before, they both rest on the iron socket fastened to the front edge of the upper steps. Next, the horfe *o* is folded by the side of the upper steps, and then both they and the horfe fall down within the table frame; and it must be observed, that in folding

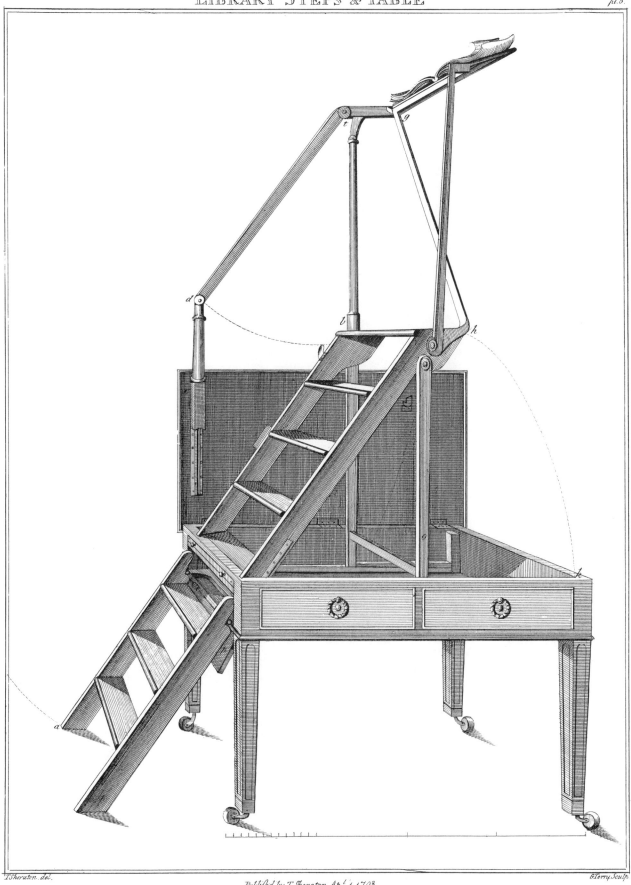

T.Sheraton.del.

Publish'd by T.Sheraton Apl 1.1793.

G.Terry.Sculp.

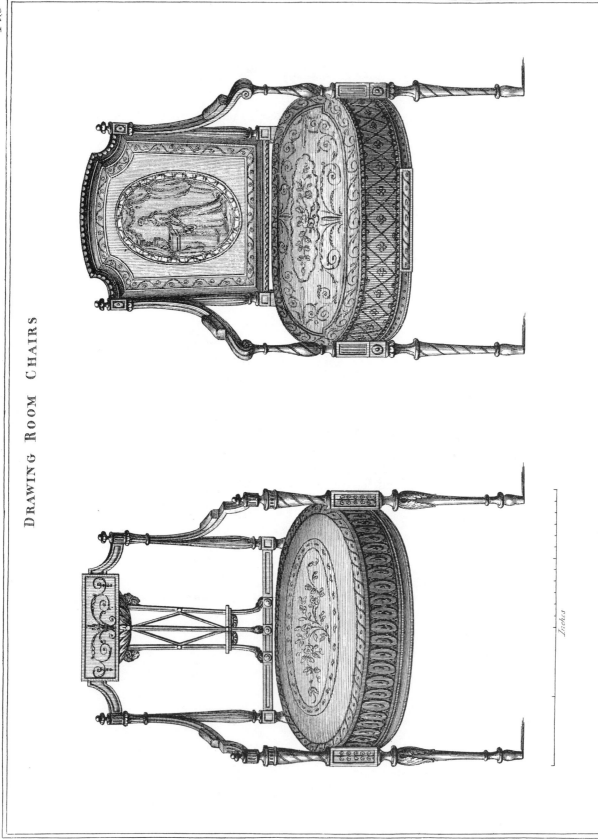

Pl.6

DRAWING ROOM CHAIRS

Inches

T. Sheraton Del.

Published as the Act Directs by T. Sheraton

J. Caldwall Sculp.

ing down the fteps, the hand-rail and ftandard, which refted for a while on the focket faftened to the front of the fteps, fall into another focket of the fame kind faftened to the under fide of the table top, where they remain, and fall within the table frame when the top is folded down. Laftly, the lower fteps *a* are turned up to a horizontal pofition, and being hinged to a flider which runs in a groove, the whole flips in as a drawer, and is enclofed by the flap *p*, which turns up and appears as the front of a drawer.

Of the Drawing-room Chairs. Plate VI.

THE frame of the right-hand chair is intended to be finifhed in burnifhed gold, and the feat and back covered with printed filk.

In the front rail is a tablet, with a little carving in its pannel. The legs and ftumps have twifted flutes and fillets, done in the turning, which produce a good effect in the gold.

The chair on the left may be finifhed in japan painting, interfperfed with a little gilding in different parts of the banifter, which has a lively effect. The covering of the feat is of printed

5   chintz,

chintz, which may now be had of various patterns on purpofe for chair-feats, together with borders to fuit them.

Of *the Bidet Dreffing-Table, and Night-Table Bafon-Stand.* Plate VII.

THE dreffing-table has a real drawer under the cupboard part, and the reft are fham.

The right-hand cupboard door opens by a fpring-catch communicated to the patera handle in the center. The water-bottle is fupported by a round box, made of very thin wood, glued and canvaffed over to ftrengthen it, and fixed to the top.

The bidet legs turn up with a joint. The defign fhews only legs at one end, but the other legs are fuppofed to be folded up till the whole is taken out; and when ufed, the legs are kept to their place by iron hooks and eyes.

The fcale fhews the fize of the front, and its depth from front to back is fixteen inches and a half. The frame, to which the glafs is hinged, is fourteen inches in width.

The night-table requires no explanation, and I fhall only obferve, that the covers with rings on them are meant for

a tooth-

Pl.7.

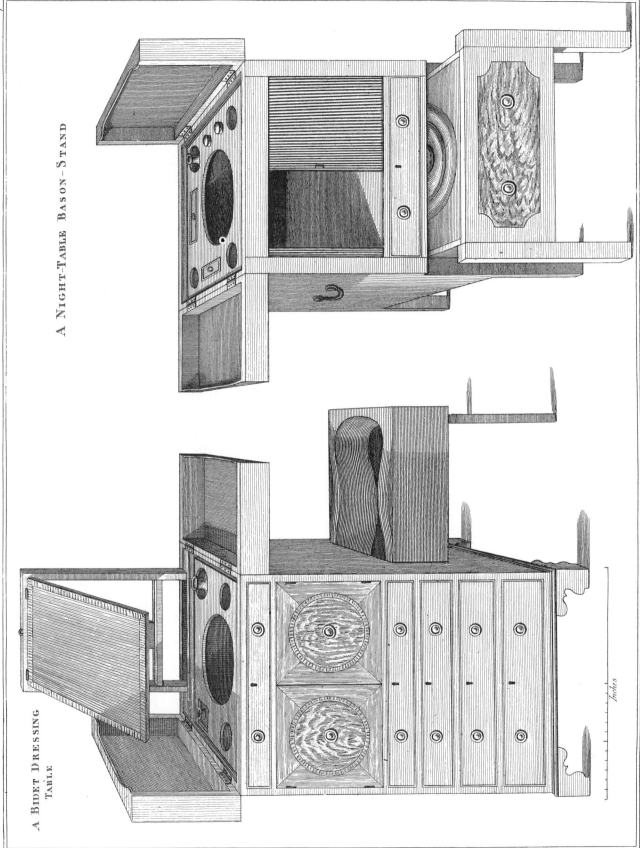

A NIGHT-TABLE BASON-STAND

A BIDET DRESSING TABLE

Inches

T.Sheraton Del.

Published as the Act. Directs by T. Sheraton April 11 1793.

J. Caldwell Sculpt

A · WARDROBE .

T. Sheraton del.

Publish'd by T. Sheraton, Ap. 14, 1793.

T. Terry, Sculp.

a tooth-brush, and the ivory boxes on the right for tooth-powder.

The scale for the dressing-table shews the size of the night-table, applied to the front, and its depth from front to back is eighteen inches.

Of *the Wardrobe*. Plate VIII.

THE upper middle-part contains six or seven clothes-press shelves, generally made about six, or six inches and an half deep, with green baize tacked to the inside of the front to cover the clothes with. The lower part consists of real drawers. The wings have each of them arms, to hang clothes on, made of beech, with a swivel in their center, which slips on to an iron rod fixed by plates screwed on to each side of the wings, as ex-pressed in the design.

The whole is made in four separate carcases. The wings by themselves, and the upper and lower middle parts separate.

The plinth is made all in one frame, and likewise the cor-nice with its freeze, and being screwed to each carcas, the whole is kept firm.

D   Obferve,

Obferve, that in the wings a bead is put up for the doors to fall againft when they are fhut to; by which means are cleared the knuckles of the hinges on the doors of the middle part.

It fhould alfo be obferved, that as the furbafe cannot go round the out ends of each wing on account of opening the doors, the moulding is returned againft the front of each door.

The furbafe on the middle part returns, and ftops againft the inner end of the wing; and the edge of the door of each wing, with the furbafe which is on them, are fcribed on to the aforefaid return, which then appears as an internal miter, and gives place to the opening of the door.

The fcale, applied to the middle part, gives its height and length. The wings are two feet, and fixteen or feventeen inches deep; and the depth of the middle part about twenty-three inches.

Of the Bed. Plate IX.

THIS defign requires no explanation, except that which relates to the tefter. The cove of the tefter is to be formed by

8   ribs;

1   2   *feet*   3   4

T. Sheraton del.

Barlow sculp.

Published as the Act directs by T. Sheraton April 16. 1793.

CONVERSATION
CHAIRS

Inches

T Sheraton Del.

Published as the Act Directs by T. Sheraton April 20 1793.

J. Caldwall Direx.t

ribs; one at each miter, and other fhort ones joined to them, with the reft about five inches apart from each other. At the upper part of the cove is a fquare tefter into which the ribs are fixed. On the edge of this tefter, which is made very light, is fixed a fmall moulding mitered all round. The cove being formed, the ribs may be covered with ftrong board-paper, both infide and out, which may either be japanned to match the furniture, or it may be covered with the furniture itfelf. The circular part about the cove is nothing more than a ftraight board fixed on to the upper tefter. For the fake of eafy conveyance, the cove may be made in four parts, mitering at each corner, and the ornament intended to be at each miter on the outfide running entirely up to the feathers, will hide the joint.

The fwags of filk line that appear on the drapery fhould be faftened to the back part of the cornice, in order that they may hang eafy. The pillars are to be japanned. The pannel that hides the fcrews is made to flip into a groove at the bottom, and when raifed up a little from their place, can be taken away to come at the fcrews. The valence and drapery both together flip on to a lath as in common.

Of

Of the Sofa and Converfation Chairs.   Plate X.

WITH refpect to this fofa, all that is neceffary to be obferved is, that in the fpace between the divifions of the back
part, it is meant that there fhould be a ground-work covered
with filk, to fuit the reft of the fofa.   Againft this ground the
two columns and the ornament are fuppofed to reft.

The converfation chairs are ufed in library or drawing-
rooms.   The parties who converfe with each other fit with
their legs acrofs the feat, and reft their arms on the top rail,
which, for this purpofe, is made about three inches and an half
wide, ftuffed and covered.

For the convenience of fitting in the manner juft mentioned, the chair is made long between front and back, and
very narrow at the back and front in proportion.   The height
of the chair to the ftuffing is three feet; at the back ten inches,
fpreading out in width to the top rail, which is twenty inches
in length.   The front is fixteen inches, and the height of the
feat as in common.

Of

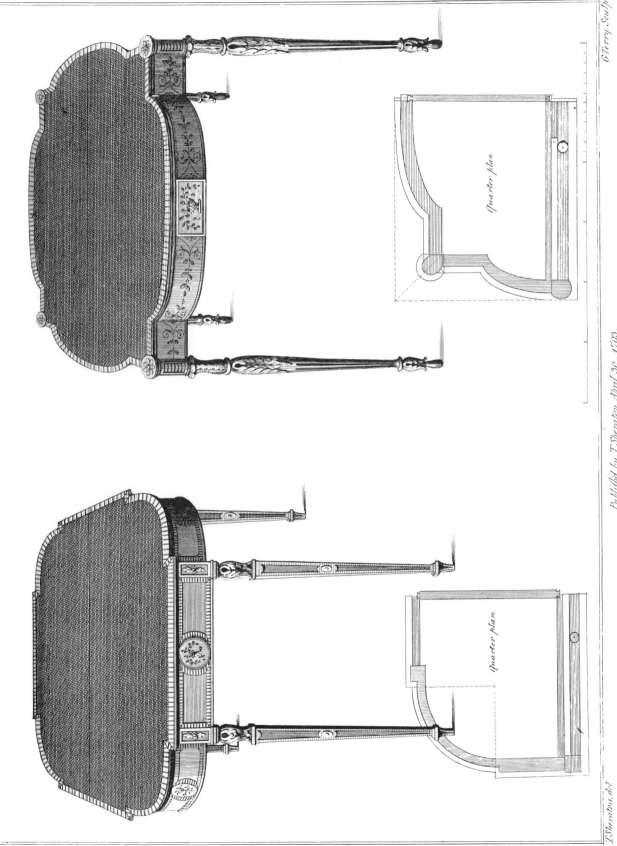

CARD TABLES

Quarter plan

Quarter plan

T.Sheraton, del.

Published by T.Sheraton, April 30, 1793.

G.Terry, Sculp.

A LIBRARY TABLE with SECRETARY DRAWER.

Half plan

T.Sheraton.del.   Publish'd by T.Sheraton.May.4.1793.   G.Terry.Sculp.

Of the Card Tables. Plate XI.

ON these tables it is scarcely neceffary to fay any thing, efpecially as the quarter plans fhew how they muft be framed; and therefore I fhall only obferve, that the ornaments may be japanned on the frames and carved in the legs. As to the method of managing the tops, I take it to be the beft to rip up dry deal, or faulty mahogany, into four inch widths, and joint them up. It matters not whether the pieces are whole lengths provided the jump-joints be croffed. Some tongue the jump-joints for ftrength.

After the tops are dry, hard mahogany is tongued into the ends of the deal, then flips are glued on the front and back, that the whole may appear folid mahogany, if a moulding is to be worked on the edge; but if the edge be crofs-banded there is in this cafe no need for tonguing in mahogany.

Of the Library Table with a Writing Drawer. Plate XII.

THIS table is intended either to fit or ftand and write at. The height of the fecretary-drawer is adjufted for fitting, and

E

the

the top of the table is high enough to ſtand and write on, eſpe-
cially if the middle top be raiſed by a horſe, as ſhewn in the deſign. This table will alſo prove very uſeful to draw on; for
when the middle part is up for drawing upon, there remains
ſufficient room at each end of the table on which to place the
neceſſary impliments for drawing; beſides, the drawers at each
end may be fitted up to hold colours of various kinds; I mean
the two upper ones, for there are drawers quite down to the
plinth. The drawers under the ſecretary will hold the large
ſheets of drawing-paper, together with the tee ſquares; and as
it will not be neceſſary to make the drawers under the ſecretary
the entire width of the table, the oppoſite front, being made
ſham to have the ſame appearance, the whole of it may be
hinged at bottom and locked at the top, and the inſide will allow depth for books. This ſham front being a conſiderable
width, it would hazard the hinges to let it reſt wholly on them
when turned down, and therefore there ſhould be iron rule-
joints at each end as ſtays.

To theſe conveniences there are alſo four cupboards in-
cloſed with doors, as ſhewn in the deſign, and the whole finiſhed in this manner, I venture to affirm, will prove as uſeful a
table as has ever been deviſed or publiſhed.

In

In refpect to the manufacturing part, it will be beft to make it in two parts. The upper part containing the fecretary, and two drawers at each end; and the lower part, four drawers under the fecretary, a book-cafe behind, and four drawers at each end, the lowermoft of which is fhewn in the defign. The top fhould be framed of inch and quarter wainfcot (as de-fcribed in page 373), containing a well for the defk part, which may be made to rife on the front as well as at the back, by forming a double horfe; but in this defign it is only intended to rife at the back by a fingle horfe, and hinged to the crofs-band at the front.

The cupboard doors may either be framed and pannelled, or glued up to their fweep in narrow flips of inch mahogany, and clamped; not by tonguing, but by a fquare joint, and pins driven through the clamps.

The management of the circular bafe-moulding and plinth may be learned in page 375.

Of the Fire Screens. Plate XIII.

THE lyre fcreen is conftructed upon an entire new plan, it being defigned to turn upon a fwivel, which fixes to the vafe

and

and paſſes through the bottom rail, ſo that the ſcreen may be turned to any poſition without moving the ſtand.

The ſcreen part, which riſes between the ſtandards or pillars, is ſuſpended by a weight in the taſſels, which are communicated to the ſcreen by a line paſſing through the pillars and over a pulley fixed to their top.

There muſt be a dovetail groove in each ſtandard, and the ſcreen made to fit into theſe; ſo that the ſtandards may keep their proper place, and not fly open at the top.

Obſerve, that the ornament on the tops of the pillars or ſtandards riſe up with the ſcreen, being fixed to it, and detached from the pillars.

It is intended that the lyre ornament be carved in bas relief, gilt and burniſhed; which, when planted on to a blue ſilk or ſatin ground, cannot fail to produce a fine effect.

The other ſcreen being common, needs no explanation, only that it is ſuſpended by little ſprings fixed in the dovetail grooves of the ſtandards.

In

Pl. 13.

Horse Fire Screens

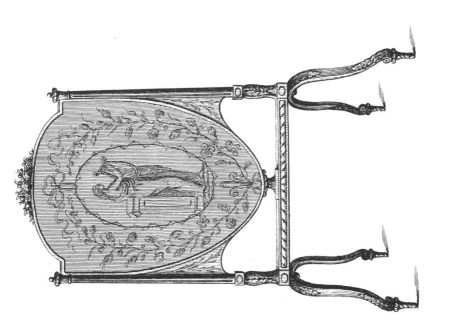

T. Sheraton Del.

Published as the Act Directs by T. Sheraton.

1   Feet   2   3

Plan

T.Sheraton.del.

G.Terry.Sculp.

Publish'd by T.Sheraton.May. 20.1793.

In refpect to the general fize of horfe fire-fcreens, about eighteen inches or nineteen may be allowed for the breadth, and three feet fix or feven inches for their height.

Of the Cabinet. Plate XIV.

THIS cabinet, I prefume, is as new as the fire-fcreen, and will have a better effect in the execution than in the defign.

The front of the cabinet is hinged to a fliding piece which runs in a groove, upon the fame principle as the writing-table page 408. The front being turned down to a horizontal pofition, it may then be flipped in till it ftops. To fupport the front thus turned down, there are two fliders which come out of the plinth on which the cabinet refts. Thefe fliders come out by relieving a fpring which is fixed in their fide, and having a common fpring behind, they are forced out fo that the fingers may lay hold to draw them quite out. They are lined with green cloth both at top and bottom to prevent fcratching. The infide of the front is alfo lined with green cloth to write on. The infide of the cabinet is fitted up in the manner fhewn in the cabinet Plate XVI.

F   Above

Above the falling front is a drawer, to the under fide of which the front locks, fo that the drawer and front are either locked or opened at one time.

Above the drawer is an ornamented freeze, japanned; and round the top, which is marble, is a brafs edging.

The flower-pot at the top is fuppofed to be real, not carved; but that on the ftretcher is carved.

The columns ftand clear, as fhewn by the plan; and they are intended to have brafs bafes and capitals, with wooden fhafts fluted.

The candle branches turn to any form in a focket, and the whole may be taken away, as they are only fcrewed into a nut fixed into the legs of the table.

There is a brafs fret fixed at each end, which finifhes at the ftandards of the candle-branches. The lower frame contains a drawer in front, and the legs being octagon, are intended to be veneered croffways as far as to the carving, which may be gilt to fuit the bafes and caps of the columns.

Of

T. Sheraton Del.

Published as the Act Directs by T. Sheraton.

J. Caldwall Direxit

A LADY'S CABINET.

Inside of the Cabinet.

Plan of the Cabinet.

feet

T. Sheraton delin.

Published as the Act directs, by T. Sheraton, May 27th 1793.

I Barlow sculp

Of the Dreſſing Cheſts. Plate XV.

THESE cheſts are alſo on a new plan, particularly as the common ſlider for merely writing on is turned into a ſhallow drawer, which contains a little writing flap which riſes behind by a horſe, and places for ink, ſand, and pens, and alſo dreſſing-boxes. When the drawer is in, it appears like a common ſlider, with a partition above and below, as that with the convex front. There is therefore no ſlip under the top, as the drawer ſides muſt run cloſe up to it. The drawer below of courſe muſt lock up into the under edge of the dreſſing-drawer, and the dreſſing drawer into the top, which is done at one time, by the bolt of the under lock forcing up that of the upper one.

The height of theſe cheſts are always governed by the ſlider, which runs thirty-two or thirty-three inches from the floor. The ſcale ſhews their length, and their breadth is twenty-two or twenty-three inches.

Of the Lady's Cabinet. Plate XVI.

THE cabinet in Plate XIV. is made in two parts, but this is entirely in one. The legs and columns are therefore all in one
piece

167

piece. The infide of the cabinet is made feparate, and flips in between the legs, and a piece of narrow wood, as a band, is fitted to fill the fpace up to the column, as the defign fhews.

The marble fhelves, with frets at each end, are for a tea equipage. Above and below thefe fhelves are drawers which turn out by a hinge. Above and below the front are alfo drawers. The drawer below may be made to fupport the front when turned down to write on, or it may be fupported by brafs joints, as fhewn in the defign for the infide of the cabinet.

The fcales and plans of each cabinet fhew their length and breadth; it remains only to mention their height, which is four feet, and four feet two.

Of the Horfe Dreffing Glaffes. Plate XVII.

THE dreffing-glafs on the left rifes to any height, by lead weights inclofed in the ftandards. The weights are fufpended fometimes to tambour glued on to webbing, which paffes over a brafs roller at the top, and fixes to a piece of thin wood, tamboured to match it. Through this piece of thin wood is put an iron pin, with a thin plate to it to fcrew it faft; which pin goes through the fide of the glafs, and faftens by a nut at the infide,

5 fo

fo that when the glafs is raifed, it may be turned to any direction. But fome ufe a kind of coloured ftrong webbing, without
the tambour, which makes it lefs troublefome, and lefs liable
to injury, though it does not look fo neat. Thofe unacquainted with the manner of gluing up the ftandards, may fee a fection of them in Plate XXX. Fig. C.

There is a brafs handle behind the ornamented top to raife
the glafs by.

The boxes on each fide are intended to hold conveniences
for dreffing. On thefe, there is a comb-tray on the left fide,
and a pin-cufhion on the right. When the dreffing-boxes are
not in ufe, they are intended to turn behind the glafs. For this
purpofe they are fixed to a brafs focket, which turns upon a
fhort brafs rod, and by a fcrew they may be raifed up or lowered at pleafure. See Fig. D. Plate XXX.

The other dreffing-glafs has a convenience for writing as
well as for dreffing, which convenience rifes by a little horfe.
The dreffing-boxes are made with clofe covers, and a flider inclofes the whole, fo that when the whole is turned up nothing
can come out of its place. The glafs does not rife as the other,
but fixes in centers, fo as to move in any pofition either back
or forward.

G

And

And obferve, that when the dreffing-flap is turned up it locks into the top rail, and the glafs of courfe falls to its own place. The under fide of the flap being the front when turned up, it may be japanned and banded. The lower parts of the ftandards are fhaped like a lyre; and to form the ftrings, brafs wire is let in, which has a pretty effect.

Of *the Chaife Longus*. Plate XVIII.

THESE have their name from the French, which imports a long chair. Their ufe is to reft or loll upon after dinner, and in fome cafes the lower one will ferve for a fofa. The drapery under the rail is tacked to a rabbet left on purpofe. The upper one is framed firft in two parts. The end, or chair part, is made to receive the ftool part within its fides; and the fides of the ftool part fcrew in againft the infide of the chair. As to any other particular, the defigns themfelves are fufficient to point them out.

Of *the Englifh State Bed*. Plate XIX.

IN giving a defign for an Englifh ftate-bed, or fuch an one as is fuitable to the dignity of a prince, and worthy the notice of a king, I conceived it neceffary to cultivate as much as I could

the

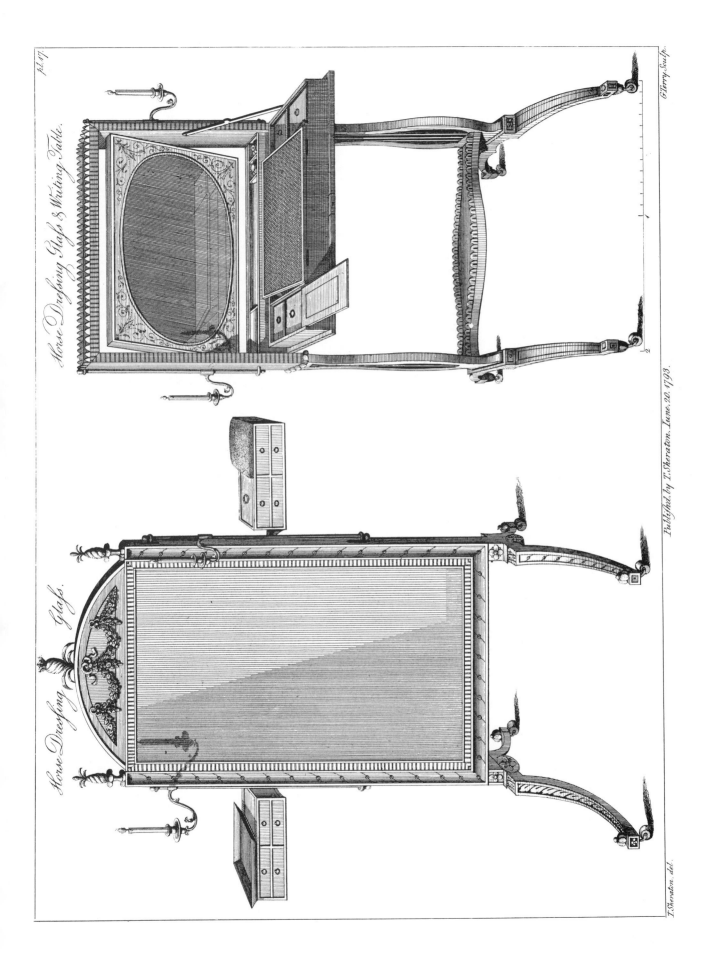

Pl. 47.

Horse Dressing Glass & Writing Table.

Horse Dressing Glass.

T. Sheraton. del.

Published by T. Sheraton. June. 20. 1793.

G.Terry. Sculp.

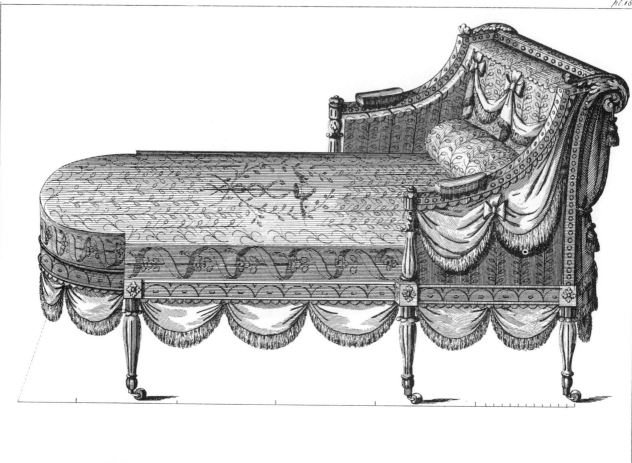

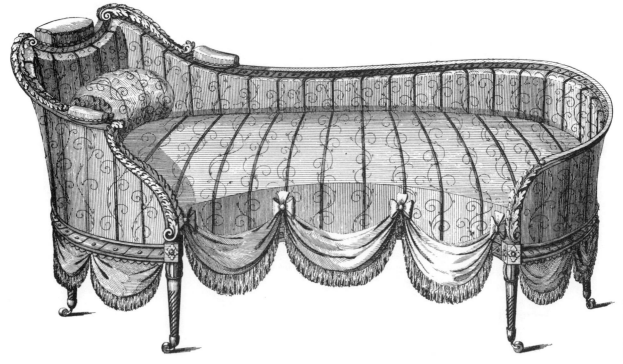

T.Sheraton.del.

Publ^d by T.Sheraton Iune.25.1793.

G.Terry.Sculp.

the moſt exalted ideas, unfettered and unreſtrained with the thoughts of expenſiveneſs, which naturally produces meanneſs of compoſition, and in many caſes injures the ingenious in their deſigns.

For ornament to a bed of this kind, it ſtruck me that nothing could be more ſuitable and charaſteriſtic than ſuch as expreſſed ſymbolically the different parts of our government, together with thoſe virtues and principles which ought to be the ſupport of regal authority, and the ruling maxims of every good government of whatever kind, whether monarchical, ariſtocratical, or democratical. Emblems of war have been avoided as much as poſſible, being inconſiſtent ornaments for a bed, and becauſe good kings ought not to delight in war, but in peace, unity, and the love of men and their ſubjects.

As our government is compoſed of three diſtinct branches, the figure on the right hand bed-pillar is intended to repreſent the democratic part of it, or the power of the people inveſted in their repreſentatives in parliament.

In iconology*, democracy† is repreſented by the figure of

---

* Iconology, from εικον, *eikon*, an image; and λεγω, *lego*, I ſpeak. The interpretation of ancient images, monuments, and emblems.

† Democracy, from δημος, *demos*, people; and κρατειν, *kratein*, to command or govern; is when the ſovereign power is lodged in the body of the people.

a woman

a woman dreffed in a homely garment, and crowned with vine leaves. In her right hand fhe holds a pomegranate, which denotes affemblies of the people on matters of importance. In her left hand is a clufter of ferpents, which expreffes the winding and flow progreffion of democratic ftates, owing to the inability of the common people to govern. Her ftanding on the two facks of corn which reft on the pedeftal, fignifies that democratic government is more attentive to the obtaining of neceffary provifions, than the increafe of fame, or the acquifition of honours. If this be a juft reprefentation, and founded on fact, the reader will, no doubt, confider the democratic branch a very important one, and for which reafon it is here placed near the groundwork.

The figure, oppofite, on the left pillar, reprefents the ariftocratic branch. Ariftocracy* is defcribed by the figure of an elderly lady, in a fumptuous drefs, with a crown of gold upon her head. Painters reprefent her fitting on a throne; which is a pofition confonant to lawgivers, but which I could not make fuitable to this fituation. In her right hand fhe holds the confular fafces, that is, a number of elm rods tied in a bundle, with a hatchet in the middle, which, originally, were the enfigns of

---

* Ariftocracy, from αριτος, *ariftos*, the beft; and κρατιω, *kratio*, I command or govern; is when the fupreme power is lodged in a fenate, compofed of the principal perfons of a ftate, either for their nobility, capacity, or probity.

5   fovereign

fovereign dignity, but in after times the hatchet was taken out, and they were carried before the confuls or magiftrates of Rome, to denote their authority. Thefe rods are entwined with a crown of laurels, a fymbol of reward due to thofe who have maintained the public welfare, and have performed great actions for the good of the ftate. In her left hand is a fteel cap, at her feet a hatchet, a plate, and purfe with money, all which denote that arms and finances are neceffary fupports of ftates. And I would here obferve, that it is not abfolutely neceffary to confider the fteel cap and hatchet as fymbols of war, but of the executive power requifite in all governments for the maintenance of peace, and the punifhment of evil doers.

The figure in the center of the upper cornice is intended to reprefent the monarchical branch of our government.

Monarchy * is characterized by the figure of a young woman of grave countenance, feated on a terreftrial globe, holding four fcepters, to denote dominion and power. The other hand being uplifted, denotes her authority in giving command. The rays of light furrounding her head, denote luftre, and the refpect due to her greatnefs. The lion on each fide fymbolizes the

* Monarchy, from μονος, *monos*, alone; and αρχη, *arche*, government; is when the fupreme power is invefted in one perfon, commonly termed the King.

H   power

power which fhe poffeffes and requires of others in order to her fupport. Painters, however, defcribe her with trophies of war, and a crowned head chained down as a captive at her feet, which I have here omitted, hoping that conqueft and war are not the prominent features in our government.

Thefe three figures in their fituation to each other form a triangle, whofe bafe is democracy and ariftocracy, and whofe fummit is monarchy; denoting that monarchical power and ho-nour are originally derived from the people, and that without their fupport, monarchy in its moft exalted ftate muft fall.

The lions which fupport the bed, with oak foliage and leaves on the bed-frame and round the fhafts of each pillar, are emblems of the ftrength and permanent nature of our govern-ment. The acorns being the fruit of the oak, denote, that by long progreffive improvements it is arrived to a good degree of maturity.

The ferpents in the cornice, which mutually entwine them-felves round Mercury's rod, denote the unity, prudence, and wifdom, requifite to monarchs in the exercife of their impor-tant charge. The trumpets and laural crown are expreffive of the fame which the Englifh ftate has acquired through the mildnefs of its government. The beads under the cornice denote

174

note its riches. The baſkets of fruit on each capital, and in the quadrantal pannels, ſymbolize the proſperous ſtate of the nation, and the plenty we enjoy. In the arch of each quadrant are marked the degrees, to denote that navigation has contributed greatly to our riches and ſafety. The lyre and trumpets on the pedeſtal above the cap, ſignify the flouriſhing ſtate of the arts; and the ſpreading oak leaves and roſes, are meant to expreſs the deſigner's wiſh and hopes, that the uſeful arts may long continue to grow and ſpread themſelves under the munificence of our government.

The coronets round the dome are thoſe of the immediate ſons and daughters of the king of Great Britain, of which there are thirteen; but the dome being divided into ſixteen compartments, ſtill leaves room for an increaſe of the royal family, to denote that the ſubjects of Great Britain ſhould hope for a long ſucceſſion of a mild and good government. The feſtoons of flowers denote that happineſs and proſperity are wiſhed to ſurround each branch of the royal offspring.

The crown of England is ſupported on the top of the dome by three figures, intended to repreſent Juſtice, Clemency, and Liberty; for notwithſtanding theſe may, in ſome inſtances, be ſullied in our government, yet ſcarcely any nation can boaſt of more than that which we have long enjoyed.

3   Juſtice,

Juftice, which ought to be the moving principle of civil government, is by painters defcribed by the figure of a woman dreffed in white robes; holding in her left hand a fword, to punifh criminals; and in her right a pair of fcales, to give that which is due to every one without partiality; which impartiality is denoted by a bandage over her eyes. In this fituation the fword and fcales may be fuppofed to lie on the other fide of the dome ready for ufe.

Clemency is a neceffary quality or principle in government, by which thofe in authority are enabled to take into confideration, and to effect the relief of the miferies of the helplefs and infolvent. In the exercife of this virtue, he who is ready to be cut afunder by the uplifted hand of juftice can be faved, and the rotting infolvent prifoner can be abfolved and releafed. Such actions beget gratitude in the minds of the fubjects, and are as a pillar to the crown; while cruelty and tyranny have often proved fatal to princes.

Painters defcribe this virtue by the figure of a woman crowned with olives, as a mark of her peaceful and gentle temper; and dreffed in a purple robe, which denotes her eminence. She is characterifed by the mildnefs of her countenance, and fitting on a lion (which I could not here introduce.) She alfo holds a laurel branch of honour and refpect in her right hand.
She

She is said to have a spear by her side, so that when her mercy is abused she may in justice revenge it.

The other figure, Liberty, on the other side of the dome, is an essential principle to good government. It supposes a disposition in those possessing supreme authority to allow subjects to enjoy their natural, moral, and religious rights. In the possession of these we are delivered from slavery; the yoke is broken. Therefore painters represent liberty by the figure of a woman, with a broken yoke-stick in her left hand, and trampling upon it as a mark of resentment. She is dressed in white robes, to denote the blessings which she confers on mankind; and in her right hand she holds a sceptre as a sign of independence. She has also a cap of liberty on her head, in allusion to the custom of the Romans, in setting their slaves free; who also shaved their heads, and permitted them to be covered in the presence of those who gave them liberty *.

The figures on the other side, and at the end of the bed may be the same, not merely for uniformity's sake, but to convey the sentiment expressed by the allegory with more weight, as it is well known that repetition is some-

* Richardson's Iconology, from whose work I am indebted for several ideas on this subject.

I   times

times introduced to give force and energy to a subject. However, if any should think it necessary to vary the figures on the different sides, there are plenty of subjects suitable enough.

Fortitude may be placed on the center of the cornice, opposite to monarchy; to denote a quality of mind so highly necessary in those who rule. The emblem of this quality is a woman resting on the shaft of a column and its base, having a brown robe and part of a military dress, with a lion on one side of her; but she may have one at each side, to make the outline more agreeable to the figure of monarchy. Her military dress conveys the idea of courage; and resting on a column, steadiness and firmness; and the lion, strength of mind.

On the bed-pillar, opposite to the figure which represents the aristocratic branch of our government, should be Counsel, to denote the wisdom and ability necessary in those who make up that branch.

Counsel is represented by the figure of a grave old man, having a long beard, dressed in long robes of violate colour. His age denotes that experience requires length of time, and that wisdom is the result of experience. His long robes denote

his

T. Sheraton Del.

J. Caldwall Dirext.

Published as the Act Directs by T. Sheraton Aug.t 24. 1793.

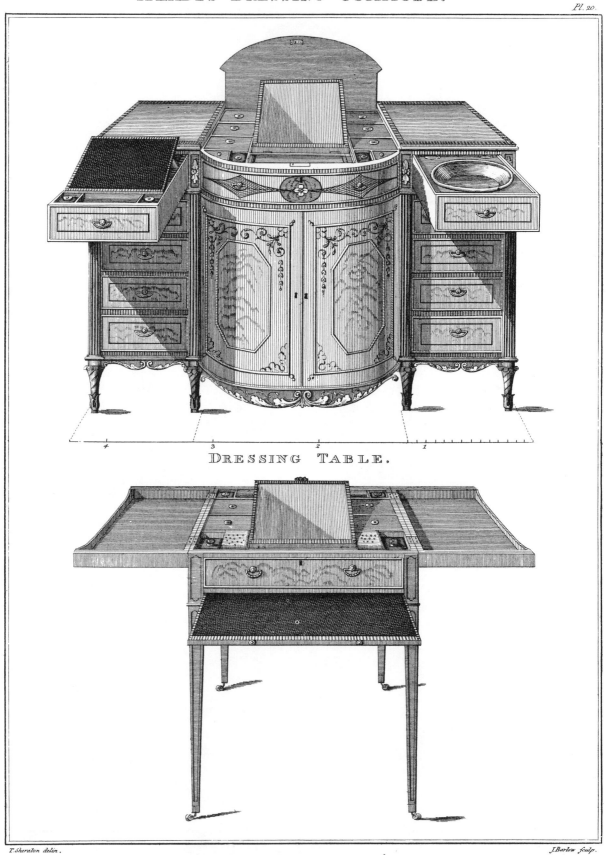

DRESSING TABLE.

T. Sheraton delin.

J. Barlow sculp.

Published as the Act directs, by T. Sheraton July 24.th 1793.

his high character, and their colour his gravity. He is reprefented fitting, to fhew his authority; and with a chain of gold
round his neck, to which is fufpended a human heart, to denote
his integrity. In his right hand is a book, to fhew he has regard to law, and that from literature he obtains his knowledge.
He may, however, in this fituation be ftanding, as the bed-pillar
will not fo well admit of a fitting attitude; and in this attitude
he may have a mirror in his left hand, furrounded with ferpents, to denote prudence and fpeculation, as neceffary to good
counfel.

On the other pillar, oppofite to the figure which reprefents
the democratic branch of our government, there may be the
emblem of Law, to denote that the members of parliament, as
the reprefentatives of the people, ought to be acquainted with
the rights and interefts of their conftituents; and alfo, that in
their debates on thefe fubjects, they ought to regard the laws of
the conftitution.

Law is reprefented by the figure of a refpectable elderly
lady, fitting on a tribunal chair. Her age denotes that law is an
ancient fubject; fhe is feated to denote eminence, and holds
a fceptre in her right hand to denote authority. In her left
hand fhe holds an imperial crown, allufive to the law of nations,

4   importing

importing that no nation can exist without laws. Her head is adorned with diamonds, to signify that law is most precious, and that its origin was from God.

At the end of the bed, and next to law, Obedience or Subjection may be introduced, to denote the duty and respect which the people owe to their representatives whom they have appointed, and particularly to signify that subjects ought not to rebel against government.

Obedience is described by the figure of a humble woman, in an upright position, with her eyes towards heaven, to denote her regard to its commands as the Appointer of government. Her upright position not only shews her willingness to obey, but that government was never appointed to oppress or bow down the backs of those who are willing to obey just laws. She is dressed in white robes, denoting innocence; and across her shoulders is a yoke, the emblem of patience and obedience. By her side may be represented a dog, which is a symbol of obedience and faithfulness.

On the center of the cornice may be represented Authority, to denote that without its influence law is rejected and contemned,—obedience is without foundation, and therefore government could not exist.

Authority

Authority is reprefented by the figure of a matron, or old lady, to fhew that the inftitution of authority which gives effect to laws is ancient as law itfelf. She is feated on a regal chair, becaufe princes and magiftrates generally perform their office fitting, indicating tranquillity of mind. She holds a fceptre in her left hand, denoting regal power and authority; and by her fide are arms, to fignify her power to punifh the licentious, and protect the obedient. In her right hand is a book, refting on her knee, to denote that civil authority is of divine origin*.

On the other pillar may be the reprefentation of Tyranny chained down, with her back bowed, to fignify that thofe in authority ought to fupprefs rather than cherifh it; and to fhew that tyranny ought, in all good governments, to be at the foot of power, to prevent its baneful effects in a ftate. The emblem of this noxious quality is a pale, proud, and cruel-looking woman, dreffed in armour, and purple drapery, to denote her readinefs to fhed blood in the defence of her arbitrary meafures. In her left hand is a yoke, and in her right an uplifted fword, to fhew that fhe is ready to enflave mankind, and punifh them if they will not put on the yoke. She wears an iron crown, to fhew that the authority which tyrants feek is for bafe purpofes and cruelty.

* See Rom. xiii. 1.

K

To

To make thefe three figures harmonize—Authority, at the top of the cornice, may be reprefented as looking towards Obedience with an eye of approbation; and the book lying on her lap, with the right hand fhe may hold a dart pointed directly to Tyranny below. And to reprefent Tyranny in the moft wretched ftate, her iron crown may appear to tumble off her head, her yoke broken, and her fword pointed to her own breaft, to fhew that in the end tyranny is her own executioner. Thus, I think, the end of the bed will exhibit emblematically the end of civil government, which is to protect the innocent and obedient, to fupprefs cruelty and oppreffion, which are the life and foul of tyranny. The front fide fhews the nature of our government, the dome the principles which fupport it, and the back fide the way in which government is managed.

The ornaments on the head-board are emblems of love and continency, expreffed by the figure of Cupid, Chaftity, and a trophy below. Cupid is reprefented as drawing his bow to guard Chaftity from the violent attempts of Impurity, whofe figure, partly a woman and partly a monkey, is behind the curtain, to denote that fuch as practife it lurk in fecret.

The emblem of Chaftity is the figure of a young woman in white robes, to denote purity and innocence. Her head is crowned with a garland of cinnamon, a pleafant and coftly plant,

5   to

to fignify that Chaftity is a virtue both pleafant and valuable. She is veiled, to exprefs her modefty; and in her right hand holds a fcepter, as a fign of her conqueft over luft. In her left fhe holds a turtle dove, which is an emblem of continence.

With refpect to the manufacturing part of this bed, it fhould be obferved, that the curtains draw up by a pulley at the feveral corners, detached from the drapery valence which is fixed to the cornice.

The tefter on which the dome refts, is made perfectly ftraight, and forms an even furface on both fides; which, in the infide, is pannelled out with gilt moulding at each angle.

The quadrantal pannels recede back from the cornice, and are framed into the top of the pillars, which are left fquare. The ground of thefe pannels being continued the whole length, from pillar to pillar, ferves as a facia on which to fix the cornice. Then obferve, that the bafket of fruit and the lyre being in one piece, they are fixed to the pillar, and meet in a miter with the other fide.

The oak foliage is in one entire piece, and fcrewed up to the bed-fides, after the drapery valence is tacked to a rabbet made for that purpofe.

Every

183

Every other particular muſt naturally occur to the workman, after what has already been ſaid on the other beds in this
work. Upon the whole, though a bed of this kind is not likely
to be executed according to this deſign, except under the munificence of a royal order, yet I am not without hopes that uſeful ideas may be gathered from it, and applied to beds of a more
general kind.

Of the Dreſſing Commode. Plate XX.

WITH reſpect to the dreſſing part of this commode, it may
be made either fixed faſt, or to be brought forward in the manner of a drawer, with leapers to keep it to its place. If it is
made to be fixed faſt, the doors may be opened to form the
knee hole.

The top which covers and encloſes the dreſſing part, ſlides
down behind, in the manner deſcribed in page 407, to which I
refer the reader; only obſerve, that in this top there are miters
to fit the ſtraight moulding in front when the top is put down.
A bottle of water, and a pot to receive it when dirty, can both
be kept in the cupboard part.

The dreſſing-table below can require no explanation, except what relates to the ſize, which from front to back is
eighteen

eighteen inches, thirty-four the whole height, and two feet four the length of the front.

Of the Sideboard, with Vafe Knife-cafes. Plate XXI.

THE pedeſtal parts of this ſideboard may be made ſeparate, and then ſcrewed to the ſideboard. The top extends the whole length, in one entire piece, and is ſcrewed down to the pedeſtals. The hollow plinths of the vaſes are worked in one length, and mitered round. The top of the plinth is then blocked on at the under ſide, and the vaſe part is made to ſcrew into it, ſo that the vaſes may occaſionally be taken off. A croſs band is meant to be mitered all round the hollow plinths, coming forward to the edge of the top; ſo that if the top be veneered, it will only require the length between the two plinths. Within the front is a tambour cupboard, which is both uſeful, and has a good effect in its appearance; almoſt any workman will know how to manage this, ſo that I need not explain it. The ornament behind is braſs, intended as a ſtay to ſilver plate, and has branches for three lights. The circle in the center may have a glaſs luſtre hung within it, as an ornament. For any other particular relative to ſideboards in general, ſee page 363, where the common principles of this uſeful piece of furniture are explained.

L

Of

Of the Library Steps. Plate XXII.

THESE fteps are confiderably more fimple than thofe already defcribed; and though not fo generally ufeful, will come vaftly cheaper. The upper flight of fteps turn down upon the under ones, both of which rife up and flide in as a drawer; after which a flap, which is fhewn in the defign, is turned up, and has the appearance of a drawer front. Obferve, that the refting poft at the top folds down to the fide of the fteps by means of an iron joint. The horfe has green cloth under its feet, to prevent its fcratching the top. The defign fhews that the two fteps are connected together by hinges, fo made as to clear the edge of the table-top; and alfo, that there is a fliding board to which the under flight is hinged, which fliding-board runs in a groove.

The length of the table is three feet fix inches, its width twenty-two inches. The table is thirty inches high, the upper flight is thirty perpendicular, and the refting-poft thirty-three. This, and the other defign for library fteps, have obtained a patent; yet any part being materially altered, will evade the act, though the whole be nearly the fame. Thofe mafters, however, who do not think it worth their while to be at the trouble

8

of

A SIDE BOARD.

with VASE KNIFE CASES.

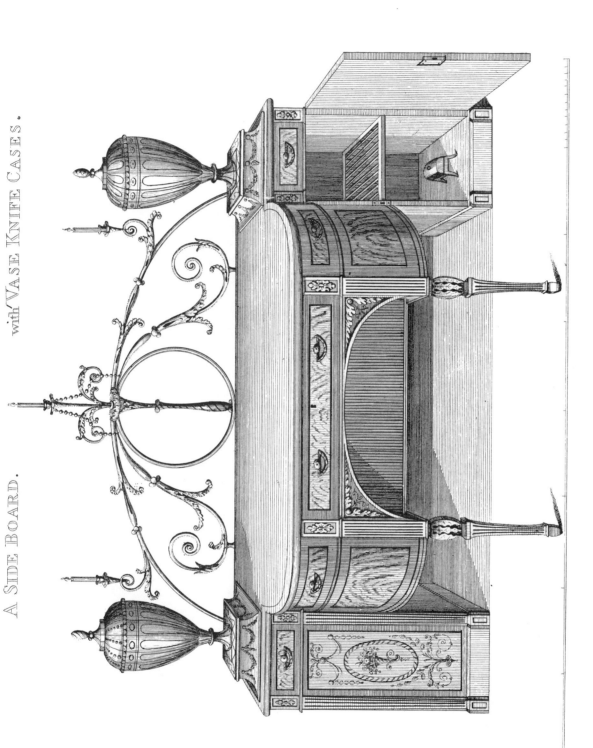

T.Sheraton.del.

Publish'd by T.Sheraton July 25.1793.

G.Terry.Sculp.

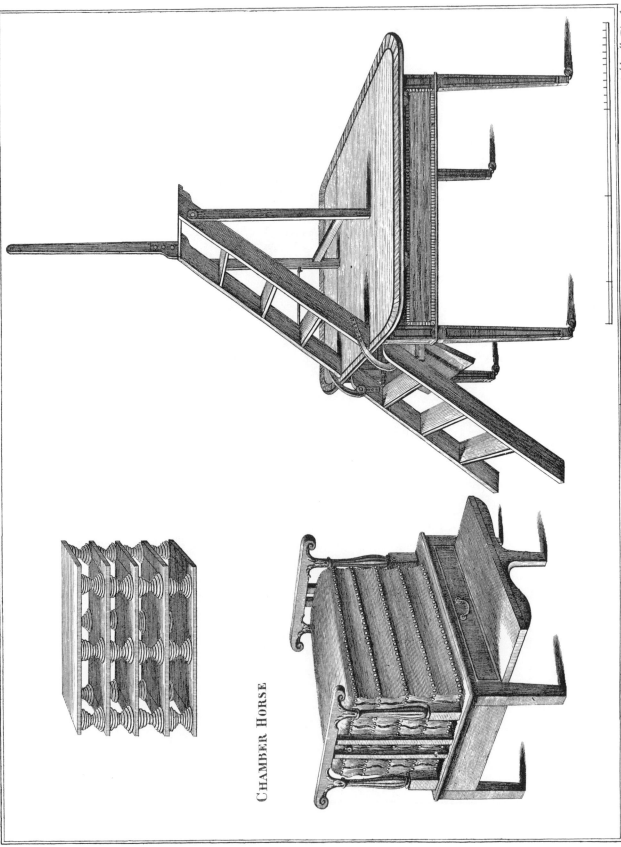

Pl.22.

LIBRARY STEPS *and* PEMBROKE TABLE

CHAMBER HORSE

J. Caldwall Dirext.

Published as the Act Directs by T. Sheraton. July 27. 1793.

T. Sheraton Del.

of introducing any effential alteration in them may have thefe fteps from Mr. Robert Campbell and Son, Mary-le-bone Street, London, with a fufficient allowance for felling them again.

Of the Chamber Horfe.

THE upper figure fhews the infide when the leather is off, which confifts of five wainfcoat inch boards, clamped at the ends; to which are fixed ftrong wire twifted round a block in regular gradation, fo that when the wire is compreffed by the weight of thofe who exercife, each turn of it may clear itfelf and fall within each other.

The top board is ftuffed with hair as a chair feat, and the leather is fixed to each board with brafs nails, tacked all round. The leather at each end is cut in flits to give vent to the air, which would otherwife refift the motion downwards.

The workman fhould alfo obferve, that a wooden or iron pin is fixed at each end of the middle board, for the purpofe of guiding the whole feat as it plays up and down. This pin runs between the two upright pieces which are framed into the arms at each end, as the defign fhews.

The

The length of the horfe is twenty-nine inches, the width twenty, its height thirty-two. To the top of the foot board is eight inches, and to the board whereon the feat is fixed is thirteen.

Of the Corner Night Tables. Plate XXIII.

THAT on the right requires no explanation, except that the doors may be hinged to turn in, if it is thought moft convenient.

The table on the left is intended to anfwer the purpofe of a wafh-hand ftand occafionally. To anfwer this end the top part is framed together of itfelf, and fixed by an iron or ftrong wooden pin, into the back corner of the lower part, which contains a focket, fo that the top part can be turned to one fide, as fhewn in the defign, or as much further as is neceffary to clear the hole.

Obferve alfo, that on the front is worked a groove, in which a pin paffes that is fixed to the front of the bottom of the upper part, and prevents the top part from turning quite off from the bottom, which would endanger the pin on which the top part turns; it fhould have caftors at the brackets, that when the night

Pl.23.

CORNER NIGHT TABLES

Plan

T.Sheraton Del.

J.Caldwall Dirext.

Published as the Act Directs by T.Sheraton Augt. 14. 1793.

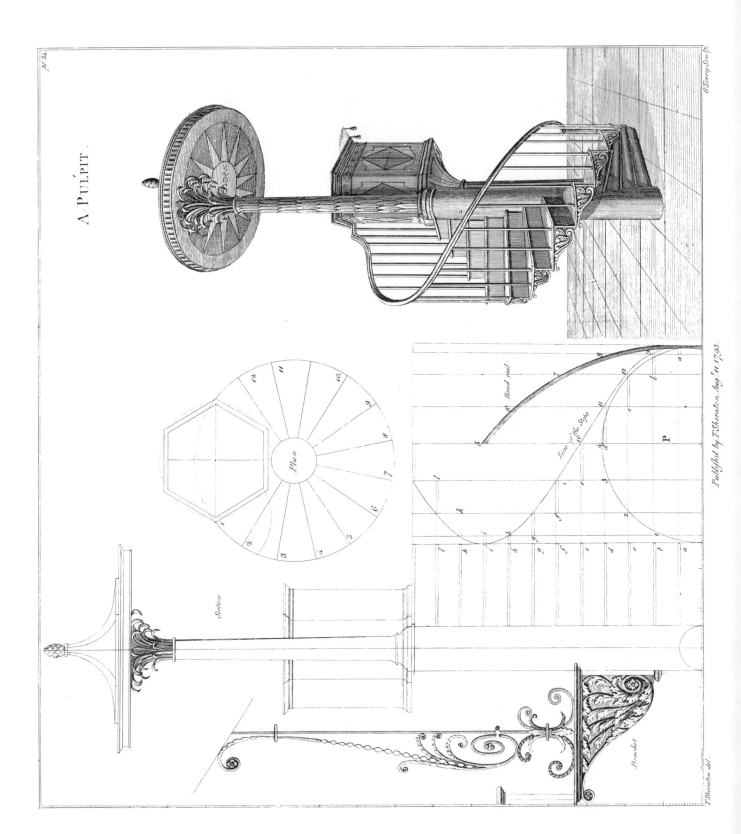

A PULPIT.

Plan

Section

Bracket

G.Terry Sculp.

T.Sheraton del.

Publifhed by T.Sheraton, Aug.st 11.1793.

night table is wanted, it may be drawn a little forward from the corner of the room to give place for turning round the upper part. It fhould be about thirty-four inches to the top of the bafon fhelf. The height of the feat fixteen inches and a half, and its other dimenfions are known from the plan. The bottom drawer may be made neat, and drawn out by means of a dovetail groove in the middle of the drawer, and a piece to fit it fixed acrofs the bottom of the carcafe.

Of the Pulpit. Plate XXIV.

THE defign of introducing a pulpit into this work was to afford fome affiftance to the cabinet-maker, who in the country is generally employed on fuch occafions. In erecting a pulpit of this kind, three particulars ought principally to be regarded. Firft, the plan; fecondly, the manner of conducting the fteps and hand-rail round the column; and, laftly, to fix the whole firm, fo that it may not by fhaking produce a difagreeable fenfation to the preacher.

The plan of this pulpit is a regular hexagon, which to me is the moft beautiful and compact of any. One of its fides is occupied by the door, and one for the back of the preacher, another to reft his arm, and the remaining three for the cufhion.

M   The

The plan of the fteps is a circle, which is moft convenient where there is a want of room. The plan fhould be divided according to the number of fteps neceffary for attaining to a proper height, which in this cafe is twelve, as one, two, three, &c. in the plan.

A fection fhould then be drawn, and the height of the rifers adjufted to the number of the fteps, as in the fection *a*, *b*, *c*, &c.

Draw the femi plan P, and divide the circumference into eight equal parts, as 1, 2, 3, 4, &c. becaufe, that in the plan there are fo many fteps contained in its femi. Draw from 1, 2, 3, 4, &c. lines perpendicular, and continue them to the uppermoft ftep. From *a*, the firft ftep, draw a line to *a* on the plan P. Do the fame from *b* to *b*, *c* to *c*, and fo of all the others, which will defcribe the fteps and rifers as they revolve on a cylinder. The face mould for the hand-rail, when it is cut out of the folid, is found as follows. See Plate XXX. Draw a quarter plan as there defcribed, divide the chord line into any number of equal parts, as 1, 3, 5; from which raife perpendiculars to interfect the circumference; draw next the rake or pitch-board of the fteps at Fig. R, by taking the breadth of the ftep on the plan, and repeating it 1, 2, 3, 4; then take

the

the height of four rifers, as from *x* to *y*, and draw the line *y* 4, which line will be the chord for the face mould; therefore take *y* 4, and divide it into fix, as in the plan of the hand-rail. Take the perpendicular heights as 1 2, 3 4, and 5 6, of the plan, and transfer them to the correfpondent perpendiculars on the face mould, which will give points through which the curve is to pafs, to form the face mould, as the figure fhews. Three of thefe lengths will be wanted to complete the hand-rail, including the ramp and knee.

Thefe hand-rails are however fometimes glued up in thin pieces round a cylinder in one entire length, after which a crofs banding is put on the top, and rounded off. In this cafe a cylinder is formed in deal, and the line of the fteps is traced out as defcribed Plate XXIV. which is the guide for the thin mahogany to be bent round. In fixing the fteps, I prefume it will be found the beft method to mortice and dovetail the rifers of each ftep into the pillar: this may be done by making the mortice as much wider than the breadth of the rifer as the dovetail is intended to be in depth, fo that when the rifer is put into the mortice, it may be forced up to its place by a wedge driven in at the under edge of the rifer. By this means it will be impoffible that the fteps fhould work when they are tongued and blocked together. The foffits of the fteps are in the form of an

ogee,

ogee, anfwerable to the brackets, and are fitted up feparately afterwards.

In fixing the pillar it muft be noticed, that it is firft tenoned into tranfverfe pieces of oak timber, which are funk a
good depth into the ground, fo that when the clay is beat in
folidly about the pillar it cannot work; yet it is eafy to conceive,
that in the pulpit it will be liable to fpring when the preacher
is in it; to prevent which I have introduced a light fmall column, fituated in the center of the pulpit, and connected with it
by a cove, on which the pulpit refts. The found board is made
as light as poffible, which finifhes in an octave cove at the top,
and is fixed to the pillar by a ftrong fcrew and nut, together
with a tenon, which is funk into the found board. The bannif-
ters of the hand-rail may be ftraight bars of brafs, made very
light, dovetailed into the ends of the fteps, and let into a plate
of thin iron at top, which is fcrewed to the under fide of the
hand-rail.

Obferve, that on the left fide of the plate is a fcale of feet
and inches, from which the various meafurements may be
taken.

N. B. Plates 25 and 27, 28 and 29, require no explanations;
they are therefore omitted.

8

Of

BACKS FOR PAINTED CHAIRS.

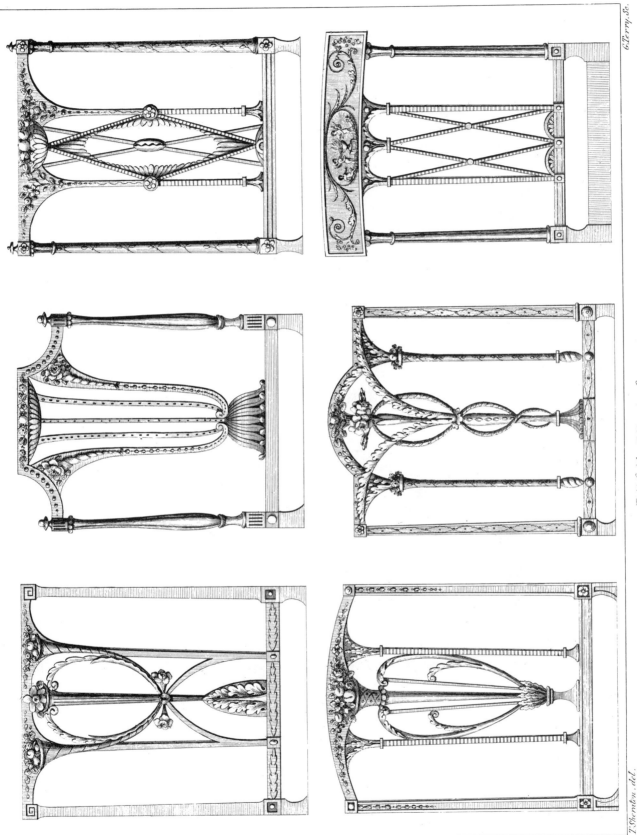

6.Terry. Sc.

T.Sheraton. del.

Publifhed by. T.Sheraton. Sep:1. 1793.

Pl. 26.

LADIES WORK TABLES.

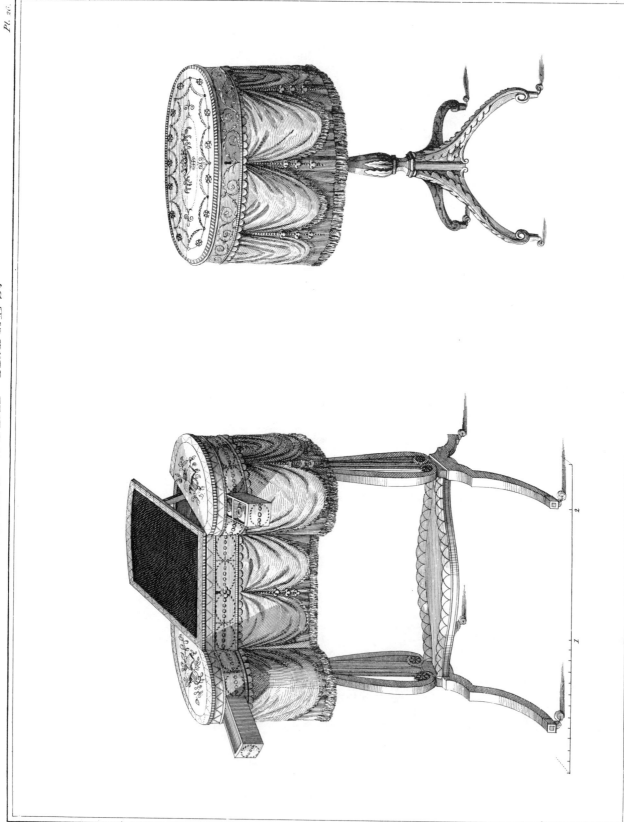

T. Sheraton delin.

Published as the Act directs, by T. Sheraton Sep.ʳ 1. 1793.

I. Barlow sculp.

Pl. 27.

DOORS FOR BOOKCASES

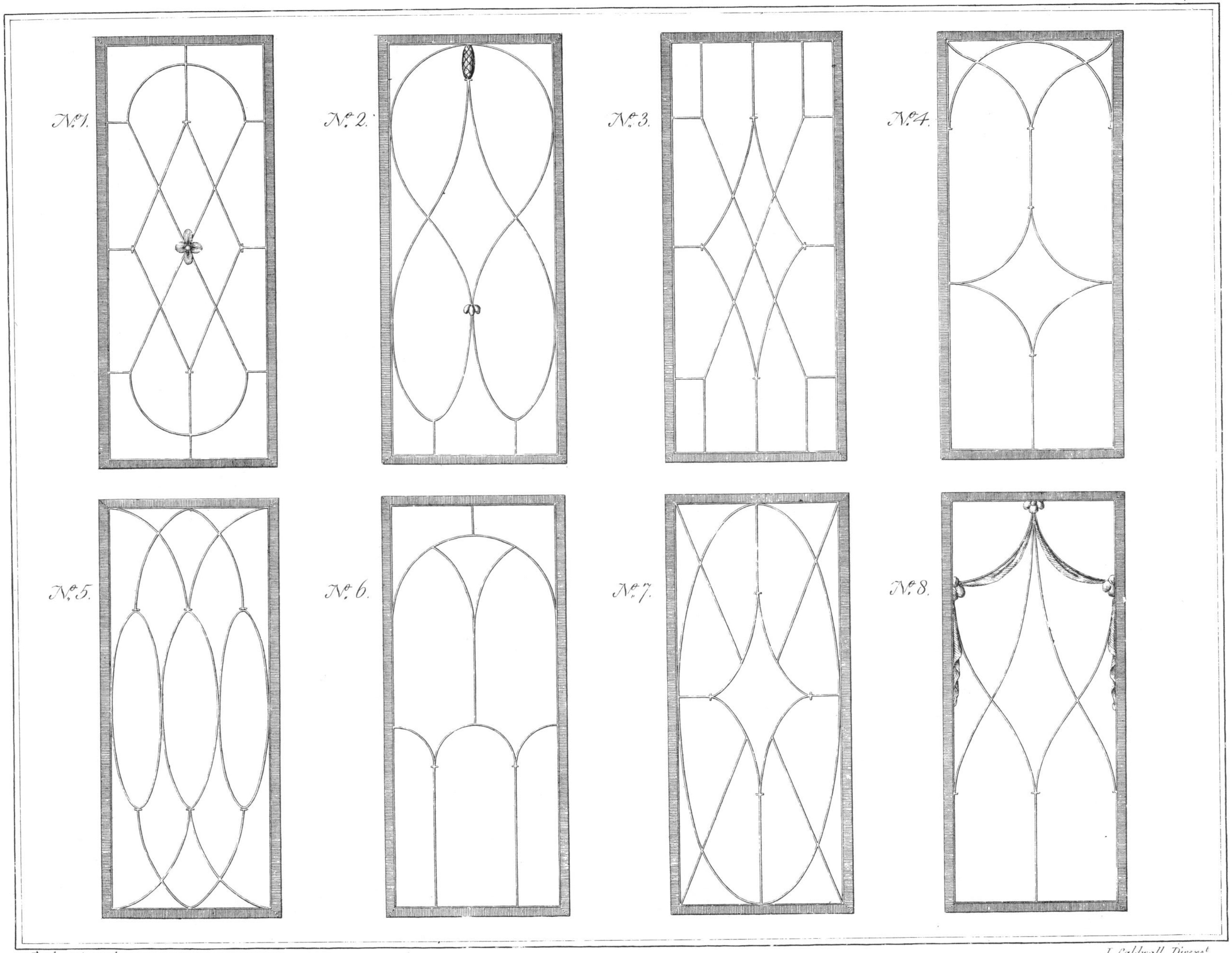

N.º 4.

N.º 8.

N.º 3.

N.º 7.

N.º 2.

N.º 6.

N.º 1.

N.º 5.

T. Sheraton Del.

Publifhed as the Act Directs by T. Sheraton. Sep.t 7. 1793.

J. Caldwall Dirext.

Pl.28.

BACKS for PARLOUR CHAIRS

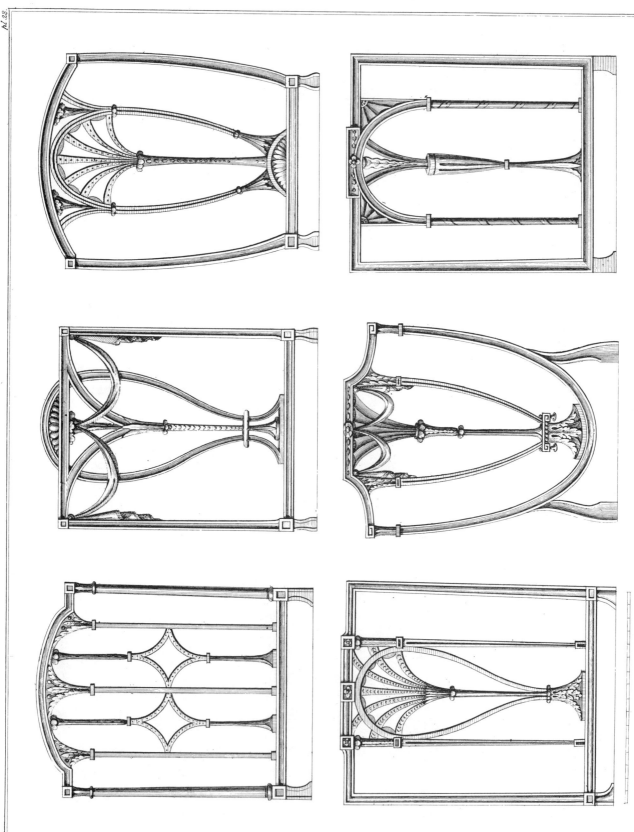

G.Terry, Sculp.

Publishd by T. Sheraton, Oct. 27. 1793.

T. Sheraton, del.

T. Sheraton. Del.

Published as the Act Directs by T. Sheraton. Oct. 24. 1793.

J. Caldwall. Dirext.

T. Sheraton Del.

J. Caldwall Dirext

Published as the Act Directs by T. Sheraton Oct. 5. 1793.

Of the Ladies' Work Tables. Plate XXVI.

THE table on the left is intended to afford conveniences for writing, by having a part of the top hinged in front to rife up. This rifing top when it is let down locks into the frame, and fecures the bag where the work is. The ftandards on which the table frame refts have tranfverfe pieces tenoned on, which fcrew to the under fide of the frame. The drapery which hides the work-bag is tacked to a rabbet at the under edge of the frame all round.

The defign on the right is fimply a work table; the upper frame, to which the top is hinged, is about two inches broad, made feparate. The pillar is fixed to the bottom of the bag, which is a round frame made of wainfcot, with a ftretcher acrofs each way, for the purpofe of fixing the pillar to it, and to ftrengthen the frame. The upper frame, already mentioned, is connected with the lower one by fmall upright pieces tenoned in, after which the bag is formed of filk, and tacked to each frame, and ornamented on the outfide with drapery.

Of the Drawing Table. Plate XXX.

THIS table will be found highly ufeful to fuch as draw, it being defigned from my own experience of what is neceffary

N

for

for thofe who practife this art. The top of this table is made to rife by a double horfe, that the defigner may ftand if he pleafe, or he may fit, and have the top raifed to any direction. As it is fometimes neceffary to copy from models or flower-pots, &c. a fmall flap is made to draw out of the top, which may be raifed by a little horfe to fuit any direction that the top may be in, fo that the model or flower-pot may ftand level. The fliders at each end are neceffary for the inftruments of drawing, and for a light to ftand on. The long drawer holds paper, fquare and broad, and thofe drawers which form the knee hole are fitted up for colours.

Of *the Drawing Room.* Plate XXXI. and XXXII.

WITH refpect to the fection, it is only neceffary to obferve, that the pier table under the glafs is richly ornamented in gold. The top is marble, and alfo the fhelf at each end; the back of it is compofed of three pannels of glafs, the Chinefe figure fitting on a cufhion is metal and painted. The candle branches are gilt metal, the pannels painted in the ftyle of the Chinefe; the whole producing a brilliant effect.

The view, Plate XXXII. contains an otomon, or long feat, extending the whole width of the room, and returning at each

5   end

Pl. 30.

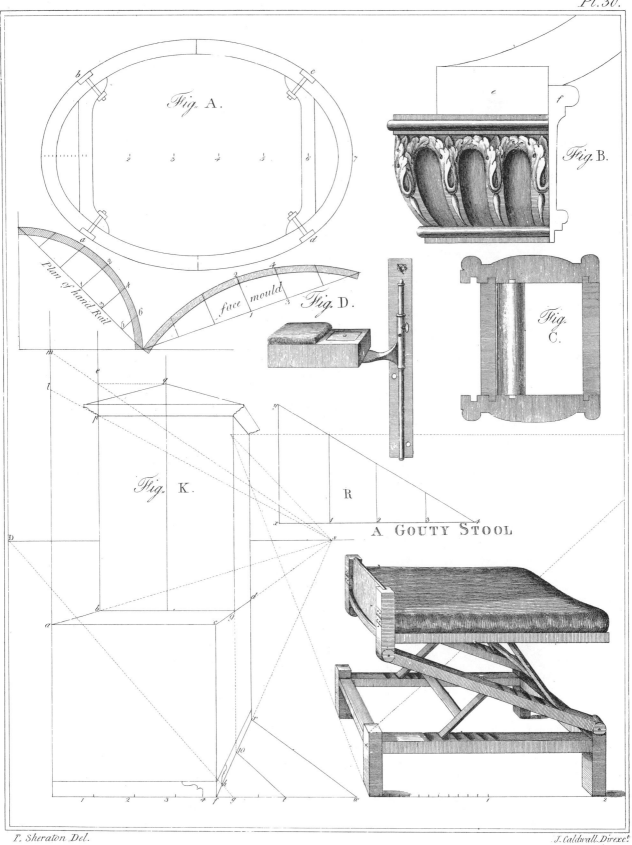

Fig. A.

Plan of hand Rail

face mould   Fig. D.

Fig. B.

Fig. C.

Fig. K.

R

A GOUTY STOOL

T. Sheraton Del.   J. Caldwall Direxet.

Published as the Act Directs by T. Sheraton. Sept.ʳ 7, 1793.

Pl. 31.

A VIEW OF THE SOUTH END OF THE PRINCE OF WALES'S CHINESE DRAWING ROOM.

T. Sheraton del.

Published as the Act directs, by T. Sheraton Oct.r 6, 1793.

J. Barlow sculp.

Pl. 32.

A VIEW OF THE PRINCE OF WALES'S CHINESE DRAWING ROOM.

T. Sheraton delin.

J. Barlow sculp.

Published as the Act directs, by T. Sheraton Nov.ʳ 1,ˢᵗ 1793.

end about five feet. The Chinefe columns are on the front of this feat, and mark out its boundaries. The upholftery work is very richly executed in figured fatin, with extremely rich borders, all worked to fuit the ftyle of the room. Within this otomon are two grand tripod candle-ftands, with heating urns at the top, that the feat may be kept in a proper temperature in cold weather. On the front of the otomon before the columns are two cenfers containing perfumes, by which an agreeable fmell may be diffufed to every part of the room, preventing that of a contrary nature, which is the confequence of lighting a number of candles.

The chimney-piece is rich, adorned with a valuable time-piece, and two lights fupported by two Chinefe figures; on each fide of the fire-place is alfo a Chinefe figure, anfwerable to thofe which fupport a table on the oppofite fide, under which is feated a Chinefe figure. Over each table, the fire-place, and in the center of the otomon, is a glafs, which by their reflections greatly enliven the whole. The fubjects painted on the pannels of each wall are Chinefe views, and little fcenes. The carpet is worked in one entire piece, with a border round it, and the whole in effect, though it may appear extravagant to a vulgar eye, is but fuitable to the dignity of the proprietor.

N. B. In

N. B. In addition to what has been faid on perfpective in the firft work, I would here annex a few remarks on taking the geometrical or original meafurements of a piece of furniture drawn in perfpective, fuppofed to be deftitute of any lines or fcales.

In Plate XXX. is therefore inferted a view of a bookcafe, figure K, which the reader muft imagine to be without any lines except thofe which form the outline of the piece. It muft, however, be premifed, that a workman is acquainted with the proportion of fome one or other of its parts, without which nothing can be done or afcertained. He muft alfo be acquainted with fo much of perfpective as to know that a line paffing through the diagonal of any fquare, if produced, cuts the horizontal line in the point of diftance. Thefe being known, proceed firft to find the horizontal or vanifhing line by producing $c\ d$, the top of, and $f\ r$, the bottom of the under part, till they meet in a point, as at s, which will be the point of fight; through s draw a line parallel to the front of the bookcafe, which will be the horizontal line fought for. From the point of fight draw at random lines forward from p, and e, or any other point that may be neceffary. Next find out the point of diftance, without which the depth of the ends cannot be known: in order to this, the workman muft recollect that the brackets are

always

always as long at the ends as on the front, and that therefore they form a fquare block; wherefore take 4 *f*, and place it from *f* to *g*, and from *g* to *h*, the end bracket will be the diagonal of a fquare, whofe fide is 4 *f*; produce the line *g h*, which will cut the horizon at D; the diftance, as the line on the leg of the gouty ftool, paffes to the diftance which is out of the plate. Laftly; from D draw lines forward through *r* and 10, or any other part, till they cut the front line, as at *t w*, by which will be difcovered the proportion that the ends bear with the front, and how much the lower part projects before the bookcafe. Now if there be a fcale of the front already to the defign, then the whole can be determined; for by taking the compaffes extended to a foot, and repeating it on the perpendicular line from *a* to *l*, the height of the doors are known, and by the fame rule the height of the pediment from *l* to *m*. Then if the fame compafs be applied from *f* to *w*, the depth of the lower part, it will be found vaftly out of proportion with the front, which I have done on purpofe, to fhew that by a comparifon of this fort the errors of a defign in point of perfpective may be difcovered. If, however, there be no fcale to the defign, then it will be neceffary to affign a certain portion for a foot, as near as we can judge, by confidering the common ength of a bracket, from *f* to 4, which in general is about four and a half or four inches, which repeated three times, finds a foot, as in this cafe, and then

O   it

it appears that the front is four feet long, and better than four feet high, that the doors are five feet nine high, and fo of the reft. But if there be no bracket, any other part may be taken whofe meafure is known, as the partition of a drawer, which is generally feven eighths thick, the height of a slider, about thirty-two inches, or the depth of a fecretary drawer, about ten inches. The ufefulnefs of this method is not confined to pieces of furniture, but may be applied to any kind of regular perfpective.

A Defcription of the Additional New Plates in the Second Edition of the Cabinet-Maker and Upholfterer's Drawing Book.

Plate XXXI. *A Sideboard.*

THIS defign is intended to have a brafs rod behind, containing lights in the center and at each end.

There is alfo a narrow mahogany fhelf about three inches and an half wide, fixed againft the middle of the rod at the back; on which fhelf a channel is worked by a plane, for the purpofe of keeping up fmall difhes placed in the fpaces between the larger ones which reft on the fideboard top.

The frame of this table is richly carved out of the folid wood

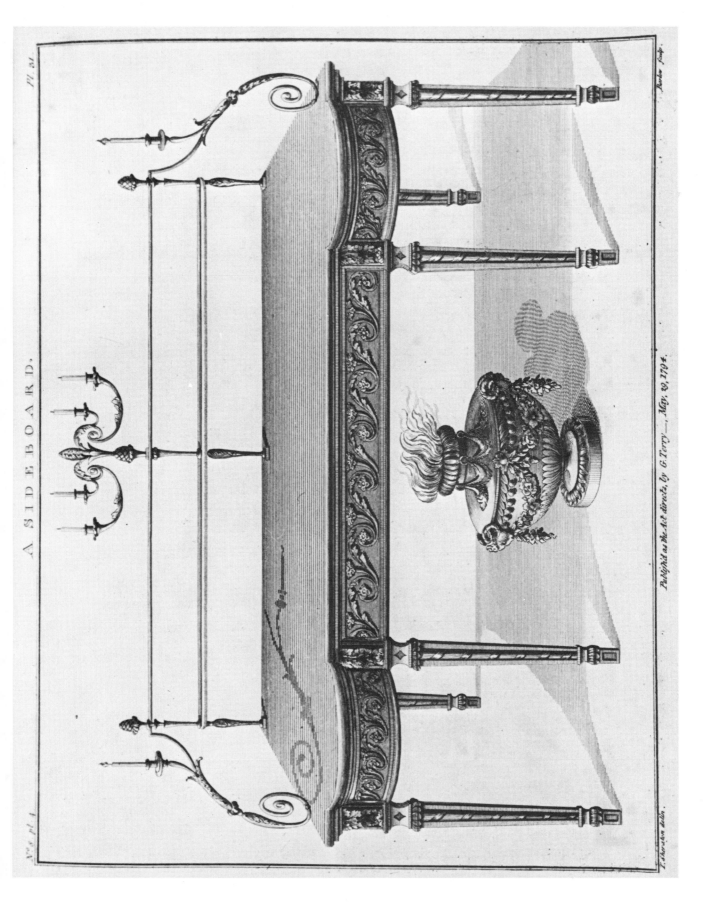

A SIDEBOARD.

Publish'd as the Act directs, by G.Terry—, May. 29, 1794.

A NEW DESIGN of a BOOKCASE & WRITING DRAWER.

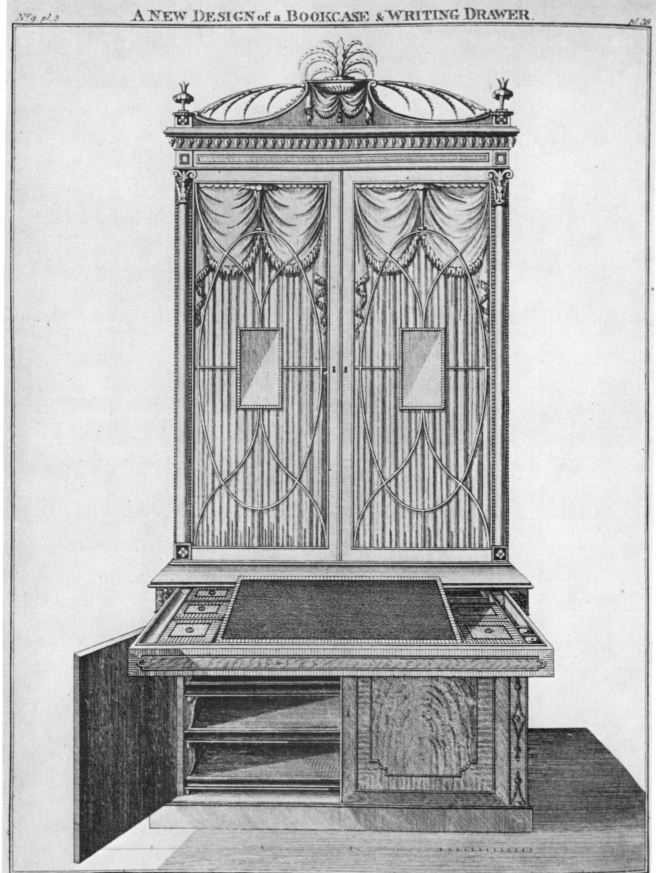

T. Sheraton. del.

Publish'd as the Act directs by G. Terry. June. 20. 1794.

G. Terry. Sculp.

wood, and the ornament of that part of the legs which crofs the frame, is formed in imitation of a trufs leaf.

The vafe under the table may be of mahogany, and fitted up in the infide to hold wine bottles, or it may be confidered merely as ornamental.

Plate XXXIX. *A Bookcafe with Writing Drawer.*

THE writing drawer reprefented out, has only the appearance of a frieze when in, it being but one inch and three quarters or two inches deep. This drawer is thrown out by a fpring fixed on the back framing, and when in, is retained by a fpring thumb-catch, which ftrikes into a plate fixed on the fide of the drawer. The place where the thumb preffes is the center of the patera at each end of the drawer, as fhewn in the defign, which relieves the fpring behind, and confequently the drawer comes forward, fo much as to afford hold for the hands to draw it entirely out.

The drawer is locked by the door lock below, which is fo contrived as to fend the bolt upwards into the under edge of it.

In the lower part are clothes-prefs fhelves, and the glafs doors above are intended to have looking-glafs in the center fquares.

Laftly,

Laftly, the drapery is of green filk, fixed firft to the curtain, and then both are pinned on to the infide of the doorframing together.

Plate XLIX. *New Defigns of Chair-backs.*

LITTLE needs to be obferved refpecting thefe, as the plate of itfelf fufficiently expreffes what they are; if, however, any of thefe be thought too crowded with work, they may be reduced to a ftate fufficiently plain without doing the leaft injury to the outline of the whole, as in the following manner:

No. 1 is intended for painting, but may have the drapery left out under the top rail, by means of fubftituting a plain upright bar in the middle.

No. 2 may be reduced by taking away the fide foliage, and making the bottom of the banifter plain.

No. 3 may be either a drawing-room chair painted, or it may be made a handfome parlour chair, by taking out the top drapery and making the bottom of the banifter plain; if for a parlour chair, the top rail is intended to be ftuffed and covered with red or green leather, or it may be entirely of mahogany pannelled out of the folid; but if a drawing-room chair, it muft be ftuffed and covered to fuit the feat.

No.

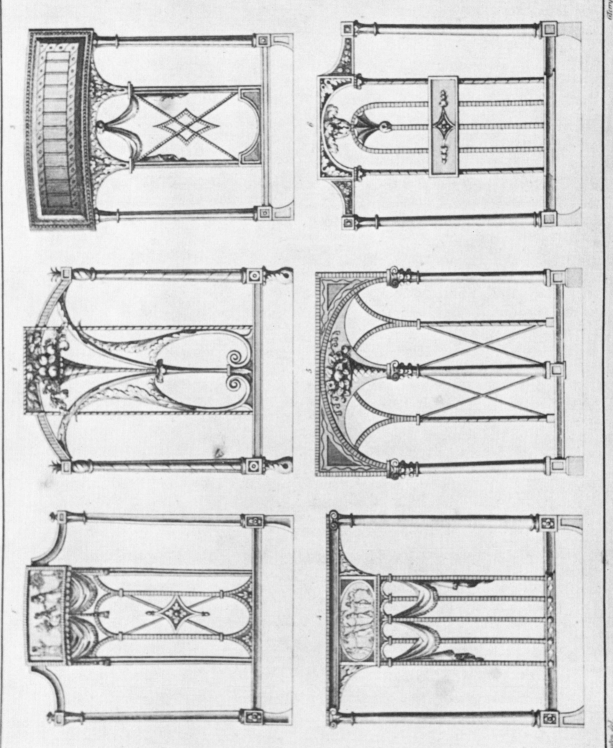

CHAIR BACKS.

Published as the Act directs by G Terry July 20 1794

Pl.52

A TURKEY SOFA

Published as the Act Directs by G. Terry ___ Augt 10 1794

No. 4 is a painted chair, with the back feet at top, formed in imitation of the Ionic capital.

The drapery in this also may be taken away without hurt done to the general outline.

No. 5 is a painted chair, and may be subject to a variety of alterations; it may be executed with good effect without any thing, except the three composite columns, and two arches in the top rail. The remaining part of the rail on each fide of the basket of flowers may be neatly pannelled in the painting; or the diamond part may be retrenched, and the two smaller pillars with their arches retained.

No. 6 cannot well be subject to any alteration, excepting that the ornament in the arch may be turned into a straight bar.

No. LII. *A Turkey Sofa.*

THESE are genteel seats introduced in the most fashionable houses, and are an imitation of the Turkish mode of fitting. They are therefore made very low, scarcely exceeding a foot to the upper fide of the cushion.

The frame may be made of beech, and must be webbed and strained with canvas to support the cushions.

P

The

The back cushions in this design have spaces between them, with drapery inserted, but they are generally made to fill close up without leaving any intervals. In rooms where there are no columns nor architrave suitable for such a feat, these may easily be put up in a temporary way, so that, if requisite, they may be taken down without any injury to the room. The back of the sofa, by which I mean the whole height of the wall, from surbase to cornice, must have a deal frame fixed to it, against which the canvas, drapery at the top, and the fluting, must be tacked.

Plate LXVI. *A Commode.*

THE top of this commode is intended to be white statuary marble. The ornaments are painted on satin wood, or other ground; at each end is formed a niche in which may be placed antique figures. The legs of the commode stand clear. The doors at each end are made to stand about three inches clear of the feet, so that the door will open square out. The internal part is merely plain shelves, as these pieces are never intended for use but for ornament.

Plate LXXV. *Bed Steps.*

THE design on the right contains a bidet behind, which runs in as a drawer. For the purpose of raising the bidet

drawer

A COMMODE

J. Sheraton. del.

Published as the Act directs by G Terry — May 25. 1794.

G Terry. Sculp.

NEW BED STEPS.

Feet

Published by G. Terry. Feby. 27. 1794.

Shearton del.

Terry sc.

Pl.41.

A LIBRARY BOOKCASE.

Publish'd as the Act directs, by Geo: Terry, September 11th. 1794.

J. Barlow sculp.

T. Sheraton delin.

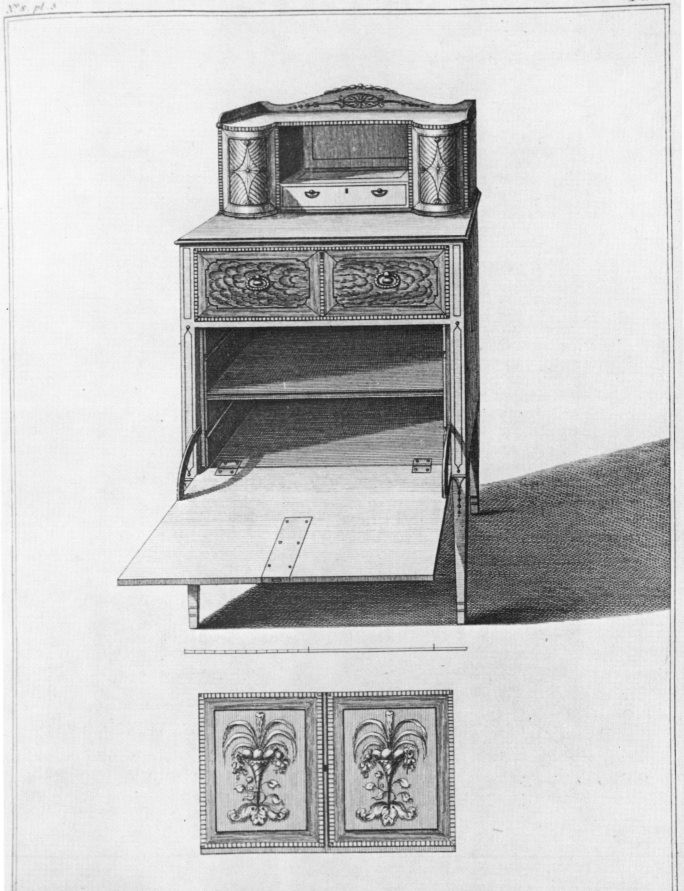

T. Sheraton Del.   J. Caldwall Direc.ᵗ

Published as the Act Directs by G. Terry __ Apᵗ 21. 1794.

drawer to a proper height, the cafe is made double, one fitting within the other, as fhewn in the plate: for provided the outer cafe is made nine inches deep, the inner one, being at leaft eight, would, when raifed up, make it eighteen inches high, which is fufficient.

The inner cafe is kept up by a couple of wooden fprings, one at each end, which are fo made and fixed to the infide of the outer-cafe, that the thumb may relieve them fo that the bidet will fettle down even with the edge of the cafe. The fecond ftep, which forms the night-table part draws out, and the ftep which covers it rifes up and falls againft the upper ftep, which forms a pot cupboard. The fteps and rifers are ufually covered with carpet, and the fides caned.

The defign on the left, when the top is down, forms only two fteps. The front of the upper ftep is hinged to the top, and the top to the back; and to keep it in its place when down, the workman will obferve, that a groove is cut in the ends, not in a ftraight direction, but near the bottom; the groove is perpendicular to the feat; a pin is then fixed to the under fide of the front at each end, which works in the aforefaid grooves, and the perpendicular part of the groove, which is obvious in the defign, affifts in throwing the front upright when it is down upon the feat.

Plate

Plate   *A Library Bookcaſe.*

THE middle lower part of this bookcaſe may have wardrobe ſhelves, the reſt is furniſhed with plain sliding shelves
for books only. The circular wings of the upper part may
be glazed, or finiſhed without glaſs, by a green ſilk curtain
only, with its drapery at the top. The diamond part is intended
to have looking-glaſs inſerted, which has a pretty effect.
The pannels of the lower doors do not come fluſh with their
framing by a ſtrong eighth of an inch, which both looks
better, and is more calculated to hide the defects, if the pannel ſhould ſhrink. The workman muſt obſerve, that the
plinth, ſurbaſe, and cornice frames, are made and finiſhed
entirely ſeparate from the carcaſes, and are ſcrewed to them
to keep the whole together.

A N

ACCOMPANIMENT

TO THE

CABINET-MAKER AND UPHOLSTERER'S

DRAWING-BOOK.

CONTAINING

A VARIETY OF ORNAMENTS USEFUL FOR LEARNERS TO COPY FROM, BUT PARTICULARLY ADAPTED TO THE CABINET AND CHAIR BRANCHES:

EXHIBITING

ORIGINAL AND NEW DESIGNS

OF

CHAIR LEGS, BED PILLARS, WINDOW CORNICES, CHAIR SPLADS, AND OTHER ORNAMENTS, CALCULATED TO ASSIST IN THE DECORATIONS OF THE ABOVE BRANCHES; TOGETHER WITH INSTRUCTIONS IN LETTER-PRESS.

By THOMAS SHERATON,
CABINET-MAKER.

LONDON:

PRINTED BY T. BENSLEY, FOR THE AUTHOR,
Nᵒ 106, WARDOUR-STREET, SOHO.

Of whom may be had, feparate, in Forty-two Numbers, price 2*l.* 3*s.* 6*d.* The CABINET-MAKER and UPHOLSTERER's DRAWING-BOOK, containing a great Variety of New Defigns in Houfehold Furniture.

205

AN ACCOMPANIMENT, &c.

Inftructions for Drawing Ornaments.

As a proficiency in the art of drawing ornaments depends chiefly on the habit of copying and the natural turn of genius in this way, a few hints only are neceffary for the affiftance of the learner.

Some inftructions, however, are certainly neceffary, as appears from the frequent applications that are made to mafters for their information. And though no written inftructions can fully fupply all that may be derived from a mafter *, yet fuch directions may be given, in letter-prefs, as greatly to facilitate the attainment of this ufeful branch of drawing without a mafter's help.

The principal art of every branch of drawing is included in the difpofition of a few fimple lines of but two different fpecies,

---

* One very material advantage derived from a mafter is, that the pupil fees how he practifes, by which he may acquire his manner and ftyle.

the

the right line and the curve. Of thefe two are compofed all that infinite variety of fhapes that we are able to fee and conceive.

I will, therefore, propofe to the learner, firft to begin with drawing, by the hand, right lines a tolerable length parallel to each other in all directions; firft, inclined to the right, as approaching neareft to the art of writing; fecondly, perpendicular; thirdly, inclined to the left; and laftly, horizontal and at right angles with thofe perpendiculars, and paffing through their center. A proficiency in this is certainly the firft ftep in drawing, and is not fo eafily attained as may be imagined.

Secondly, let the learner then proceed to draw by the hand a circle, as large as poffibly he can without moving the wrift. And it will be proper for the learner to obferve, that in being able to draw a circle by the hand and eye he thereby draws curve lines in all poffible pofitions, as perpendicular, inclined to the right and left, and horizontal. In addition to this practice it will be neceffary to draw one circle concentric with another; that is, as when two or more circles of different diameters are drawn from one center. This becomes ufeful when any thing is to be defcribed in the fhape of volutes, as the running foliage frequently introduced in friezes and pilafters. What has here been faid of the circle will alfo apply to the practice of drawing an

ellipfis

ellipſis by hand. An ellipſis may be confidered as a curve con-
fiſting of a number of ſegments of circles compound, whoſe
radii differ in length. Of this kind of curve are many of the
turns in ornament, and therefore the practice of drawing them
will be found worthy the attention of the learner. To practiſe
as has been deſcribed I confider as indiſpenſably requifite to a
ready and perfect attainment in the art of drawing ornaments;
and ought particularly to be recommended to youth, as a help
to their writing any kind of hand, or drawing the Roman
letters.

The learner who is advanced in years will not, perhaps,
ſubmit to this kind of teaching: but if he cannot already draw
right lines, of ſome length, parallel in all poſitions, and a circle
tolerably near by the eye, he ought not to be above learning
it, becauſe the time that is ſpent in this, will be deducted in
future by a more ſpeedy progreſs in the art of drawing ornaments. And however this may be thought of by ſome as a
thing of no merit, yet we will venture to affirm, that the hand
of a real maſter may be certainly diſtinguiſhed by the manner
of drawing theſe.

Of

Of Copying Ornaments. Plate I.

SUPPOSE C to be the example to copy from. Take a black-lead pencil, and draw at B the principal curve-line at the bottom very faint *. Then proceed to form a rude fketch of the out-line, obferving carefully each projecting part of C, that a fuf-ficient breadth or fpace may be taken within the out-line, in which may be formed all the diftinct parts of B, without re-ducing their proportion.

Upon this procefs correctnefs and difpatch very much de-pend. Therefore, if upon the firft attempt of this there fhould appear any defect, it will be beft to take out the lines with the India rubber, and make them perfect.

A carver or fculptor proceeds upon this principle until merely the maffive parts are made out; and it is well known that thofe of the greateft fkill in thefe profeffions are always employed in this part of carving and fculpture.

After having done this, proceed to give the diftinct forms of each leaf and rofe in faint touches, that if there fhould be any caufe for alteration it may be more eafily effected. The

---

* To handle a pencil is, in many cafes of drawing, different from the manner of hold-ing a pen. In handling a pen, the ends of the fourth and fifth fingers reft on the paper; but in managing a pencil, the hand is turned over more to the right, and refts on the knuckles of the little finger.

8   learner

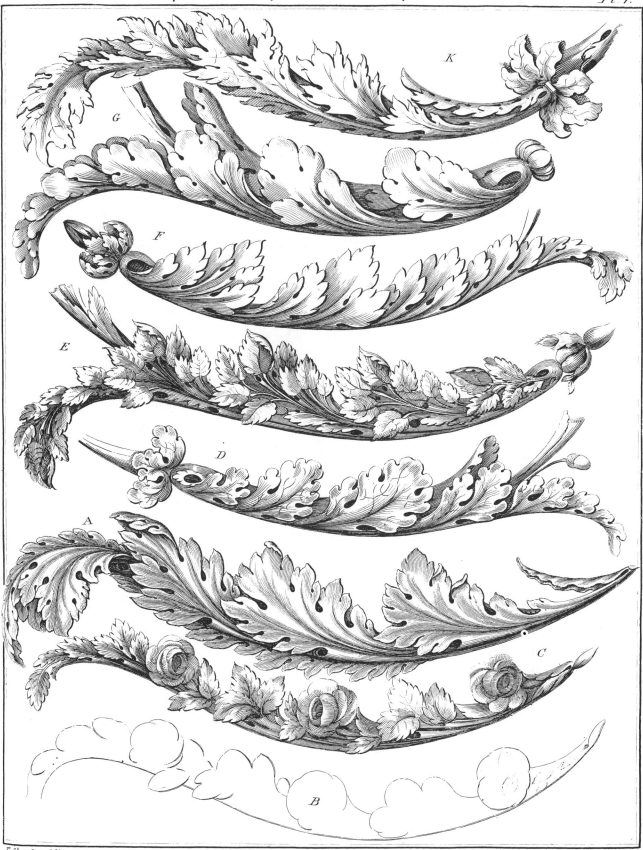

T. Sheraton delin. Publifhed as the Act directs, by T. Sheraton July 4. 1793. J. Barlow sculp.

Pl. 2.

CHAIR LEGS

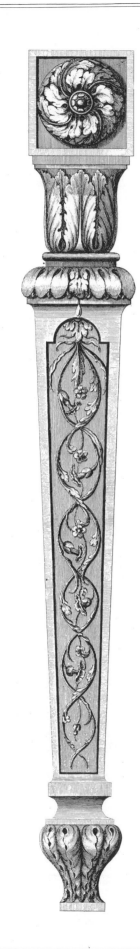 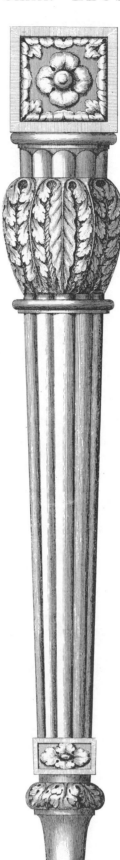 

T. Sheraton Del.

Publish'd as the Act Directs by T. Sheraton Aug.t 30. 1793.

I. Caldwall Dirext.

learner fhould, in doing this, carefully obferve and touch the fibres of each leaf, and give the proper lead to each ftem, fo that they do not cut each other.

Laftly, take a view of the whole, and confider in what point the light is to ftrike on the ornament; and on that edge of the leaves and rofes oppofite to it, retouch and ftrengthen the outline in fuch a way as to give relief and effect to the whole, even upon fuppofition that the drawing is to remain a mere outline.

Of *Shading Ornaments*.

IF the ornament is to be fhaded with Indian ink, mix fome of it thin and clear, and take a crow-quill pen, or fine camel-hair pencil, and touch the outlines very faintly, fo as fcarcely to be feen on the light edges of the ornament; becaufe in nature there is, in reality, no outline on the light fides of objects, efpecially if the fun is fuppofed to fhine on them. After this, touch the ftronger parts of each ftem and fibre, that they may not be loft when the pencil marks are expunged.

Having cleaned your drawing, take a large camel-hair pencil, and dip it till it flow freely with Indian ink very thin and clear. And obferve, that if the ink do not work with freedom on a piece of wafte paper, which fhould be kept for the pur-

pofe

pofe of trying the pencils, the brufh in this ftate ought not to be applied, but fhould again be well worked in the thin Indian ink, fo that it work eafy, without leaving white fpots on the paper. In this ftate apply the pencil to the ornament, and give a general tint to thofe parts fuppofed to be all in fhadow; at the fame time a partial tint may be given to the objects partly in the light. This firft courfe of fhadowing is the great bafis of all real effect; for if the maffes of light and fhadow are not properly parted, but confounded, the drawing will look heavy, intelligible, and boyifh.

When the drawing is properly dry, the laft tints are to be given with great delicacy and care, left the whole be over done, and, as it were, tormented with harfh dabs. The intention of this laft tint is only to give reflected lights to thofe parts which lie in the mafs of fhadow, and fharpnefs to the partial fhadows directly oppofed to the light.

It is natural for the learner, in giving the laft tint, to think of thickening his ink; but this muft be avoided, as dangerous to the effect of ornament; for if the ink at firft ufed be again repeated on the former tint, it will give fufficient colour, except the openings of the fibres, which may be touched with ftronger ink.

Effect

Effect to ornament may alſo be given by a pen, in imitation of etching; which, if well executed, is more pleaſing in ornament than Indian ink.

Italian chalk is ſometimes uſed along with a black-lead pencil, which may be done with extremely good effect.

The learner, being furniſhed with theſe inſtructions, may proceed in the ſame way with the reſt of the ſpecimens in foliage, the principal variety of which is here exhibited.

K, is the thiſtle leaf, ſharply pointed and irregular.

G, is the Roman-leaf, round and maſſy.

F, the parſley leaf, light and rather ſharp pointed.

E, the roſe leaf, formed into groups.

D, The oak-leaf, broad and maſſy, ſcolloped on the edge, with ſmall partings.

A, Is a fancy leaf, rather ſharp, with large partings.

C, roſes and leaves alternately.

B   With

With thefe fpecimens the learner ought to be well acquaint-ed, before he proceed to draw running ornaments, that he may give fufficient variety in each turn.

The regular leaves, in Plate XI, fhould alfo be copied, as they are much in ufe in carving and japanning.

Next proceed with the borders in Plate III, which are in-tended for japanning or inlaying; and fo on with any other of the Plates, as Plate V. VII. and IV. as they may appear moft fuit-able to his abilities in drawing; obferving in all cafes to make a very light pencil-fketch of the whole defign, before any thing is attempted to be finifhed.

Of *Qualifications neceſſary for Compoſition.*

To qualify the learner for compofition, he ought, in fome meafure, to be acquainted with the proportions of human figures, efpecially thofe taken from the antiques. My very li-mited plan in publifhing thefe ornaments affords me no oppor-tunity of doing any thing in this way by example. I will, how-ever, give a few hints refpecting their proportions, for the af-fiftance of thofe who have no opportunity of confulting the beft mafters.

The

The proportion of the male figure, according to Mr. Brif-
bane's Anatomy, from Albinus, will be near enough, as follows:
If the perpendicular height of the intended figure be divided into
ten equal parts, and one of thefe parts into four, the proportions
will run thus with refpect to length : the head, from the crown to
the chin, one tenth and one fourth; the neck rather more than
one third of the head; from the fummit of the fhoulders to the
bottom of the belly, three tenths; from the bottom of the belly
to the center of the knee-joints, two tenths and one half; and
the fame from the center of the knee-joints to the bottom of the
feet. Obferve, the height of the hips are fix tenths and one
third from the ground, and the length of the arm four tenths
and rather more than one half.

In thicknefs as follows.—Over the fhoulders, two tenths and
one fourth; over the hips, one tenth and rather more than
three fourths; over the thick part of the thigh, one tenth; the
fmall part, near two thirds. Thefe principal parts being attended to, the reft will follow of courfe, by practifing a little
upon the different parts of the body from examples. When the
proportion of any male figure is to be proved, take the thicknefs of the thigh as one tenth of its height, and by remember-
ing the above proportions any figure may be examined. By
thefe proportions I have examined a figure engraved from the
famous Raphael, an Italian painter, and found them to agree

B 2   exactly.

exactly. In refpect to the female figure there is fome difference in the proportions; the whole is more flender and elegant; the fhoulders are not fo broad; the trunk or body is fhorter; the hips broader, and in proportion higher from the ground; and the mufcular parts are not fo ftrong and prominent. As female figures are frequently interfperfed in the compofing of orna-ments, it is proper to obferve, that much depends on the ma-nagement of the drapery with which they are clothed. It ought to hang with freedom and eafe, and in fome parts to lie clofe, fo as to difcover fome of the principal fhapes. To effect this, it is beft, firft, to draw the figure by the pencil as if entirely def-titute of drapery, and afterwards to lay the drapery gently over with Indian ink, or colour, as may be required; fo that the lines which marked out the parts of the body, now covered, may be expunged. This method gives true effect to the dra-pery, by enabling us to determine where there ought to be ftrong, where flight, and where no folds at all. On the pro-minent parts of the body there are no folds in the drapery; but after having juft paffed over thefe, the folds commence in ten-der marks, and increafe into ftrong folds where the drapery is detached from the body.

In examining Cipriani's figures, I find, that if the affigned height of the female figure be divided into ten equal parts, from the ground to the waift, where the drapery is fometimes tied round,

round, is feven tenths; from the waift to the top of the fhoulders, one tenth and an half; the neck a quarter, the head one tenth and a quarter, and over the fhoulders rather more than two tenths.

As boys or cupids are frequently introduced in ornaments, it is proper that the learner fhould take notice of their proportions and general appearance, as different from thofe already defcribed. Cipriani's boys are of the following proportions:—If the affigned height be, as before, divided into ten equal parts, the head will be full two tenths in height; the neck very fhort; from the top of the fhoulders to the bottom of the belly, four tenths; from the bottom of the belly to the knee-joint, full two tenths; and from the knee to the ground, bare two tenths; the arms, when hanging perpendicular, come not quite to the middle of the thigh; the breadth of the fhoulders not quite three tenths; and, laftly, the thick part of the thigh, one tenth and an half, which will of courfe give the proportion of the leg. The learner fhould obferve the general caft of thefe figures; the head is large and round; the neck fcarcely diftinguifhable between the head and fhoulders; no joints appearing in the arms or legs fcarcely; the ankle covered with flefh, and the whole leg thick and maffy.

But, befide the human figures, there are others of an ima-
ginary

ginary kind employed by the antiques in their decorations. Thefe are ftill, and ever will be retained in ornaments lefs or more. The moft tafty of thefe were felected by Raphael, and painted by his pupils on the walls and ceilings of the Vatican Library at Rome, and which are handed down to us, by the Italians, in mafterly engravings; which, in the courfe of this work, I have confulted, and from which I have extracted fome of my ideas, as well as from fome French works.

In the Vatican are figures whofe upper part is female, and the lower of foliage entwifting round. Other female figures have their lower part of a fifh, and fome of a greyhound. Others fhew only a human head, with foliage fpringing from it in different forms, anfwering for wings, and for a covering of the lower parts. In it, we fee fometimes a dolphin fifh with an ornamented tail; a lion's head and an eagle's leg and talons brought into a fmooth outline by the help of foliage: at other times a tiger's head and paw formed in the fame manner. Some, again, are partly a horfe with wings and two fore legs, and partly the tail of a fifh; all which are now a namelefs generation, but once the offspring, I prefume, of the ancient metamorphofes, either what they termed real or apparent.

Befides thefe, are to be feen, in the above work, the fphinx, a figure of much fame amongft the ancients, whofe upper part

is

is a woman's head and breasts, and the wings of a bird; the lower part the body of a dog, and the claws of a lion. This monster is said to be the production of two deities, and sent as a scourge to the Thebans. Its business, on a mountain at Thebes, was to propose dark questions to passengers, and if not answered to devour them. It is said that the Egyptians used the sphinx as a symbol of religion, on account of the mysteries which it was capable of interpreting. The Romans therefore placed it on the porches of their temples.

The centaur, partly a man, and partly a horse, used as one of the signs of the zodiac, in which the man part is represented shooting with a bow.

This being is also said to be the offspring of a deity in conjunction with a cloud. They inhabited Thessaly; and, engaging in hostilities with the bow, were vanquished by Theseus. As they seem to have been a rebellious race, they may be introduced into such subjects as are intended to shew the odium of such conduct.

The griffon is another fabulous being, existing only in the vain imaginations of the ancient heathen poets, as do the two former. They represent it partly an eagle, and partly a lion; that is, the lower part of it. They suppose it to watch over

golden

golden mines and hid treafures. It was confecrated to the fun, whofe chariot was drawn by a number of them. And thefe, if you pleafe, may be introduced into fubjects intended to reprefent covetoufnefs; or they may be placed over cabinets where trea-fure is kept.

It will be proper that the learner fhould ftudy to compofe thefe, if he intends being a proficient in ornaments. In fhort, to be fully qualified for ornamental decorations, is to be ac-quainted with every branch of drawing.

And, further, to compofe to much purpofe, it requires to have a general infight into works of this nature, and particular-ly to fee the painted walls in noblemen's houfes, in many of which the art is exhibited to its utmoft perfection; and in none more fo than in the printed and painted filks executed of late by Mr. Eckhardt, at his manufactory at Chelfea, adapted for the purpofe of ornamenting pannels, and the walls of the moft ele-gant and noble houfes.

Of Compofition.

AFTER the ideas of the pupil are extenfively furnifhed in the manner now defcribed, it will be proper to begin with fome fmall ground to compofe on, fuch as the frieze of a cornice;
and

and to confider its fituation with the eye, whether it be intended to be much above it, fo that the parts of the ornaments may fuit the fuppofed diftance of the eye from it. It is of no effect to put a number of fmall ornaments in, to be viewed at a great diftance. In this cafe the parts fhould be fimple, entire, and rather maffy, to produce a proper effect. If the frieze be near the eye, it may then be divided into fmaller parts; but to crowd it in any cafe ought ftudioufly to be avoided. And obferve, the tablets of friezes ought to be diverfe to the other ornaments in it.

I would then recommend to compofe on the ground-work of a pilafter not very broad; for it is to be obferved, that the difficulty increafes in proportion to the width, more than in the height of a ground-work. The ornaments in a pilafter or pan- nel is confidered as growing upwards, and therefore it ought to take its rife from fomething principal at the bafe, and grow rather lighter towards the top, as in every inftance is fhewn in nature. But this does not confine the compofer to fuppofe that every thing is to be faftened or tied to each other as in ftrict nature, for this would fometimes be the fource of heavinefs in ornaments; nor do I fee it practifed in the Vatican, or by any of the beft artifts in this way. But certain it is, that the beft compofitions are thofe which keep the parts moft connected in one entire piece. The more we attain to this, whilft we avoid a

C   heavy

heavy repetition of the fame parts, the nearer do we arrive at perfection in this art.

The ornaments of a pilafter ought to fill regularly on each fide, and not to leave much naked ground. And efpecially we ought to obferve, not to have the ground alternately crowded and naked. If we begin in an open ftyle, leaving much naked ground, this fhould be continued uniformly all the way up, and, if any thing, only to grow more open at the fummit. The laws of harmony in every art, where time, motion, and fpace are obferved, require this.

If the furface to be ornamented be horizontal, and is liable to be viewed alike in all points, as in a ceiling, the fubject fhould be regular, and formed into pannels and groups, furrounded with foliage of the fame kind and form on all fides. Nature exemplifies a regularity in moft flowers, and in other things that grow horizontal.

Laftly, to compofe ornaments for a large upright pannel, as in rooms, is by far the moft difficult tafk in this art. Here it is required that the artift collect and arrange all his ideas; and thofe fcattered fragments which exift in his mind through long and repeated obfervation on the works of the beft mafters, muft now be collected to form an entire whole, by a general concourfe

I   or or affemblage of every branch of drawing. In this large field, architecture, perfpective, figures, landfcape, foliage, and fruit, may vie with each other, and fhew the mafter's fkill.

Attempts of this nature may be made by the learner, and with fuccefs, though he fall vaftly fhort of a perfect difplay of all thefe different branches of drawing; for it is to be obferved, that the rule for judging in works of this nature is not to look for eminence in each and every diftinct branch, but to difcern fine tafte and juftnefs of compofition in the whole.

In compofitions of this nature fomething fpreading and maffy ought to be at the bottom of the pannel, except the ornament be only intended to occupy the center, in which cafe the principal part of the ornament fhould be in the middle; but where the entire pannel is to be filled up, we fhould begin as above, that there may be an opportunity of giving breadth to the foliage, for the purpofe of filling up the ground regularly from one beginning only, for two defigns muft not be entwined with each other in the manner of cyphers. This deftroys the beauty of fimplicity, which confifts in fewnefs of parts, and entirenefs of forms, without which all is a jumble.

This obfervation will teach us to avoid that kind of croffing and cutting each other, fomething like the rigging of a fhip,

C 2

which

which may be obferved in fome ornaments, even of French production as well as Englifh. A practice this, which always denotes bad compofition, and a barrennefs of thought. It is done with a defign to enrich, but it only turns out to be a filling up to the prejudice of the whole. The learner muft therefore ftudy to enrich by a variety of thought fpringing from fomething, yet without interfering with each other.

He fhould alfo be careful in avoiding the appearance of ftraight lines continued from bottom to top, which is formal and bad. Some continuance of a right line is beautiful; but it ought quickly to be broken in thefe compofitions, whether perpendicular or horizontal.

Obferve breadth in the parts, fhun niggling and meannefs, and ftick at nothing that will have a comely and pleafant appearance.

An Explanation of the Plates.

PLATE II. are chair legs. That on the left is intended for japanning, and is formed fquare. The other two on the right are turned, carved, and gilt.

Obferve,

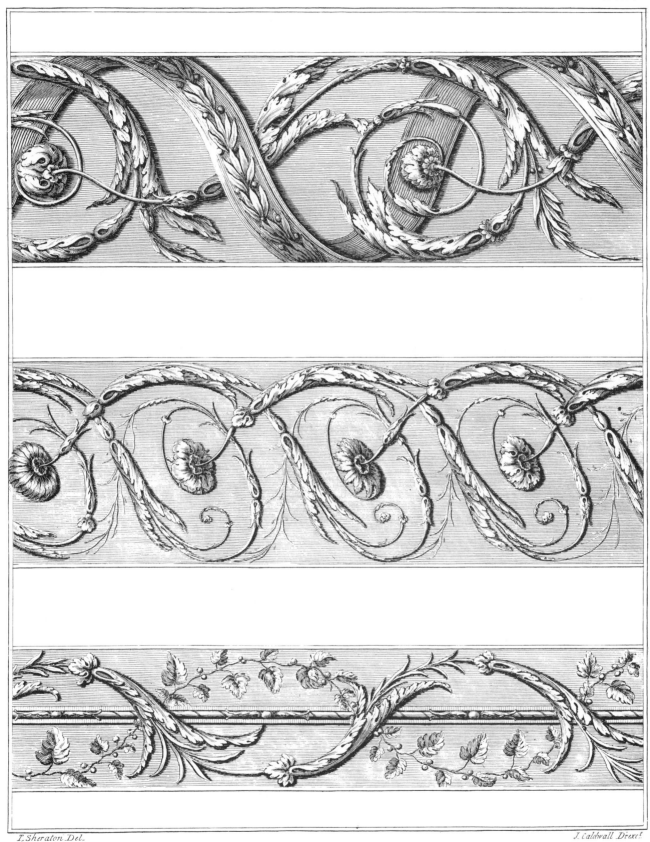

T. Sheraton Del.

J. Caldwall Dirext.

Published as the Act Directs by T. Sheraton Nov. 5 1793.

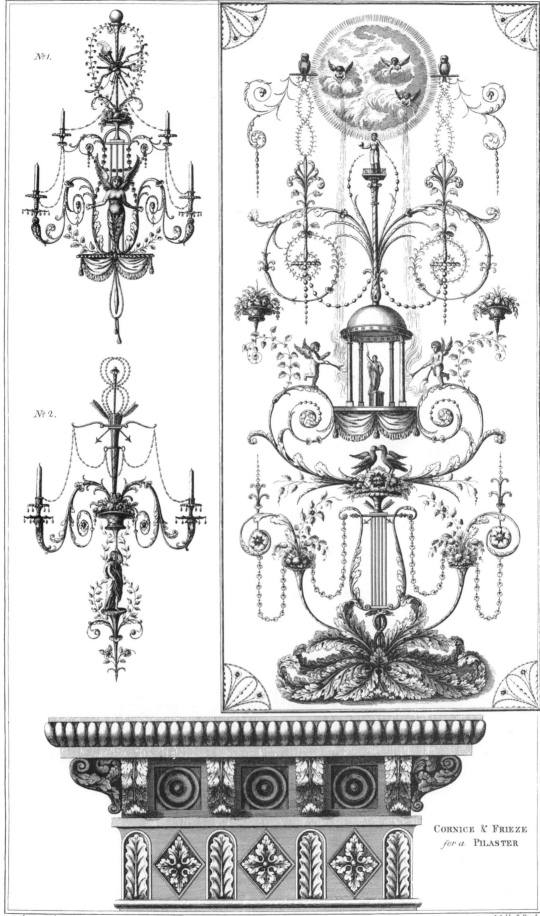

N°1.

N°2.

CORNICE & FRIEZE
for a PILASTER

T. Sheraton Del.   J. Caldwall Dirext.

Published as the Act Directs by T. Sheraton Nov.* 5. 1793.

Pl. 9

ORNAMENT for the TABLET of a PIER TABLE

CORNICES
with Ornamental
FRIEZES

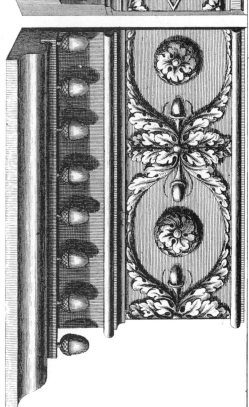

T. Sheraton. Del.

Publiſhed as the Act Directs by T. Sheraton. Nov.r 23, 1793.

I. Caldwall Dirext.

BED PILLARS

Pl. 6.

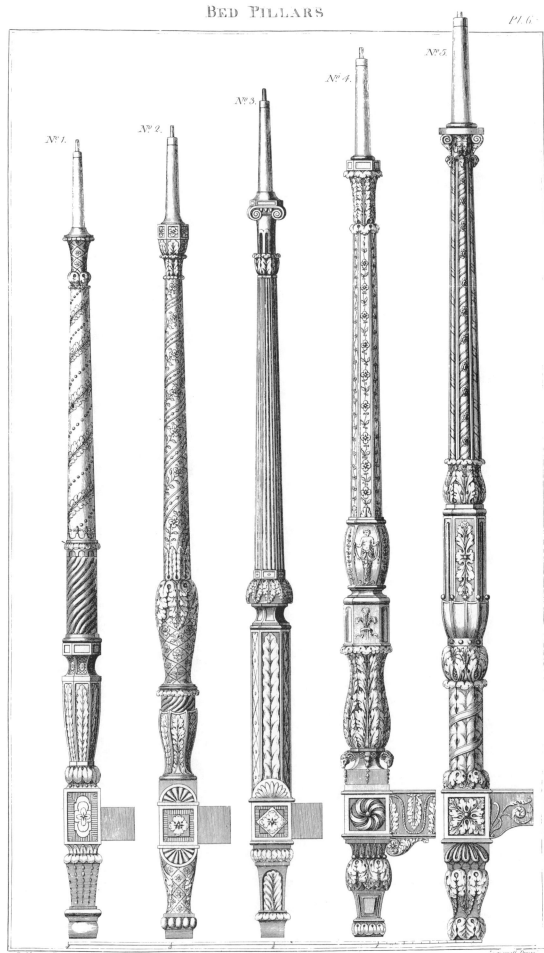

Nᵒ 1.   Nᵒ 2.   Nᵒ 3.   Nᵒ 4.   Nᵒ 5.

T. Sheraton Del.   Published as the Act Directs by T. Sheraton Novʳ 25. 1793.

Obferve, the plinth of the center foot is left fquare, and pannelled out.

If the leg on the right be thought to have too much work, the hufks in the flutes and the drapery on the plinth may be omitted.

Plate III. Borders for japanning or inlaying.

Plate IV. Ornament for a pannel. The whole fprings from a fpreading leaf at the bottom, from which a ferpent attempts to come at the doves on the fruit. In the center is a temple not dedicated to the interefts of the cupids, for which reafon they are burning it with their torches. The figure on the top of the column, in refentment, means to pelt them with ftones; and the geniufes above are pouring down water to quench the flames. The owls are emblematic of the night, at which feafon thefe mifchiefs are generally carried on. The other defigns in this plate require no remark.

Plate V. Ornament for a tablet, intended for painting on a grey or blue ground, as beft calculated to throw forward the figure and fruit.

In the cornices, the acorns in one, and hufk in the other,

are

are turned with a pin; by which they are fixed into the large projecting fquare.

I would advife to work the upper part of the cornice fepa-rate, by which means the acorns will be more eafily fixed. The frieze may be carved, painted, or inlaid.

Plate VI.   Defigns for Bed-pillars.

No. 1 and 2 are to be painted; No. 3 carved in mahogany; and No. 4 and 5 are intended for rich ftate-beds, carved in white and gold.   The fcale of feet and inches at the bottom will give the heights, and other proportions.

The pateras which cover the fcrew heads are on loofe pan-nels let into the pillars, and which fettle down into a groove at the bottom, by which means they are kept in their place, and eafily taken out.

Plate VII. Ornaments for the center of a pembroke and pier table needs no explanation.

Plate VIII. Of chair fplads.

No. 1, 2, 3, and 6, are intended for parlour chairs, carved in mahogany.

No.

Pl. 7

CENTER *for a* PEMBROKE TABLE

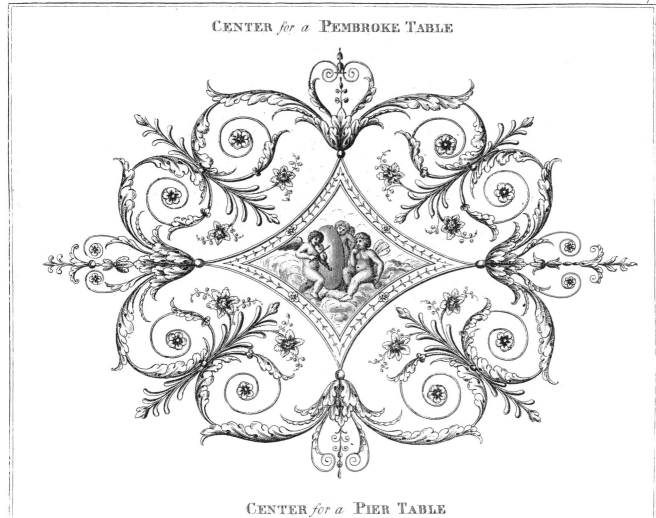

CENTER *for a* PIER TABLE

C. Sheraton Del.

J. Caldwall Dirext.

Published as the Act Directs by T. Sheraton Dec.ʳ 23. 1793.

N.º 4.

N.º 3.

N.º 2.

N.º 5.

N.º 6.

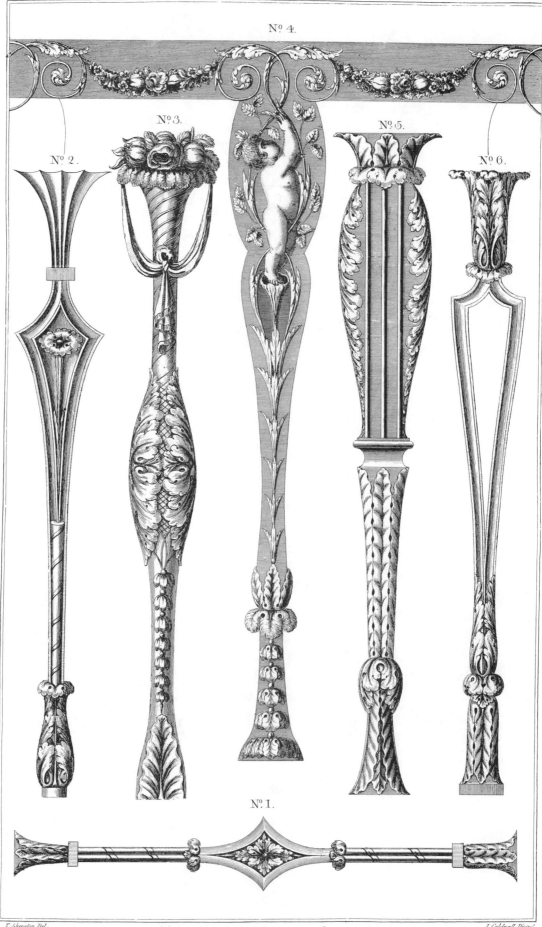

N.º 1.

T. Sheraton Del.

Publifhed as the Act Directs by T. Sheraton Dec.ʳ 23 1792.

I. Caldwall Dirext

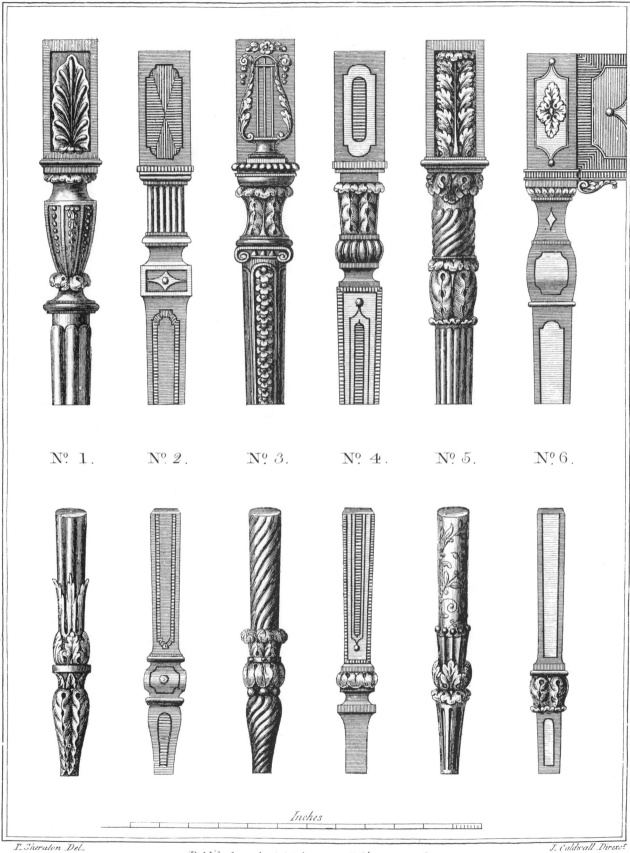

Nº 1.　　Nº 2.　　Nº 3.　　Nº 4.　　Nº 5.　　Nº 6.

Inches

T. Sheraton Del.

J. Caldwall Dirext.

Published as the Act Directs by T. Sheraton Janʸ 14. 1794.

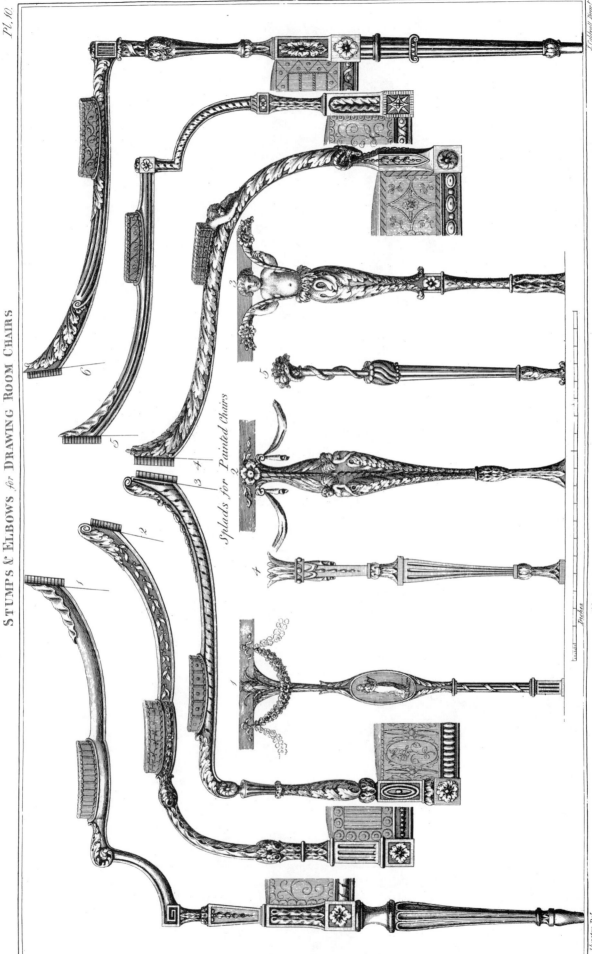

Pl. 10.

STUMPS & ELBOWS for DRAWING ROOM CHAIRS

Splads for Painted Chairs

Inches

Published as the Act Directs by T. Sheraton Jan.ʳ 14. 1794.

T. Sheraton Del.

I. Caldwell Denn F.

No. 3 and 4 are for painted chairs. Obferve, the curve lines which come from the top rail at No. 2 and 6 are intended to fhew where the outfide fplads in a complete back will come in, anfwerable to No. 4.

Plate IX. Of toes and knees for pier and card tables.

No. 1, 3, 5, are meant for pier tables, the ornaments of which are intended to be carved and gilt.

No. 2, 4, 6, are for card tables, with ftringing and pannels let in.

Plate X. Of chair elbows, with part of the feat, together with fplads for chair backs.

The fplads are all intended for japanning, except No. 4, which may be worked in mahogany.

The elbows are meant chiefly to be carved and gilt; but the mere outlines of any of them will ferve as patterns either for painted or mahogany chairs, by leaving out the ornaments for the mahogany, and retaining fome of them, or even all of them may be adapted for painting.

It

It may be proper to obferve, that as high as the ftuffing of the feat a rabbet fhould be left on the ftump to ftuff againft; which is eafily done, as the ftump is made fmaller above the rail. The cufhions on the arms are formed by cutting a rabbet in the arm, or leaving the wood a little above the furface. Some, however, bring the rabbet fquare down at each end, covering the wood entirely, except a fillet, which is left at the bottom and continues round the cufhion.

Plate XI. Ornament for a tablet intended for a painting, but which might be enlarged very well.

The fubject is a faint moonlight fcene, reprefenting Diana in a vifit to Endymion; who, as the ftory goes, having offended Juno, was condemned by Jupiter to a thirty years fleep. It may not be improper to advertife fome, that thefe, with a thoufand other of the fame kind of ftories, are merely the fabrications of ancient poets and idolaters, forming to themfelves innumerable gods, according to their vain imaginations, and which now, only ferve to try the painter's fkill in decorating our walls. And in oppofition to thefe vanities, I cannot well omit whifpering into the ear of the reader, that " To us there is but one God, the Father, of whom are all things." I Cor. viii. 6.

Plate

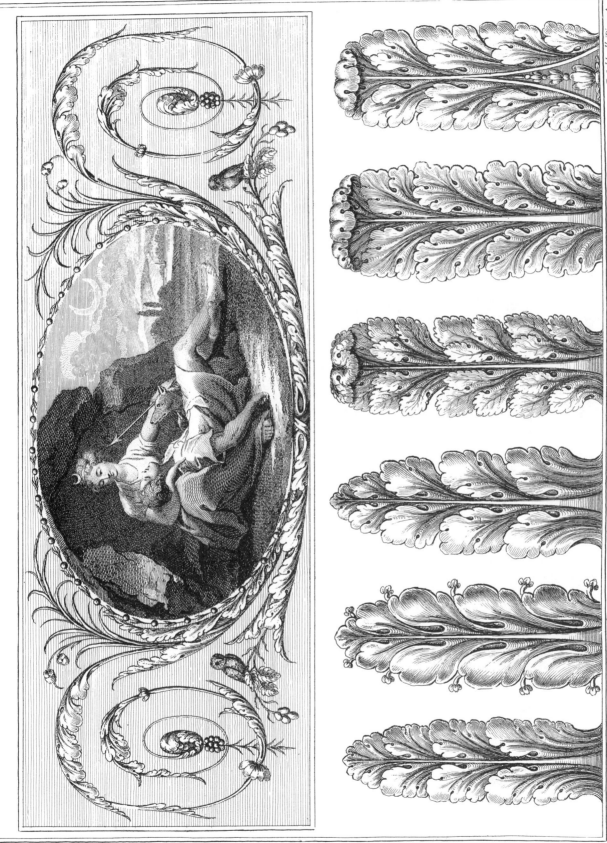

Pl. II.

ORNAMENT FOR A TABLET & VARIOUS LEAVES

T. Sheraton. Del.

I. Caldwell. Direct.

Publifhed as the Act Directs by T. Sheraton. Feb.ᵞ 7. 1794.

Pl. 12.

WINDOW CORNICES

Nº 4

Nº 3

Nº 2

Nº 1

I. Sheraton Del.

Published as the Act Directs by T. Sheraton Feb. 10 1794

J. Caldwall Direct.

Plate XII. Cornices for Windows.

The one acrofs the plate is intended for japanning, the upper one for carving and gilding, and the two under ones may be either carved or japanned.

The circular ends of this cornice are fometimes formed of a faintifh curve, and fometimes of a quick one. When they are of a faint fweep, they ought to be made fomewhat longer at each end than the outfide of the architraves, to give place to the curtain rods, fo that they may be brought fufficiently forward on the lath, and not leave too great a vacancy between the rod and cornice leaves, otherwife the lath will be feen when there is no drapery. In making thefe cornices, it is beft to plough and tongue in the leaves to the under fide of the facia of the cornice. The ends may be formed by gluing blocks of deal one on another till they come nearly to the fweep; and after having formed the outfide curve, I would then advife to gage on for the plough-groove for the leaves, before the wood in the infide is brought to its form, that the pieces for the leaves may be put in without fplitting off the groove. After thefe are well dried, then the fuperfluous wood on the infide can be taken away.

D

When

When the cornices are made at each end with a quick curve, the whole is firft worked in ftraight mouldings, and mitered together at each end, the fame as if intended to be fquare, according to the old fafhion. When they are glued in the miters, get out blocks of deal, about two inches and an half fquare, and cut them down anglewife, and let their length be equal to the width of the cornice and length of the leaves.

After thefe blockings are dry, cut off as much of the old miter as is fufficient to form the curve, and work the mouldings again by hand; and obferve, that as the block was left long enough, the curved leaf is intended to reft againft it, by which it will be much ftrengthened.

The cornices made thus, with a quick curve, needs not be made longer than ufual, becaufe the quick curve admits the rod to come forward more eafily than the other.

Plate XIII.   Pilafters for Commodes.

Thefe may be painted, inlaid, or gilt in gold behind glafs, and the glafs being then beded in the pilafter, it is fecure, and has a good effeƈt.

7   Plate

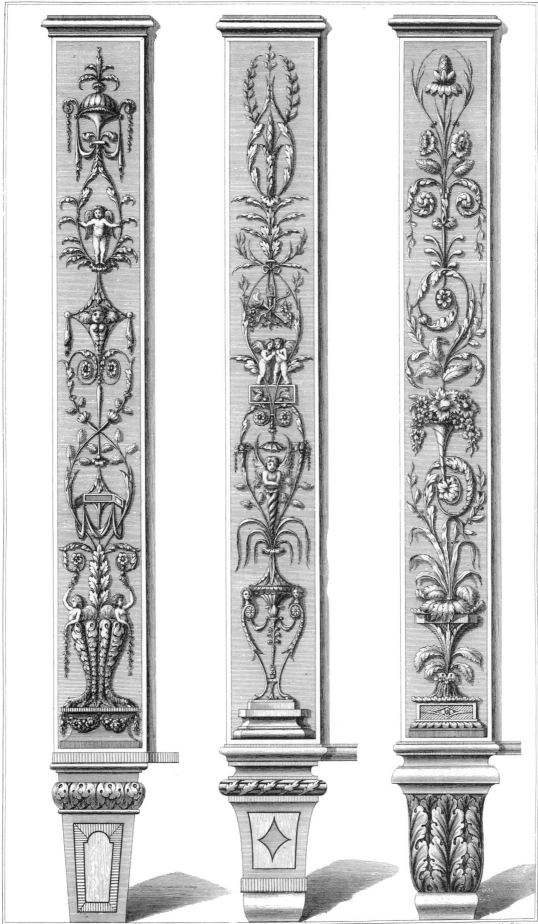

T. Sheraton Del.

Published as the Act Directs, by T. Sheraton, Feb.ᵗ 24 1804.

J. Caldwall Direx.ᵗ

CHAIR LEGS

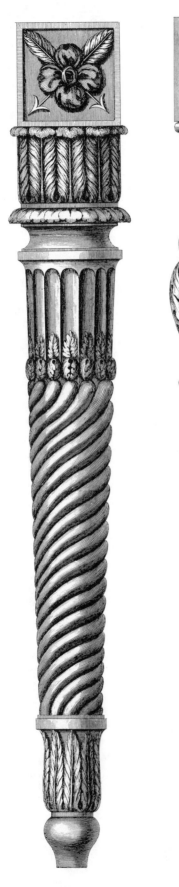

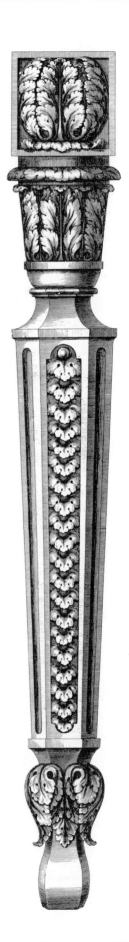

T. Sheraton Del.

Published as the Act Directs by T. Sheraton Aug.ᵗ 1793.

J. Caldwall Direx.

(27)

Plate XIV. Chair Legs.

The center leg is worked fquare; that on the right is octagon, except the vafe at the knee; and that on the left, round. Thefe may, in the view of fome, be thought too full of work; but the fkilful workman will eafily fee how to reduce their richnefs, and accommodate them to his purpofe.

A

DESCRIPTIVE INDEX

TO

THE SEVERAL PIECES OF CABINET FURNITURE

CONTAINED IN THE WORK;

INCLUDING

THE NEW AND ORIGINAL DESIGNS,

ADDED IN THE SECOND EDITION,

ALPHABETICALLY ARRANGED.

BEDS.

DESCRIPTIVE INDEX.

DESCRIPTIVE INDEX.

DESCRIPTIVE INDEX.

R

DESCRIPTIVE INDEX.

236

A
DESCRIPTIVE INDEX

TO

THE ACCOMPANIMENT

TO THE

CABINET-MAKER AND UPHOLSTERER's DRAWING-BOOK,

CONSISTING OF VARIOUS ORNAMENTS.

———————

DESCRIPTIVE INDEX.